Expanding Horizons

T0373801

ROYAL INSTITUTE OF PHILOSOPHY SUPPLEMENT: 93

EDITED BY

Julian Baggini

CAMBRIDGE UNIVERSITY PRESS

PUBLISHED BY THE PRESS SYNDICATE OF THE UNIVERSITY OF CAMBRIDGE
The Pitt Building, Trumpington Street, Cambridge, CB2 1RP,
United Kingdom

CAMBRIDGE UNIVERSITY PRESS
Shaftesbury Road, Cambridge CB2 8EA, United Kingdom
32 Avenue of the Americas, New York, NY 10013–2473, USA
477 Williamstown Road, Port Melbourne, VIC 3207, Australia
C/Orense, 4, planta 13, 28020 Madrid, Spain
Lower Ground Floor, Nautica Building, The Water Club, Beach Road,
Granger Bay, 8005 Cape Town, South Africa

Printed and bound by CPI Group (UK) Ltd, Croydon, CR0 4YY
Typeset by Techset Composition Ltd, Salisbury, UK

A catalogue record for this book is available from the British Library

ISBN 9781009418577
ISSN 1358-2461

Contents

Notes on the Contributors

Amy Olberding (aolberding@ou.edu) is Presidential Professor of Philosophy at the University of Oklahoma. Her most recent book is *The Wrong of Rudeness* (Oxford University Press, 2019) and she is currently working on a book on bereavement.

Nilanjan Das (nilanjan.das@utoronto.ca) is Associate Professor in Philosophy at the University of Toronto Mississauga. He works on the connections between self-knowledge and irrationality and also on debates between Buddhist and Brahmanical thinkers on the nature of the self, knowledge, and self-knowledge. Currently, he is also writing a book on the twelfth-century Indian philosopher and poet Śrīharṣa.

Noburu Notomi (noburunotomi@gmail.com) is Professor in Philosophy at the Graduate School of Humanities and Sociology at the University of Tokyo. He specializes in Western ancient philosophy and during his career he has visited and studied at numerous universities, including the University of Cambridge where he completed his PhD in Classics. He is the author of various works published in Japanese. In English his most notable work is *The Unity of Plato's Sophist: Between the Sophist and the Philosopher* (Cambridge University Press, 1999).

Leah Kalmanson (leah.kalmanson@unt.edu) is Associate Professor and Bhagwan Adinath Professor of Jain Studies at the University of North Texas. She is the author of *Cross-Cultural Existentialism: On the Meaning of Life in Asian and Western Thought* (Bloomsbury, 2020) and co-author with Monika Kirloskar-Steinbach of *A Practical Guide to World Philosophies: Selves, Worlds, and Ways of Knowing* (Bloomsbury, 2021).

Roger T. Ames (rtames@hawaii.edu) is Humanities Chair Professor in the Department of Philosophy and Religion at Peking University. His recent publications include *Human Becomings: Theorizing Persons for Confucian Role Ethics* (State University of New York Press, 2021) and *A Conceptual Lexicon for Classical Confucian Philosophy* (State University of New York Press, 2022).

doi:10.1017/S1358246123000176   © The Royal Institute of Philosophy and the contributors 2023

Royal Institute of Philosophy Supplement **93** 2023   v

Notes on the Contributors

Chike Jeffers (chike.jeffers@dal.ca) is Associate Professor in the Department of Philosophy at Dalhousie University. He is the co-presenter of the Africana philosophy editions of the *History of Philosophy without Any Gaps* podcast and has two forthcoming books based on it. He is also the co-author of *What is Race? Four Philosophical Views* (Oxford University Press, 2019) and editor of *Listening to Ourselves: A Multilingual Anthology of African Philosophy* (State University of New York Press, 2013).

Lewis R. Gordon (lewis.gordon@uconn.edu) is Professor and Head of the Department of Philosophy at UCONN-Storrs; Honorary President of the Global Center for Advanced Studies; Honorary Professor in the Unit for the Humanities at Rhodes University, South Africa; and Distinguished Scholar at The Most Honourable P.J. Patterson Centre for Africa-Caribbean Advocacy at The University of the West Indies, Mona. He co-edits the journal *Philosophy and Global Affairs*, the Rowman and Littlefield book series *Global Critical Caribbean Thought*, and the Routledge-India book series *Academics, Politics and Society in the Post-Covid World*. He is the author of a number of books, including most recently *Freedom, Justice, and Decolonization* (Routledge, 2021) and *Fear of Black Consciousness* (Penguin Books, 2022). In 2022 he received the Eminent Scholar Award from the Global Development Studies division of the International Studies Association.

Joanna Burch-Brown (j.burch-brown@bristol.ac.uk) is Senior Lecturer in Philosophy at the University of Bristol. Her work has focused on issues of contested heritage and public memory. She is founding director of social enterprise Bridging Histories, academic director for the Fulbright Summer Institute on 'Arts, Activism and Social Justice', and has served on the Bristol History Commission.

María del Rosario Acosta López (mariadea@ucr.edu) is Professor at the Department of Hispanic Studies at the University of California Riverside where she is also a co-operating faculty member of the Department of Philosophy. Her teaching and research are in areas around romanticism and German idealism, aesthetics, contemporary political European philosophy, and more recently on questions of decolonial and Latin American studies with an emphasis on questions of memory and trauma in the Americas.

Helen De Cruz (helen.decruz@slu.edu) holds the Danforth Chair in the Humanities at Saint Louis University. Her main areas of specialization are philosophy of cognitive science and philosophy of religion, and she also works in general philosophy of science, epistemology, aesthetics, and metaphilosophy. She is the co-editor of *Philosophy through Science Fiction Stories* (Bloomsbury, 2021), editor and illustrator of *Philosophy Illustrated* (Oxford University Press, 2021), and author of the forthcoming monograph *Wonderstruck. How Awe and Wonder Shape the Way We Think* (Princeton University Press).

Jonardon Ganeri (jonardon.ganeri@utoronto.ca) holds the Bimal Matilal Distinguished Professorship in Philosophy at the University of Toronto. His work draws on a variety of philosophical traditions to construct new positions in philosophy of mind, metaphysics, and theory of knowledge. He is a great advocate for an expanded role for cross-cultural methodologies and his research subjects include consciousness, self, attention, the idea of philosophy as a practice, and philosophy's relationship to literature. His books include *Attention, Not Self* (Oxford University Press, 2017), *Inwardness: An Outsider's Guide* (Columbia University Press, 2012), and most recently *Virtual Subjects, Fugitive Selves: Fernando Pessoa and His Philosophy* (Oxford University Press, 2020).

Eileen John (eileen.john@warwick.ac.uk) is Professor of Philosophy at the University of Warwick and works in aesthetics and philosophy of literature. Two of her recent papers are 'Meals, Art and Meaning' (*Crítica: Revista Hispanoamericana de Filosofía*, 2021) and 'Learning from Aesthetic Disagreement and Flawed Artworks' (*The Journal of Aesthetics and Art Criticism*, 2020). She co-directs Warwick's Centre for Research in Philosophy, Literature and the Arts.

Tamara Albertini (tamaraa@hawaii.edu) is a philosopher with a Swiss-Italian father and a Serbian mother. She grew up in hospitable Tunisia, married a Bulgarian-Macedonian-American dissident, and later in life became a US citizen. She is yet to find out whether she is a go-between, a multiple host-guest, or both. She is Professor and Chair at the Department of Philosophy and the Director of Islamic Studies at the University of Hawai'i at Mānoa. In more recent years, she has begun to host Renaissance, Islamic, and contemporary Arab concepts in her responses to contemporary philosophical questions such as hospitality, digital presence, and women in comparative philosophy.

Introduction: How Can and Should Philosophy Be Expanding its Horizons?

JULIAN BAGGINI

Abstract
The Royal Institute of Philosophy volume of which this paper is an introduction is on the theme of 'Expanding Horizons'. But what does it mean for philosophy to fruitfully expand its horizons? The contributions to the volume suggest at least five profitable ways. First, by looking to other philosophical traditions for new perspectives on familiar questions and alternative methods, questions, and ways of understanding. Second, by looking to what has been neglected or overlooked in our own histories of thought. Third, by developing novel methods, in addition to argument, for investigating philosophical issues. Fourth, by embracing different modalities for doing philology, such as the literary. Fifth, by reflecting on the practice of comparative philosophy to better understand the extent to which philosophy can and should be universal. Together, these approaches both increase the range of voices heard in philosophy and the scope and ambition of the discipline.

There are not many intellectual or cultural practices which enjoyed their most fertile periods when they settled into widely agreed and established ways of doing things. In the Western history of ideas, Ancient Athens, Renaissance Italy, Enlightenment Amsterdam, Edinburgh, and Paris all stand out largely because those were times when new ideas flourished, marking a break from the past. Art forms of all kinds are divided into periods, each of which began with a new way of working.

In the late twentieth century, however, Anglophone philosophy seemed to have settled into a comfortable groove, happy to pursue a familiar range of questions, drawing on a canon of classic texts and a narrow corpus of contemporary academics' work. It rarely looked to other disciplines or cultures.

Perhaps one reason for this was that it was too influenced by a precedent that looked in some ways like an exception to the general rule, but which was actually another example of it. Natural science had flourished to such an extent that it had in most people's eyes seized philosophy's crown as 'queen of the sciences', a throne philosophy had in turn taken from theology. Science was becoming a runaway

doi:10.1017/S1358246123000140

Julian Baggini

success, it seems, because it had settled on a general method of experimentation and observation that its practitioners all agreed on. Could philosophy flourish as much if only it could find its own special methods and domain of enquiry?

In mainstream academic philosophy in Britain and America throughout much of the twentieth century the generally accepted answer seemed to be yes, even if assent was generally implicit. Philosophy used the tools of logical and conceptual analysis to answer fundamental but non-empirical questions, such as the meaning of 'meaning', the nature of causation, the basis of morality, the principles of justice, and so on. These tools had been honed over millennia and there was no need to borrow any from other disciplines or traditions.

Much good work was produced under this programme. But as the century drew to a close, more and more people were concerned that philosophy had become too narrow, too parochial. One danger was that it was spending too much time answering questions only other philosophers were asking. Another was that it was dealing only with artificially demarcated sub-questions and not the larger, more important ones. Philosophical debates about free will, time, justice, causation, identity and so on were just leaving out a lot of what makes those issues so interesting and important.

It was time for philosophy to expand its horizons. That process has been underway for some years and it was our intention in this volume, and in the lecture series on which it is based, to both encourage and celebrate it.

But what does 'expanding horizons' mean and how is it to be achieved? Just as an open mind is not a virtue if it uncritically lets everything fall into it unfiltered, so expanding horizons is a futile quest if it takes you anywhere and everywhere without discrimination. The essays in this volume provide examples of what expanding horizons should mean and why it matters.

The most obvious horizon-stretcher is almost literally geographical: look to what has been done in the name of philosophy in distant lands. It surprises many that Western philosophy has not routinely done that for centuries. It had its reasons, it just turns out they weren't very good ones. Ignorance, prejudice, and a sense of cultural superiority explains much, but not all of it. More recently, one root cause is that same conviction that Western philosophy had found its own, distinctive *modus operandi*, its key questions and canonical texts. When practitioners glanced at Chinese, Indian, East Asian, African, indigenous American philosophy and so on, they saw diverse disciplines separated by a common disciplinary label, not philosophy as we know and do it.

Belatedly, this dismissiveness has been shown to be unfounded. There is more common ground than first glances suggest, as five papers in this volume ably demonstrate.

First, non-Western philosophers can provide fresh ways of looking at (too) familiar questions. Noburu Notomi for instance, reveals how Japanese philosophers often read Plato very differently from their contemporary Western counterparts. When these Western philosophers read Plato, Notomi claims, they make four background assumptions concerning the primacy of empirical science for understanding reality, the absolute centrality of the 'I' in experience, a devaluation of representation and imagination, and a confinement of philosophy to academic research. Notomi's critique is challenging in at least two senses of the word: these assumptions are so deep-rooted that it is hard to see them for what they are, and to even countenance the idea that they might be wrong threatens to undermine our image of what philosophy is.

Nilanjan Das looks at a question that has been highly salient in the West for decades now, but from a very old Buddhist perspective. The nature of the self and its identity was put centre stage by Derek Parfit in his 1971 paper 'Personal Identity' and later his book *Reasons and Persons* (1984). In that book, Parfit has a short, one page appendix, in which he says it has been pointed out to him that his view has striking similarities with that of the Buddha. Parfit goes no further with this and simply notes with pleasure that the Buddha would have agreed with him. In retrospect, it seems extraordinary that such a tireless reader and researcher never thought it worth his while to go away and study the Buddhist texts in question.

Das provides us with an account of some of what Parfit might have found in his discussion of the *Commentary on the Treasury of Abhidharma* (*Abhidharmakośabhāṣya*), by the 4th to 5th-century Abhidharma Buddhist philosopher Vasubandhu. Vasubandhu is clearly grappling with one of the very same questions Parfit and his critics had to deal with: if there is no singular, self-contained, indivisible, unchanging self, only the flux of experiences, how can we even talk about an 'I'? Das's essay is a real I-opener.

Amy Olberding casts fresh light on familiar issues by showing how early Confucian philosophy provides a way of thinking about troublesome emotions that is very different from the template set out by the Ancient Greeks, which set the agenda for Western philosophy to come. The dominant Greek approach, exemplified by Socrates and the Stoics, is, broadly speaking, to avoid feelings like anger or even grief by coming to appreciate their futility and irrationality. The title of Olberding's essay captures the Confucian alternative

Julian Baggini

pithily: 'Getting Good at Bad Emotions'. The point is not to avoid discomforting or difficult emotions but to get better at dealing with them. This is not just a challenge to Western philosophy but to dominant ideas in Western culture.

With all the three contributions mentioned so far, it's easy enough to recognise the common ground, even as we see how very differently it is cultivated. In contrast, Leah Kalmanson shows how non-Western traditions have considered issues that have gone almost unnoticed in the West. The methods of philosophy in the West are all to do with forms of reasoning. In Asia, however, there is a whole different set of tools in the kit: contemplative practices. What we generally lump together as 'meditation' can be ways to prepare for rational thought or attempts to do something different from it: achieve a kind of acute or heightened awareness that allows us to see more clearly. For too long such ideas have been dismissed by analytic philosophers as having nothing to do with reasoning as we know it. Kalmanson suggests this is wrong.

Roger Ames's challenge is even more fundamental. Western philosophy has generally been characterised by forms of 'substance ontologies', meaning accounts of the grounds of being that postulate some kind of unchanging substance, be it material or mental. Chinese thought, however, is less concerned with such metaphysical substances. Events are more fundamental than things, while creatures such as ourselves are not so much 'beings' as 'becomings'. Borrowing the Greek word *zoe* or 'life', Ames creates the neologism 'zoetology', the art of living, as an alternative cosmological focus to ontology. Again, to those trained in the Western tradition this might sound more like New Age woo-woo than philosophy. One hint that this is far from the truth is that a similar, Eastern-inspired process understanding of nature can be found in the very empirical and rational physics of Carlo Rovelli.

Horizons can also be expanded without leaving for foreign shores. One lively family of research areas looks again at what has been missed within our own cultures and traditions. The somewhat crude but not entirely inaccurate way to characterise what has been left out is: pretty much everything not led by the thinking of white men. Chike Jeffers offers one example of this in his exploration of the work of W.E.B. Du Bois, 'long known as an African American intellectual and activist of towering importance' but only recently 'recognised as a philosopher of uncommon depth and historical significance'. One reason why Du Bois has been ignored is that the issues he wrote about were not even recognised as essentially philosophical ones. This is curious since there is a long tradition of thinking about justice in philosophy. Why should racial justice not be included?

Lewis Gordon takes this challenge to rethink the structural and institutional racism of philosophy further in his call to 'decolonise' philosophy. Campaigns to decolonise academic curricula have received a lot of media attention, much of it ill informed, some of it downright hysterical. Certainly the framing of the issue as a 'culture war' of the 'woke' against either the defenders of bigotry or common sense, depending on your point of view, is not helpful. Gordon's essay is essential reading for anyone who wants to go beyond the polarised social media debate and dig into the substance of the issue.

So far, all the forms of expanding horizons mentioned have essentially been about letting hitherto unheard voices be heard. Both Joanna Burch-Brown and María del Rosario Acosta López look to further this goal, but with an emphasis not only on whom we hear but the methods we use to hear them. Burch-Brown considers how philosophers might contribute to important social debates concerning historical injustices and how to rectify them. It is tempting for philosophers to think they can do this simply by applying their expertise to the question in hand. For example, if the issue is reparations for past racial injustice, they can simply think through the ethics of reparations and decide how it applies to the case in point. Burch-Brown argues that this is far too limited. By engaging with people directly affected by the issues, philosophers can come to appreciate the force of more arguments than they could dream up in their studies and seminar rooms. Only then will they be able to use their skills to formalise the arguments in their strongest forms and be able to present arguments for or against, and genuinely help participants in the debate to clarify their positions.

Listening to those directly involved is all central to Acosta López's project of doing justice to testimonies of traumatic experiences, with particular reference to those suffered in Colombia's recent civil conflicts. Traditional philosophical methods are not up to the task. They assume that utterances reveal their 'semantic content' or 'truth conditions' transparently, when trauma makes such clear, objective, and dispassionate speech impossible. We need new 'grammars of listening' or '*gramáticas de lo inaudito*' in order to hear these experiences on their own terms. Otherwise, philosophical accounts of justice and what it requires simply cannot connect with urgent, real-world issues of injustice.

Acosta López's approach suggests that there is – or should be – more for philosophy to do than simply pronounce on the validity and soundness of arguments. Philosophy is at its most basic level a way to help us build a better, more accurate picture of the world.

Julian Baggini

There are more tools to help us do that other than logic and argument, as Helen De Cruz and Jonardon Ganeri show. Both suggest that there can be a more literary approach to philosophy, one which shows rather than tells. Logical proofs are sometimes called 'demonstrations' but stories and fictions can be other forms of demonstrations of how the world is.

De Cruz's provocative suggestion is that more matters in philosophical writing than the truth and falsity of its propositions. Texts also have 'moods' and these can be important not only because they affect how we read the arguments, 'scaffolding the reader's attunement', as she puts it. The purpose of a piece of philosophy may be to transform us, to make us see the world differently. Hence, 'Mood is not just window dressing but an important element of philosophical writing and understanding, which cannot be reduced to the cogency of arguments'.

Jonardon Ganeri makes the case that the great Portuguese poet and writer Fernando Pessoa is also a philosopher in his own right. Pessoa wrote through the voices of various 'heteronyms', which Ganeri describes as 'another I, a self that is not one's own'. This is not the same as writing pseudonymously, where one writes as an another. Heteronyms are aspects of the writer's self, expanded into fully formed personalities. Ganeri makes a compelling case that Pessoa's heteronymic writings provide a unique and revelatory insight into the nature of subjectivity.

Expanding our philosophical horizons opens up many doors. But it might be worried it opens up too much. What are we to make of all this diversity? Must we give up on any aspiration for universal truth? The last two contributions to this volume address this challenge in different ways.

Eileen John considers its relevance to one specific area of philosophy: aesthetics, which theorises artistic and sensory experience. She asks whether there can be a global aesthetics or whether a proper appreciation of the different approaches taken in different times and places leaves us with an irreducible plurality. John refuses to rush to a neat answer. Rightly so: it is more than enough to set out many of the unexplored questions and issues. Tentatively, however, she concludes that although 'the universalising ambition' that characterises philosophy cannot be entirely given up, it 'has to be held loosely, self-consciously, and self-critically'.

The final contribution, by Tamara Albertini, is an invitation to think differently about how we undertake the whole project of comparative philosophy. She argues that we must go beyond 'intercultural dialogue' and become guardians of each other's traditions.

This requires a profound intellectual hospitality, 'a world where civilizations are each other's cultural and spiritual "food"'. It is a beautiful dream, albeit one Albertini accepts we are far from fulfilling.

I would like to note that one lecture from the series did not manage to make the transition to a contribution to this volume due to circumstances beyond the author's control. You can, however, watch Owen Flanagan's talk 'The Ethics of Anger and Shame' on the Royal Institute of Philosophy's YouTube channel, along with the other lectures in the series. Many have been developed a great deal for this volume, some are almost completely different. It is as though our speakers have modelled what it means to live with ever expanding horizons by showing how even over the course of a few months their own thinking has grown and evolved.

Philosophy in the English-speaking world today is marvellously diverse. Some of what is currently flowering may bloom for a short while and then disappear. But at the risk of stretching the horticultural metaphor too far, much of what is planted will take strong root, and much will cross-pollinate to create yet more new branches of enquiry. The ground on which philosophy grows is wider and more fertile than ever. But the work of cultivation is never done. That which ceases to grow, dies.

Community Practices and Getting Good at Bad Emotions

AMY OLBERDING

Abstract
Early Confucian philosophy is remarkable in its attention to everyday social interactions and their power to steer our emotional lives. Their work on the social dimensions of our moral-emotional lives is enormously promising for thinking through our own context and struggles, particularly, I argue, the ways that public rhetoric and practices may steer us away from some emotions it can be important to have, especially negative emotions. Some of our emotions are bad – unpleasant to experience, reflective of dissatisfactions or even heartbreak – but nonetheless quite important to express and, more basically, to feel. Grief is like this, for example. So, too, is disappointment. In this essay, I explore how our current social practices may fail to support expressions of disappointment and thus suppress our ability to feel it well.

In the popular imagination, philosophers are often associated with equanimity. Whatever people may imagine philosophers to be, they tend to expect philosophers to manage the ordinary struggles of human life with greater composure and, indeed, may expect that philosophers *should be* wise in ways that afford protection from the negative emotions that bedevil the rest of us. While anyone who personally knows a philosopher will know better than this, this perception that wisdom can or should guard against negative emotion has some historical purchase. Models such as Socrates or traditions such as Stoicism do align wisdom with protection from conventional sorrows and struggles. Early Confucianism, particularly Confucius himself and, later, Xunzi, offer a striking and, I believe, heartening counterpoint.

While Confucius and Xunzi do suggest that wisdom affords an improved capacity to navigate the travails of life, they find substantial place within wisdom for negative emotions. A wise person will also sometimes feel quite bad, and part of pursuing wisdom amounts to getting good at bad emotions. Much of what improvement of our bad emotions entails is internal work, adjustments to our thinking and framing of experience. But much of it is also social, and it is to the social aspects of our emotions that I want to attend here. One important aspect of early Confucian philosophy is its refusal to isolate wisdom, or the wise, from the social, communal, and familial dimensions of experience. Wisdom is found *in* these aspects of experience

doi:10.1017/S1358246123000036   © The Royal Institute of Philosophy and the contributors 2023

and is importantly supported by them. If we will be better at feeling bad, then, we do well to see how our emotions are inflected and influenced by our environment. My own interest in these matters is not scholastic, but born of a sense that much in our present culture fails to well support us in emotions we would do well to feel. So while I first detail the early Confucian approach to our negative emotions, my more pressing target is considering what they may offer us.

The negative emotions to which the Confucians most closely attend are not, significantly, unusual or uncommon emotions. Rather, they are strikingly ordinary and commonplace, just the sorts of negative emotions that will and do arise in the course of experiences most typical of human beings. Just as wisdom may be found in our ordinary lives with and among other people, so, too, some of the emotions that importantly matter to our wisdom are found just there. For example, unlike their ancient counterparts in Greece and Rome, the early Confucians, and indeed most early Chinese philosophers, made much of the struggles of grief. Where Western philosophers largely ignored bereavement or counselled against grief, early Chinese philosophy is rich with sensitive reflections on loss and even heated debates about funerary ritual. The Confucians, in particular, focused their closest attention on that most ubiquitous form of bereavement: the deaths of parents.[1] Most of us have or someday will endure this sorrow. Indeed, a life that goes the way that both we and our parents would wish must include it, for the alternative is surely counted worse. In short, the experience of losing parents is both terribly common and aligned with an order of life we prefer. Even so, as the Confucians recognized, the change this loss enforces can be seismic, the struggle it entails fierce. So in their reflections on death and loss, we find close attention to this most common of human heartbreaks and strategies for honouring its place in our lives.

Just as the Confucians attended to the prosaic struggles of losing beloved elders, they also, as Wenhui Xie argues, paid attention to worry, to the ways that caring about other people and about the world entails courting some distress (Xie, forthcoming). Here, too, the relation between parent and child can serve as a touchstone. Much is often made of the Confucian tradition's extolling of filial piety, of its emphasis on children deferring to elders. But in one of the tradition's oldest texts, the *Analects*, Confucius sometimes and tellingly references the worries that reside in close parent-child relations, attaching filiality to care for how we, parents and children

---

[1]   I cannot here do justice to the intricacies of the Confucian position regarding the loss of parents. For more on this, see Olberding (2011).

both, worry each other. He counsels children to give their parents no cause for anxiety beyond their health (Eno, 2015, 2.6), and he remarks on how a child whose parents have grown old will find this a joy, but also a source of great trepidation (Eno, 2015, 4.21). In these passages, Confucius acknowledges that even when the parent-child relation is at its best, it will include anxieties. Parents will worry for their children's well-being, and children who bear witness to their parents' decline come to know this worry too. Most broadly, to care for another is to want for her health, well-being, and flourishing – and to worry about just such matters. As Xie argues, Confucius' approach to such realities is not to deny the worth of worry or to seek its eradication in favour of personal peace, but to learn to worry well. A wise person seeks to worry where it is well spent, as a measure of affection and care, while keeping in view what matters we can control and what we cannot, and while schooling herself to favour worries that reflect her profoundest values and commitments.

In their attention to prosaic experiences such as the loss of parents and the worries we bear for those we love, the early Confucians pick out some of the most commonplace human experiences and make them a philosophical focus. They appear to grant that a well-lived life will include distress and unpleasant emotions. Their work appears predicated on the idea that some of what it takes to live well – caring well and deeply for others, in particular – will exact costs that we should not seek to dodge. Love of others will induce worry, and it will induce grief. These are bad emotions – unpleasant, distressing, sometimes miserable – but they are also important. For they originate in relations that constitute much of the value life may offer us. To fly from such emotions or seek their eradication, as some of the Western ancients recommend, is to lose something of the humanity we achieve in caring for and about beloved others. Because of this, what the Confucians sought were ways that one can endure well and perhaps even come to valorize some of our bad emotions – to see them as regrettable elements of a life that, nonetheless and in its totality, is exquisitely rewarding.

Of course, if one will extol the value of emotions most find both negative and unpleasant, one will need to take care. Grief can sometimes be romanticized and is quite often actively damaging; worry can abduct us and separate us from the goods that love of others affords. Recognizing just such hazards in part motivates those philosophers, such as the Stoics, who exhort us to train ourselves out of bad emotions. The Confucians, too, see the peril. Their response to it, in its most basic form, is to seek skilfulness in managing one's emotion and to seek a society that supports us in just this.

Amy Olberding

Managing negative emotion well entails some substantial tending to our own internal workings. We should both seek and sustain an internal mental life that seats distressing emotion in values we circumspectly endorse. The internal effort here is naturally quite complicated and indeed intricate, worthy of its own study. This is but what we would expect, as philosophers of all sorts who recommend ways to seek our own flourishing turn us inward toward adjustments to our thinking and reflecting. But I wish to focus instead on an aspect of managing negative emotion less often philosophically addressed: the impact of social experience on emotion.

In the everydayness that pervades the Confucians' work, they understood that even as we may experience grief or worry as our own internal workings, there is a social side to both. Emotions develop not just internally, but also socially. They are coloured, influenced, and steered by the communities and social environments we inhabit. And how our emotions go for us will often have much to do with what our society supports or fails to support, what it invites us to cultivate and what it disdains, or, most basically of all, what it attends to and what it ignores. The social practices and rhetorics surrounding familiar experiences can function to steer what we feel and how. The frameworks we employ for understanding our experiences – from what they mean to how they ought to be countenanced – are shaped by the social narratives and practices that structure our communal lives. Likewise, whether we can make our emotions intelligible, both to ourselves and others, will ride in part on whether we have, ready to hand, shared linguistic and behavioural resources for their expression. The fullest development of this view is in Xunzi's work.

Xunzi understood that our social and cultural practices function as paths tracing out what reactions and responses to events are acceptable and reflect our values. We are shaped by others and by a variety of social forces – our shared manners and mores, our interactional norms and practices, and the social rhetorics we employ. Xunzi's primary interest was in articulating a moral system that would foster virtue through the joint effects of good role models (Hutton, 2014, chapter 1) and robust ritual practices (Hutton, 2014, chapter 23). He argues that well-devised, shared social practices are key to both social and personal well-being. On Xunzi's view, the human being is like bent wood that may be made straight where it is brought under the correcting influence of appropriate ritual (Hutton, 2014, p. 267). Xunzi's account of moral and social life takes its own shape under the influence of a society riven by war, corruption, and decline, circumstances Xunzi seeks to remedy with a return to traditional practices. What interests me here, however, are the wider dynamics on which he rests his recommendations, his emphasis on the shaping power of social practice and environment.

The first chapter of the *Xunzi*, called 'An Exhortation to Learning', begins with a series of images that vividly capture the significance of setting and environment (Hutton, 2014, pp. 2–3). There is a bird whose nests tend to fail at the slightest wind because she builds them on frail branches. There is a short plant that enjoys the view of vast vistas because it grows along mountaintops. A sprawling, curving vine grows straight because it is set among upright hemp. A famously 'sweet-smelling' plant becomes offensively malodorous because it is set in foul water. In each of these cases, circumstance and setting, for good or ill, exert a shaping pressure. So it is with human beings as well. We, too, enjoy the view and adopt the contours that our social positioning makes possible. We, too, take on the odour of the social waters we are 'soaked' in. Much of what influences us and gives us our shape will be the behavioural and emotional patterns most evident in our society's practices, both formal and informal. And much of this influence will transpire below conscious awareness.

Xunzi's work remarkably anticipates concepts now common in psychology – the effects of peer influence and emotional contagion, the ways we absorb and mirror the moods and emotional states of others. As Xunzi puts it, we are akin to animals in this, such that when one horse neighs, the others neigh responsively (Hutton, 2014, p. 19). Our nature is to be receptive and give uptake to the emotional and behavioural states of our fellows. The most direct form of this is of course the face-to-face encounter, those occasions when we catch and mirror the mood of one with whom we interact. But at a wider level, our commonplace social practices and patterns operate as settings influencing and constraining our responses. Our social practices and patterns will inflect what sorts of 'neighs' we make and so, also, what sort of 'neighs' we find in answer. Where ethically important negative emotions are concerned, the early Confucians recommend social practices that, optimally, support our healthy development of these emotions or, minimally, do not discourage such emotions. Here, too, grief can serve as illustration.

If we exist in a society that publicly recognizes loss and subsequent mourning as a period of great fragility for the bereaved – through forms of ritual and suspension of more routine business – we will find grief an emotion more natural to express and even to feel. Where mourners are socially recognized as such – say, by the adoption of symbolic dress that denotes their status – we invite a communal responsiveness to grief that functions to support those experiencing it. This dynamic is in evidence throughout the *Analects* and *Xunzi*,

Amy Olberding

where social rituals attending mourning are emphatically endorsed (e.g., Hutton, 2014, pp. 223–234), but even simple gestures are salient. In offering Confucius as a role model, the *Analects* notes his habits in the presence of mourners: he 'never ate his fill' when dining in their company (Eno, 2015, 7.9) and would incline his head in a bow or alter his expression when encountering them (Eno, 2015, 10.22). Such gestures give both recognition and sanction to a mourner's distress.

A striking contrast to the Confucian style of social practice is evident in the personal reflections of Geoffrey Gorer, describing his experience of mourning his brother in mid 20th-century England. When Gorer declined invitations to events or parties, citing his mourning status, others were palpably uncomfortable. Indeed, in Gorer's recounting, 'I got the impression that, had I stated that the invitation clashed with some esoteric debauchery I had arranged, I would have had understanding and jocular encouragement; as it was, the people whose invitations I had refused, educated and sophisticated though they were, mumbled and hurried away' (Gorer, 1965, p. xxxii). As Gorer's experience shows, if our social practices make little place for mourning, offer few public ways to acknowledge our sorrows, then what grief we feel may be discouraged – from expression, certainly, but perhaps also from feeling. What grief we experience, we may feel pressure to conceal. More forcefully, we may have incentives to 'move on', rather than to grieve. The early Confucian emphasis on our social practices may be understood to live in the contrast between these two examples.

Confucius' society is one that effectively commends grief to its members, providing sanction and forms of expression that support the emotion. Gorer's society is one that effectively discourages grief, implicitly treating it as shameful and thereby denying its members both ready forms of expression for grief and support from others. Where one seeks to grieve well, to situate one's experience of this most negative emotion in a life one can judge meaningful, a society such as Gorer's (and of course our own) will work against one's efforts.

There is much we might here say about how poorly our current social environments aid in the experiences of grief. However, I want here to focus instead on an experience and negative emotion I less often see addressed: disappointment. Put plainly, where disappointment is concerned, I think it quite important to have some. Like grief and worry both, disappointment is an emotion rooted in our caring for and connection with others. Yet I also find that disappointment is an emotional response our current social environment both discourages and makes very difficult to express. Let me sketch some of what I mean by 'disappointment' by first offering an example.

The state in which I live has one of the highest Covid death rates in the United States. Despite this, when my university resumed in-person classes, it refused to institute any vaccine or mask mandates. In autumn 2021, just as the Delta variant began tearing through the region, the semester began for faculty with a gust of menacing emails forbidding our doing anything that might be perceived as pressuring students into wearing masks, from any gestures that might make unmasked students feel judged or excluded. Both the university's policies and its tight restrictions on faculty classroom speech were disappointing in their own right, but I here want to speak of what followed.

Forbidden to insist on masks, yet desperate to increase the safety of their classrooms, many professors began their classes with recitations of their personal circumstances – immunocompromised spouses, unvaccinated infants, elderly relatives in their care, or health vulner-abilities of their own. These painful narrations were a last-ditch strategy to get their unmasked students to put on masks, but they largely did not work. The many who arrived unmasked mostly stayed that way, the students not just unmoved to take up masks, but gratuitously appearing so: bland looks of indifference, distracted scrolling through phones, averted looks, and even eyerolls in response to a professor's pleading. Reports circulated on campus of students even laughing at professors as those professors detailed their anxieties about their own health or loved ones.

My initial response to this phenomenon was plain shock. It had, I confess, never occurred to me that our students would behave so. I had not anticipated the open displays of contempt and indifference, nor the sheer number of students who would refuse. Once the shock abated, I found myself profoundly disappointed. Disappointment of this sort seems to me a rather complicated response to other people. Most basically, disappointment occurs when our expectations of others fail, when they do not do what we would expect them to do. But it is also more than this, more than expectations that fail. It is also about hopes that fail. Disappointment emerges through some regrettable failure of understanding and aspiration. It derives from both a knowledge problem and a hope problem. Let me address knowledge first, then hope.

Disappointment can expose underlying beliefs about people we may have assumed as knowledge. Prior to fall semester, I would not have believed so many students *could* engage in hostile disrespect of their professors in moments of self-exposure and vulnerability – in fact, I thought I *knew* such a thing wasn't possible, that it did not reside in the character of our students to behave so. When they did so behave, I was left painfully aware that I had made an error, that what I thought I knew was just wrong. This looks like an error in knowledge, but it can't simply be so. Because errors in knowledge don't inevitably produce disappointment. After all, when people turn out *better* than we expect, when they do better than we thought they could, we don't respond with disappointment. To be disappointed, one must also have some hope, however modest.

My prior understanding of my university's students was not a neutral bit of knowledge, but one laced all through with trusting optimism. It was not really about how I knew them to be, but about what I *supposed* them to be. It was rooted not just in what I saw of them, but in something more nebulous, something like a disposition to think well of them, to expect well of them even in circumstances none of us had ever experienced before.

The reality is such that life is unpredictable. We cannot forecast with reliability how people will behave in circumstances not yet encountered. What we do instead is try our best to form accurate judgments about their general character and, where we are hopefully disposed, to think well of their possibilities. We may recognize that people, so to speak, sit on a fence and can go one way or another, but opt to trust that they'll tilt the way they ought, that they will be their better selves rather than their worst selves. Disappointment emerges where we had some high degree of confidence, where we felt reasonably well grounded in the expectation that they would tilt to the good.

As I hope is clear, disappointment interlocks with doubt in important ways. On the front end, our orientation toward others is taken based on a hopeful reading of the evidence before us – that is, we can become well disposed toward others in a hope rooted in what we see of them. But this is, and must be, a position short of certainty; it can be doubted. On the back end, when others have disappointed us, doubt is of course far more forceful and unpleasant: we're left to wonder where exactly things went wrong and, above all, what now to think of others and our relations to them, what kind of relation is possible or prudent. On my account, then, disappointment originates in some uncertainty and results in even more. Experientially, disappointment doesn't yet draw a moral conclusion – it is instead the distressing state that arises where we recognize that others have failed to meet a higher expectation we have had of them.

Characterized in this way, it is possible to see why disappointment can be ethically valuable, why disappointment, despite its unpleasantness, is an emotion we might want included in the fullness of a good life. Disappointment rides on an orientation toward other people that often serves us well. Healthy personal and social relations profit where we can be well disposed toward others, where we *want* to think well of them – of their character, their capacities, and so forth. This has to do in part with the lack of any fact of the matter here. People really are an unpredictable muddle and what they can or might do will often live in an open, undetermined space. If we think well of them, they may be more likely to behave well; our thinking well of them can be social support for their being their better selves. They may rise to the higher expectations we have of them. This is in part why the Confucians recommend supportive social practices, a society that can 'soak' us in aspirational aims about what humanity can be.

Even as we recognize that disappointment can be ethically valuable, we can also see why the orientation it requires may be hard and even undesirable. To be disappointed, one must be vulnerable – vulnerable both to being wrong and to hoping for better than you will get. Longing for the better, and the disappointment to which it can give rise, invites practical risks. It is not just that we may risk being wrong, but where being wrong may leave us. One notable trouble is that frustrated hopes are not easily contained. Disappointment in one can generate wider suspicion and alienation. This explains why Confucius remarks of one of his more disappointing students that this student's untrustworthy talk led him to doubt the trustworthiness of people more generally (Eno, 2015, 5.10). Finding your hopes in one misplaced, you may come to doubt all. This is also why some faculty at my university came to feel alienated not just from the students who refused to mask, but from students generally. And, as one might imagine, experiencing disappointment in others can rather quickly transmute into becoming a disappointment oneself – as one becomes less open and well disposed, one grows less receptive to others' needs and situations. Burdened by the weight of frustrated expectation and hope, one is more likely to let others down.

Becoming good at disappointment would surely involve avoiding retraction from trying to be well disposed toward others. It would likewise involve cultivating a capacity to tolerate doubt, to holding in abeyance quick conclusions about those we perceive to have failed us and about our relation toward them. As with both grief and worry, much of the work would necessarily be internal. One needs to think hard and reflect well on the orientations that produce disappointment. When I am disappointed in other people, I need to ask: am I expecting too much of them? Have I misunderstood their capacities, attitudes, or relationship to myself? Are the hopes I had of others vain or misplaced, hopes not well grounded in understanding of what they can or should do? These – and surely other questions – are the sorts of internal considerations that should proceed when I have found myself disappointed by a friend, a colleague, or my fellow citizens.

While I don't discount the internal aspects of managing disappointment, I want to consider some of the social reasons it can be so hard to have some, to experience disappointment and to express that, out loud, where others can recognize it. My own disappointments in the last several years have been many and diverse. Perhaps because of this, I have noticed that the available social modes and moods for reactions to our present plight tend not to make much space for disappointment. We are, to be sure, permitted negative reactions to others and to our fellow citizens, but these have a direction that carries us well away from disappointment. One may, for example, freely express outrage and disdain. One may excoriate, condemn, and deride. One can confess bitter aggravation, hostility, and even enmity. Far less common are reactions that would betray that one expected better of people than they have given – that is, reactions that admit to vulnerability and thus to disappointment. Let me just target two of the more commonplace responses: outrage and cynicism. To be clear, outrage or even cynicism are not always unwarranted. There may well be circumstances in which either or both are well justified. My concern instead is with their *prevalence* and indeed their *ubiquity* as public and social responses to human failings, specifically as this can narrow or foreclose the space for expressions of disappointment.

When we receive evidence of human failings with outrage, we are of course angry and indeed angry in a form made fierce. In its most common form in our public discourse, outrage is characterized as a product of just-minded attention to the unjust structure of the world, as a righteous response to the many unrighteous ills of society. The now cliché slogan, 'If you aren't outraged, you aren't paying attention', serves not just to recommend outrage, but to implicitly condemn its absence. However, as a mode of social expression in response to human failing, outrage carries certain risks. This seems particularly the case where outrage is overused, where outrage becomes a kind of social currency that through overspending loses value it might otherwise have. Crucially, where we are socially encouraged to outrage, we may be primed to bypass any doubts that accompany disappointment, leaping to quick condemnation rather than reflection about just how failure may originate. If we presume – as I admit that I do – that human failures of all sorts tend to emerge from vexing and complex factors not easily or quickly understood, the rush to outrage may cost us understanding, and it may cost us the usually valuable connections on which disappointment rides. Outrage can operate, as it now too often does, as a distancing mechanism. Outrage is rarely directed at those for whom we care, those with whom we align ourselves. The targets of outrage are some others, people represented as our enemies or opponents. We are, put plainly, most often outraged at what *they* have done, but rarely with what *we* or *ours* have done – we do not identify or align ourselves in relation to those who so provoke us.

Like outrage, cynical responses to human failings also remark a distance between ourselves and others. In the context of my earlier example, some faculty at my university responded to our students' poor behaviour with a summary 'but of course'. The further explanations varied, but coalesced for the cynical among us as proof of what they already so well knew and never doubted, that the students were incapable of better. Both the distance and the certainties that the cynic thereby asserts are more totalizing than the outraged.

In public discourse, the cynic operates as seer, one whose knowledge of humanity is so complete that it forbids surprise. The cynic's doubts have all been settled. This sets the cynical apart not just from those who behave badly but from those who would evince surprise or harbour doubt. The cynical response will often operate as an implicit claim to special discernment, greeting each fresh ill as utterly foreseeable and predictable, an altogether too obvious twist of the ever-twisting knife of human life. In weariness with humanity, the cynic rejects ahead of time both good expectation and the hopes on which it rides. This is why the cynical response is more corrosive to our possibilities for disappointment. For it suggests that to have hoped that people could be otherwise-than-awful was naïve folly, a patently obvious mistake and error. Disappointment may, to the cynic, read as but stupidity, a failure to grant what evidence purportedly everywhere shows.

Disappointment can of course lead us into anger – the force of expectation and hope betrayed can yield to ire. Disappointment can also tempt us to be cynical, to truncate or even eliminate any higher expectations of others. Maintaining a capacity for disappointment, then, requires resisting these responses overtaking us entirely. Disappointment originates in connection to others, however tenuous that connection be, and, in its doubts, does not immediately resolve us against maintaining that connection. To be well disposed toward others is to harbour hope of them, to cast oneself toward them in some aspiration. It requires a measure, however modest, of trust

Amy Olberding

borne by connection and connectedness. It requires something of an *us* that is resistant to casting some offside as *them*, as well as resistant to expressive reactions that would assert or even finalize such separations. We must count others as connected to ourselves, and we must tolerate – indeed, maintain – a capacity to get things wrong, to expect more than we may get.

The Confucian interest in our social practices is, in part, a concern with how we make ourselves intelligible to each other morally – that is, the norms, practices, and rhetorics that we culturally share do moral work, signalling where we stand in relation to others and in relation to important values. Where expressions of outrage, cynicism, and the like dominate our shared discourse, disappointment risks losing its intelligibility, or of taking on meaning altered by the wilder reactions with which it must compete. As I have noted already, to the cynical, disappointment may but read as wilful ignorance or plain stupidity. More deeply, where disappointment loses traction in our shared catalogue of intelligible responses to human failing, it may lose traction in our internal capacities for feeling. That is, we may find it harder to feel that which cannot also be expressed. And the ways we find to hand for expressing ourselves may shape what responses we find possible. Trained to express outrage or cynicism, feeling otherwise – retaining both hope and doubt that these expressions so foreclose – grows a greater challenge.

My reasons for focusing on disappointment are, I expect, likely obvious, but let me admit just now that I have found far too much in the last few years disappointing. My shaken faiths just lately are too many here to list, but surely they can sum in saying simply that my prior expectations of the world have not been met. My expectations have been wrong, my hopes misplaced, but in their place now rises a confusion that, on my account of disappointment, comes as partner to that breach of expectation and of hope. And, in this, I have also found that too often, our public practices and rhetoric embrace responses that discourage me in this. The outraged would have my confusion sort itself into a fury. To do otherwise is to have failed to pay attention, to be wanting in those faculties of noticing all we ought. The cynical cannot bear a broken heart left to its grief. If I announce my sorrows, I should expect that some will say I earned them, that my faith in others or naïveté are my own undoing. I have not yet any explanation for my failed expectations. But neither have I much anywhere to go with my disappointment and the doubts it has induced. To the extent that you share something of this reaction, we ought to take a lesson from the Confucians and seek modes of public discourses that hold open avenues of hopeful connection, support for uncertain aspirations for humanity, and open up a tamer space for sorting out just where things have gone wrong. We ought, in short, seek to support each other in cultivating some of our bad emotions.

References

Robert Eno (trans.), *The Analects of Confucius* (2015). Published as open access: https://chinatxt.sitehost.iu.edu/Analects_of_Confucius_(Eno-2015).pdf.

Geoffrey Gorer, *Death, Grief, and Mourning* (Garden City and New York: Anchor Books, 1965).

Eric Hutton (trans.), *Xunzi: The Complete Text* (Princeton: Princeton University Press, 2014).

Amy Olberding, 'I Know Not "Seems": Grief for Parents in the *Analects*', in Amy Olberding and Philip J. Ivanhoe (eds.), *Mortality in Traditional Chinese Thought* (Albany: State University of New York Press, 2011), 153–176.

Wenhui Xie, 'Worries in my Heart', *Dao: A Journal of Comparative Philosophy* (forthcoming).

Vasubandhu on the First Person

NILANJAN DAS

Abstract

In classical South Asia, most philosophers thought that the self (if it exists at all) is what the first-person pronoun 'I' stands for. It is something that persists through time, undergoes conscious thoughts and experiences, and exercises control over actions. The Buddhists accepted the 'no self' thesis: they denied that such a self is substantially real. This gave rise to a puzzle for these Buddhists. If there is nothing substantially real that 'I' stands for, what are we talking about when we speak of ourselves? In this paper, I present one Buddhist answer to this question, an answer that emerges from the work of the Abhidharma thinker Vasubandhu (4th to 5th century CE).

1. Introduction

In Sanskrit philosophy, there is a debate between Buddhists and Brahmanical philosophers on the existence and the nature of the self (*ātman*). On both sides of the debate, the self is quite often understood as a constituent of a person – and sometimes as a person *simpliciter* – that has three characteristics. First, we can pick it out by means of the first-person pronoun 'I'. Second, it serves as a subject of mental states and as an agent who performs actions. Third, it persists through time. The Buddhists, without exception, defended the view that such a self isn't a basic constituent of reality. This is:

> *The 'No Self' Thesis*
> There is no substantially existent (*dravyasat*) or fundamentally existent (*paramārthasat*) self.

The Brahmanical thinkers – especially, those belonging to the text traditions of Nyāya and Mīmāṃsā – rejected this claim. Suppose we grant that the Buddhists are right: there is no substantially or fundamentally existent self. But, then, can the first-person pronoun 'I' refer to anything at all?

The question matters. If we want our ordinary self-ascriptions of mental states to be truth-apt, we should want the first-person pronoun to have a referent. If 'I' didn't refer to anything, self-ascriptions of mental states, like 'I am in pain', would simply be without a truth value – in the same way as 'Santa Claus lives in the

doi:10.1017/S1358246123000097   © The Royal Institute of Philosophy and the contributors 2023

Nilanjan Das

North Pole' is without a truth value. If we deny that self-ascriptions of mental states are truth-apt, it becomes hard to explain how inferences from first-person ascriptions of mental states to third-person ascriptions of mental states can be valid. For example, the conclusion, 'Nilanjan is in pain', seems to follow from the premises, 'I am in pain', and 'I am Nilanjan'. But, if the premises are not truth-apt (given that 'I' isn't a referring expression), it is difficult to explain how such inferences can be necessarily truth-preserving. But if we assign a referent to 'I', then it seems to commit us to the existence of a self.

To answer our question from a Buddhist perspective, I shall turn to the Abhidharma Buddhist philosopher Vasubandhu (4th to 5th century CE).[1] In his magisterial *Commentary on the Treasury of Abhidharma* (*Abhidharmakośabhāṣya*), Vasubandhu tried to reconcile the claim that there is no substantially or fundamentally existent self with the claim that 'I' is a referring expression. In this paper, I explain how he did so.

2. Vasubandhu on Existence, Truth, and Language

The *'No Self' Thesis* – though universally shared amongst Buddhists – is fleshed out in different ways by different factions of Buddhists, partly depending on the conception of substantial or fundamental existence that they work with. In the sixth chapter (*kośasthāna*) of the *Treasury of Abhidharma* (*Abhidharmakośa*), Vasubandhu distinguishes two modes of existence (*sattā*): fundamental (*pāramārthika*) and conventional (*sāṃvṛtika*). Roughly speaking, a fundamentally or substantially existent object is a basic constituent of reality: its nature and existence is (in some sense) independent of other entities. By contrast, a conventionally existent object isn't fundamentally existent, but rather something whose existence we accept because it is practically useful for us to do so. Here, I spell out this distinction, and explore what this view entails about the truth-aptness of our talk about ordinary objects.

---

[1]   The only other writer to have written explicitly about this topic with reference to Vasubandhu is Ganeri (2010, 2012, ch. 8). While Ganeri focuses on the Yogācāra writings of Vasubandhu, I only address the *Commentary on the Treasury of Abhidharma* (*Abhidharmakośabhāṣya*). On the controversy concerning the question whether the author of the *Commentary* is the same person as the author of these Yogācāra writings, see Gold (2014).

Vasubandhu on the First Person

In v. 6.4 of the *Treasury of Abhidharma* (*Abhidharmakośa*), Vasubandhu fleshes out the distinction between the two modes of existence as follows: 'That object, which is such that there is no awareness of it when it is divided or when there is an exclusion of other entities [from it] by means of awareness, is conventionally existent (*saṃvṛtisat*). For example, a pot [and water]. What is fundamentally existent is different' (AK 6.4).[2] On Vasubandhu's view, a conventionally existent object is something that ceases to be an object of awareness (*buddhi*),[3] i.e., an object of an experience or a thought, either (a) when it is divided or (b) when we mentally exclude other entities from it.

Vasubandhu unpacks the idea in his commentary (AKBh 334.4–6). For Vasubandhu, any fundamentally existent object (*paramārthasat*) is independent in two ways. First, it is *mereologically independent* of other things. So, it cannot be destroyed in virtue of being physically divided into parts. But an ordinary object like a pot depends on its parts for its existence. If I physically break the pot into the two pot-halves that it is made of, it will no longer exist. Then, we cannot correctly apply the concept 'pot' to the pot-halves that are left over: for example, we will no longer look at the pot-halves and think, 'That is a pot'. That is the sense in which the awareness of a pot ceases when it is physically broken down into parts. Second, any fundamentally existent object is *conceptually independent* of other things. Take water. We can mentally analyse the nature of water into other things: qualities such as visible form (*rūpa*), liquidity (*sneha*), and so on. Once we have mentally excluded these qualities from something, nothing remains of the intrinsic nature of the water. We cannot imagine

[2] The square brackets mark an emendation to the Patna edition of the text (edited by Prahlad Pradhan): the text reads '*ghaṭārthavat*' instead of '*ghaṭāmbuvat*'. For the corresponding emendation in the Varanasi edition (edited by Dvārikādāsa Śāstrī), see AKBh_D 889.12.

[3] Here, I shall translate the Sanskrit term '*jñāna*' and its synonyms such as '*buddhi*', '*pratīti*', and '*pratyaya*' as either 'awareness' or 'state of awareness'. Typically, this Sanskrit word picks out contentful occurrent mental states, like experiences and thoughts. But, often, it is translated as 'cognition' rather than 'awareness'. This is slightly misleading because in contemporary philosophy and cognitive science, the term 'cognition' is reserved for mental states, like beliefs and judgements, whose contents can be verbally reported and directly used for reasoning and the control of action. But, for at least some Sanskrit philosophers, a *jñāna* needn't be like this: non-conceptual perceptual experiences count as *jñāna*s, but do not have contents that can be verbally reported or directly used for reasoning and the control of action. So, I choose the more neutral terms 'awareness' and 'state of awareness' to refer to all *jñāna*s.

something that is devoid of the characteristic qualities of water and still think of it as water. That is the sense in which the awareness of water ceases when the characteristic qualities of water, e.g., its visible form and so on, are mentally excluded from it.

For Abhidharma Buddhists like Vasubandhu, the only fundamental constituents of reality are certain entities – called the *dharmas* – that are both mereologically and conceptually independent of other things. Typically, these Ābhidharmikas divide the *dharmas* into five kinds: (a) matter (*rūpa*), (b) mental events (*citta*), (c) associated mental factors (*caitta*), (d) conditioned factors that are dissociated from the mental (*cittaviprayuktasaṃskāra*), and (e) causally unconditioned *dharmas*. However, amongst the Ābhidharmikas, Sautrāntika philosophers like Vasubandhu think that categories (d) and (e) are empty. For instance, Vasubandhu explicitly argues that all *dharmas* are causally conditioned and momentary: they arise from a collection of causal conditions and cannot persist through time (AKBh 92.4–5 ad AK 2.55, AKBh 193.2–194.14 ad AK 4.2–3). What, then, are these causally conditioned, momentary *dharmas* according to Vasubandhu? According to one natural interpretation, such *dharmas* are *tropes* or *property-particulars*.[4] Vasubandhu takes matter to be of two kinds: (a) the *material elements* (*mahābhūta*) like the earth element, the water element, and so on, and (b) *derived matter* (*upādāyarūpa* or *bhautika*), i.e., physical qualities that are causally dependent on the material elements. The material elements are simply property-like entities: the earth element is solidity, the water element is fluidity, the fire element is heat, and the wind element is motion. Similarly, derived matter includes perceptible qualities like visible form (*rūpa*), odour (*gandha*), and flavour (*rasa*), which are derived from the material elements. By contrast, mental events are conscious or unconscious states of awareness, while the associated mental factors are those mental tropes that invariably accompany mental events, i.e., concepts or mental labels (*saṃjñā*), hedonic states (*vedanā*) like pleasure and pain, and conditioned forces (*saṃskāra*) like intention, mental habits, and so on.

Vasubandhu claims that all these fundamentally existent objects are mereologically and conceptually independent of other things (AKBh 334.7–11). Even after a visible material object has been whittled down to its mereologically simple constituents, or other entities like flavour have been mentally excluded from its nature, the awareness of the intrinsic nature of visible form doesn't cease. This is because the existence and the intrinsic nature of visible form are

---

[4]   See Ganeri (2001), Goodman (2004), and Siderits (2007).

neither mereologically reducible to simpler parts nor mentally analysable into other things. Since visible form is both mereologically and conceptually independent in this way, it can be treated as fundamentally existent. The same, according to Vasubandhu, is true of other physical and mental tropes that he regards as the fundamental constituents of reality.

For Vasubandhu, any object whose existence is practically useful for us to accept but fails to be either mereologically or conceptually independent in this way, can at best be *conventionally existent*. Most objects that we ordinarily treat as existent – tables and chairs, pots and cloths, chariots and carts – are like this. However, Vasubandhu emphasises that this distinction between the two modes of existence does not mean that we speak *falsely* when we assert the existence of conventionally existent objects like a pot or water. He says:

> However, the label 'conventional' is applied to those objects [such as a pot and water] alone. So, people who say on the basis of convention, 'The pot and the water exist', have in fact spoken the truth, not something false. Thus, this is conventional truth. (AKBh 334.6–7)

On one way of understanding the point, corresponding to the two modes of existence, there are two notions of truth. The content of a state of awareness (or a linguistic utterance) is conventionally true (*saṃvṛtisatya*) just in case that content presupposes or entails the existence of fundamentally non-existent objects, but still is practically useful for us to accept because that content indirectly reflects or tracks the way fundamentally existent objects are. By contrast, the content of a state of awareness is fundamentally true (*paramārthasatya*) just in case that content does not presuppose or entail the existence of any fundamentally non-existent objects *and* accurately reflects how things are with the fundamentally existent objects. The contents of our ordinary states of awareness – our experiences and thoughts about ordinary objects like a pot or water – can only be conventionally true. The states of awareness that represent what is ultimately true are much harder to attain.

After introducing the distinction between the modes of existence, Vasubandhu mentions a view of earlier Buddhist teachers, according to which what is ultimately true can be grasped only by means of two kinds of awareness: an *extraordinary* state of awareness (*lokottarajñāna*) and an *ordinary* state of awareness that is obtained on the basis of that extraordinary awareness (*tatpṛṣṭhalabdhajñāna*) (AKBh 334.11–13). The first is an epistemically direct (i.e., non-inferential), non-conceptual insight into reality, which arises when a Buddhist practitioner achieves meditative equipoise on the path of insight (*darśanamārga*) after having listened to Buddhist teachings and rationally reflected and meditated on them. By contrast, the second kind of awareness is an ordinary experience or thought that is influenced by that earlier direct and non-conceptual awareness. In the second kind of awareness, ordinary objects like tables and chairs might appear as real, but the practitioner will no longer assent to that false appearance.

There is an important lesson to be drawn from this discussion about how Vasubandhu understands the relationship between language and reality. For Vasubandhu, the realm of fundamentally existent objects is inaccessible to language. Contents that are conveyed by means of linguistic utterances proliferate distinctions – the distinction between qualities and substances, between properties and their bearers, between actions and their agents, and so on – which do not exist amongst fundamentally existent objects. Yet, this does not mean that language is inherently deceptive. Vasubandhu makes this point while discussing the Buddhist doctrine of dependent arising. Roughly speaking, this doctrine says that everything is causally conditioned: existent objects arise by depending on other existent objects. The Sanskrit term for 'dependent arising' is '*pratītyasa-mutpāda*': '*pratītya*' is a gerund that means 'having depended' whereas '*samutpāda*' just means 'arising'. So, the term literally means 'arising having depended on something else'. But, as a grammarian opponent notes, this implies that the object which arises, and therefore serves as the agent (*kartṛ*) with respect to the action or event (*kriyā*) of arising, does so by initially entering into a state of depending on something else. This is incoherent: since that object could not have existed before it arose, it could not have antecedently depended on something else. While commenting on the grammarians' distinction between an action (conveyed by the verb in a sentence) and the agent (conveyed by the expression declined in the nominative case), Vasubandhu says:

> Moreover, the following distinction between the agent and the action, which belongs to the grammarians (*śābdikī*), is unestablished: 'That which arises is the agent, and the arising is the action'. And, here, we do not find any action of arising which is distinct from the object that arises. Therefore, there is no deception in linguistic usage. But, in fact, the following is the meaning of the utterance: 'When this is present, the arising of this occurs; due to the arising of this, that arises'. This content is what is said to be 'dependent arising'. (AKBh 138 15–17 ad AK 3.28ab)

Even though the literal content of a linguistic utterance may be misleading insofar as it involves distinctions that are fundamentally nonexistent, nevertheless, in most cases of successful linguistic usage, it is possible to recover a content that isn't misleading to the same degree: a content that fits the way things are at the level of fundamental reality. Vasubandhu would agree with other Buddhists that the relationship between language and reality is dysfunctional: language, without some independent epistemic work on our part, cannot help us see how the world really is. But it is not so dysfunctional that we cannot recover any fundamentally true content at all from the literal contents of linguistic utterances. This idea – namely, that fundamental truths can somehow be salvaged from misleading literal contents conveyed by language – will be useful for understanding Vasubandhu's view about the first-person pronoun 'I'.

3. Reductionism about 'Self'

It's now time to return to *The 'No Self' Thesis*. In the ninth chapter of his *Commentary* – sometimes called 'The Ascertainment of the Person' (*Pudgalaviniścaya*)[5] – Vasubandhu argues that a person is nothing but a causally connected stream of momentary physical and mental tropes called the aggregates (*skandha*). There are five aggregates: matter (*rūpa*) and mental events (*citta*) along with associated mental factors such as hedonic states (*vedanā*), mental labels (*saṃjñā*), and conditioned forces (*saṃskāra*) like intentions and mental habits. These correspond to parts of the body as well as the physical and mental events that accompany it. A causally connected stream of these tropes is mereologically dependent on its constituents, and it is temporally extended. So, on Vasubandhu's view, it cannot be fundamentally existent. 'Therefore', Vasubandhu concludes, 'a person exists as a matter of conventional designation (*prajñaptisat*) just like a heap or a stream'. (AKBh 467.12–13) Where does this leave us with regard to the self?

Vasubandhu wants to reject two distinct views about the expression 'self'. Call the first *substantialism*, the view that the expression 'self' refers to a substantially or fundamentally existent object. Call the second *eliminativism*, the view that the expression 'self' refers neither to any substantially or fundamentally existent object nor to any collection of substantially or fundamentally existent objects.

---

[5]   For translations of this section, see Duerlinger (2003) and Kapstein (2003).

Nilanjan Das

The first view was defended by the Brahmanical thinkers, such as the Nyāya and Vaiśeṣika philosophers, who took the self to be a fundamentally real inner constituent of a person, which serves as the subject of mental states and as an agent of actions. By contrast, the second view was defended by other Buddhists – Mādhyamikas like Nāgārjuna (2nd century CE) and Candrakīrti (6th century CE) – who argued that the self is neither any fundamentally existent object that is distinct from aggregates, nor reducible to either the aggregates or a collection of aggregates. Vasubandhu wants to defend:

> *Reductionism about 'Self'*
> The expression 'self' does not refer to any substantially or fundamentally existent object, but does refer to a collection of substantially or fundamentally existent objects.

In a remarkable passage in the third chapter of his *Commentary*, Vasubandhu distinguishes his position from that of the Brahmanical thinkers (while implicitly distancing himself from other Buddhists):

> Now, here, the outsiders [i.e., the non-Buddhists], having accepted the theory of the self, come forward: 'If it is asserted that a sentient being passes to another world, then a self is established'. This very claim is refuted:
>
> AK 3.18a. The self doesn't exist.
>
> What sort of self [doesn't exist]? That which is imagined to make a connection with other aggregates after having thrown away these aggregates. Such an inner agent of action (*antarvyāpārapuruṣa*) doesn't exist. This has been said by the Blessed One, 'There is action, and there is maturation [of the fruits of action]. But no agent is apprehended, who throws away these aggregates and makes a connection with other aggregates elsewhere. For there is a formula pertaining to the *dharma*s (*dharmasaṃketa*). [To explain:] with respect to that [rebirth], there is this formula pertaining to the *dharma*s: namely, 'When this is present, that arises', which is just an expanded statement of dependent arising'. If this is so, what sort of self is not refuted?
>
> AK 3.18b. Just the mere aggregates alone.
>
> If the mere aggregates are figuratively described (*upacaryate*) as 'the self', then that is not refuted. (AKBh 129.5–14 ad AK 3.18ab)

Under the first conception, the self is an inner agent of activity (*antarvyāpārapuruṣa*), which exists independently of the aggregates and acquires new aggregates when it is reborn and throws away the old aggregates when it dies. But there is a second conception of the self on which there is no such inner agent of activity. On this view, the term 'self" is just figuratively or non-literally applied to the aggregates themselves. Vasubandhu emphasizes that the momentary aggregates cannot literally transmigrate (AKBh 129.14ff ad AK 3.18b). But we can figuratively say that a stream of aggregates, conditioned by afflictions, enters a womb, just as we can figuratively say that a lamp moves to a different place.

Elsewhere, Vasubandhu explains what this misleading view about the self (*ātmadṛṣṭi*) is:

> The self-view ascribes unreal selfhood to real objects – aggregates such as matter [i.e., the body] and so on – treating them as an agent, as a subject, and as being under one's control. And extreme views (*antagrāhadṛṣṭi*) [e.g., the view that the self is eternal or that the self is destroyed at death] and the rest arise from that self-view. So, they are said to be lacking any corresponding real object (*avastukāḥ*). (AKBh 375.2–4 ad AK 6.58ab)

On Vasubandhu's view, there is in fact no fundamentally existent constituent of a person that can serve as a subject of mental states at different times, or as an agent of actions, or as something over which we have perfect control. So, when we talk as if there is such a self, we must be ascribing these uninstantiated properties associated with the self to the impermanent aggregates themselves. In doing so, we are treating the aggregates as what they are not: as a subject, as an agent, as something under our control. This view that there is a substantial self (*satkāyadṛṣṭi*) forms the basis of different extreme philosophical views about the self like eternalism (*śāśvatadṛṣṭi*), i.e, the Brahmanical view that the self is a permanent substantial entity that can survive death and be reborn, and annihilationism (*ucchedavāda*), i.e., the Cārvāka or Lokāyata view that the self is just the living body and therefore endures through our lifetime but then is destroyed at death. And these extreme views about the self, in turn, give rise to certain afflictions (*kleśa*), e.g., one's love for oneself and what belongs to oneself (*ātmātmīyasneha*), that ultimately are the cause of all our physical and mental suffering. According to Vasubandhu, since these afflictions are based on an illusory awareness of the aggregates as what they are not, they can be abandoned through insight (*darśanaheya*), i.e., by seeing the aggregates as what they are.

Nilanjan Das

The Buddhist view that Vasubandhu prefers is the source of that insight. On this conception of the self, the term 'self' refers to a causally connected stream of aggregates. It steers clear of both the extremes of eternalism and annihilationism. Since the stream of aggregates consists of aggregates that are destroyed at every moment, there is no permanent fundamentally existent self. Yet, since a stream of aggregates can survive death and be reborn in virtue of new causal connections with new sets of aggregates, the self isn't destroyed at death.

Why should we accept this reductionist view of the self? Vasubandhu offers the following argument:

> [The Brahmanical opponent:] Still, how is this known, namely that the expression 'self' applies to a stream of aggregates, not to any other referent?
> [Reply:] On the basis of the absence of direct awareness (*pratyakṣa*) and inference. (AKBh 461.5–6)

The argument here should be construed as an argument from the absence of evidence.

Non-Vacuity
The expression 'self' refers to something, i.e., an entity that has the three characteristics associated with our ordinary conception of the self: (i) being the referent of 'I', (ii) subjecthood and agency, and (iii) persistence through time.

Knowability
If the expression 'self' refers to anything, then its referent can be established either by means of direct apprehension (or perception) or inference.

Absence of Evidence
Neither direct awareness nor inference can establish that there is a constituent of a person, which exists separately from the aggregates and plays the roles assigned to the referent of 'self'.

Role Sufficiency
The roles assigned to the referent of 'self' can be played by a stream of aggregates.

Conclusion
So, the expression 'self' refers to a stream of aggregates.

For now, let's assume that *Non-Vacuity* is true: the term 'self' (as we ordinarily use it) isn't empty, i.e., it does refer to something. What about *Knowability*? Vasubandhu assumes that, if the term 'self' refers to anything, its referent must be something that we can know either through direct apprehension, i.e., some form of perception, or by means of inference. To motivate this premise, Vasubandhu seems to appeal to the principle that any *dharma* that exists can be known (or knowable) by either direct apprehension (in the absence of obstructions) or inference. This principle – as stated – seems questionable. Why couldn't there be existent *dharma*s that can neither be directly apprehended nor known by means of inference? A better version of *Knowability* would be weaker; it would say that we don't have any reason to posit a *dharma* that cannot be known either by direct apprehension or by inference. That follows from a principle of parsimony: we should not populate our ontology with entities that we have no reason to posit.

Turn now to *Absence of Evidence*. Under normal conditions, the six intentional objects of the senses – the sensible qualities such as visible form – and our own conscious mental events can be directly apprehended when they aren't obstructed from us. In the case of unobservable objects such as the senses themselves, we can make a causal inference from observed phenomena. For instance, from the absence of perception in blind or deaf people and from the presence of perception in non-blind or non-deaf people, we can infer that perception requires a distinct cause, i.e., a sense, which is missing in blind or deaf people. But a self that is distinct from the five aggregates cannot be directly inferred or inferred in this way. The thought may be spelled out as follows. If we take a human body and pull it apart, we don't perceive any such thing as a self other than the physical elements that constitute it; similarly, when we introspect, we don't come across anything other than the mental factors such as hedonic states, mental labels, *etc*. Similarly, as Vasubandhu claims later, there are no observed phenomena that can only be causally explained by positing the existence of a self that is distinct from the five aggregates. This supports *Absence of Evidence*.

Together, these three premises yield the conclusion that the term 'self' doesn't refer to anything other than the aggregates themselves. It doesn't yield the conclusion that Vasubandhu wants: the claim that the term 'self' refers to a stream of aggregates. This is where the final premise – *Role Sufficiency* – becomes relevant (though it is left unstated by Vasubandhu). If we could show that a stream of aggregates can perform all or many of the roles – such as being the referent of the first person pronoun 'I', being a subject of mental states, being an agent of actions – that are associated with the referent of 'self', a stream of aggregates will indeed be one of the most natural candidates for being the referent of the term 'self'. But, then, given that the term 'self' cannot refer to anything other than the aggregates themselves, we will end up with the conclusion that it must refer to a stream of aggregates. This is precisely what *Reductionism about 'Self'* says.

This, then, could be used to derive the conclusion that Vasubandhu ends the passage with: namely, that there is no self. On the one hand, if we are working with the Brahmanical conception of the self, then there cannot be a conventionally or fundamentally existent object that answers to that conception of the self, since the term 'self' simply doesn't refer to any inner agent of activity that is distinct from the aggregates or from a stream of aggregates. On the other hand, if we are working with the thinner Abhidharma conception of the self, then there can be a conventionally existent object that answers to that conception of the self, since the term 'self' does refer to a stream of aggregates that has conventional existence. But the self still cannot be treated as fundamentally existent, because that stream of aggregates will be either mereologically dependent on its constituents, or temporally extended. In either case, there will be no fundamentally existent self.

Suppose we accept *Knowability* and *Absence of Evidence*. What we have not seen so far is any justification for either *Non-Vacuity*, i.e., the claim that the term 'self' refers to something that has three characteristics of the self – namely, being the referent of 'I', subjecthood and agency, and persistence through time – or *Role Sufficiency*, i.e., the claim that these three roles can be played by a stream of aggregates. To motivate *Non-Vacuity,* Vasubandhu would need an independent theory of linguistic reference, which explains why – despite our false beliefs about the self – our uses of the term 'self' do pick out something that plays these roles. To motivate *Role Sufficiency*, Vasubandhu would have to argue that the aggregates can indeed play these roles. In the next two sections, I consider whether he can show this.

4. The Reductionist Semantics of the First-Person Pronoun

Role Sufficiency commits Vasubandhu to a reductionist view about 'I'. If a stream of aggregates is sufficient to play the roles associated with the self, and one of those roles is being the referent of 'I', then 'I' must refer to a stream of aggregates. This yields a kind of reductionism about 'I', the view that, in any context of utterance, 'I' does not refer to a substantially or fundamentally existent object, but does refer to a collection of substantially or fundamentally existent objects. In the ninth chapter of his *Commentary on the Treasury of Abhidharma*, Vasubandhu offers two arguments for this view.

Vasubandhu's arguments occur in the context of a response to an objection raised by a Brahmanical thinker.

> [The Brahmanical opponent:] If the self doesn't exist, for the sake of what does one commence actions?
> [Vasubandhu:] For the sake of a purpose like, 'I would be happy', and 'I wouldn't suffer'.
> [The Brahmanical opponent:] What is this thing called 'I', which is the intentional object of the 'I'-awareness (*ahaṅkāra*)?
> [Vasubandhu:] That awareness has the aggregates as its intentional object. (AKBh 476.4–5)

The Brahmanical thinker asks how one could even undertake actions (intentionally) if there were no fundamentally existent self. Consider our self-interested actions, actions we undertake out of future-directed self-concern. When I walk out of my home on a rainy day, I typically take my umbrella with me so that I don't get wet later. Or, when I save a part of my salary each month, I do it precisely because I wish to be comfortable when I retire. As Vasubandhu's Brahmanical opponent notes, this kind of future-directed self-concern is driven by first-personal thoughts that take the form, 'If I were to save money now, I would be happy later', or 'If I were to take my umbrella, I wouldn't catch a cold from the rain and suffer later'. These judgements about the consequences of my actions could be accurate only if the two occurrences of 'I' – in the antecedent and the consequent of the conditional – were to refer to a self that persists through time, performs actions intentionally, and later experiences the happiness or the suffering that results from those actions. But, if there were no self, then how could we account for the contentfulness of such judgements? And, if those judgements weren't contentful, then how can we rationally plan and (in some cases, successfully) undertake actions on the basis of such judgements?

Vasubandhu's response to this challenge is to say that, even if there were no fundamentally existent self, the first-personal judgements of the form, 'I would be happy', or 'I wouldn't suffer', needn't be false or without a truth value. For the first-personal ingredient of those judgements – the 'I'-awareness – could still be directed at the aggregates. In other words, when we use the concept or expression 'I' in our thought or discourse, what we pick out are the aggregates. Vasubandhu offers two arguments for the claim that the first-person pronoun 'I' refers to the aggregates.

Nilanjan Das

> [The Brahmanical opponent:] How is this known?
> [Reply:] Because there is love (*sneha*) for them, and because there is co-referentiality [of the 'I'-awareness] with states of awareness that take the form 'fair', and so on. In states of awareness that take the form, 'I am fair', 'I am dark', 'I am fat', 'I am thin', 'I am old', and 'I am young', this 'I'-awareness is observed to be co-referential with states of awareness that take the form, 'fair', and the like. But these are not features of a self. On that basis, too, it is known that this 'I'-awareness arises with respect to the aggregates. (AKBh 476.5–8)

The first of these arguments – which Vasubandhu does not elaborate on – is what we may call the *argument from self-love*. The rough thought is that our peculiar love or affection for ourselves isn't directed at anything that is distinct from the aggregates, but rather at the aggregates themselves. When I take an umbrella with me, I do so out of concern for my future aggregates, so that this stream of aggregates won't include states of pain in the future. Similarly, when I save money, I do so out of concern for my future aggregates, so that those aggregates would be accompanied by states of pleasure arising from comfort in the future. But, presumably, whatever 'I' refers to is the object of this kind of love or affection for oneself. This, in turn, implies that the aggregates themselves – or a stream of those aggregates – is what 'I' refers to.

Turn now to Vasubandhu's second argument: it is what we may call *an argument from self-ascriptions*. It proceeds from the observation that 'I'-awareness and states of awareness that take the form 'fair' can be co-referential (*samānādhikaraṇa*), i.e., can be directed at the same intentional objects. If I ascribe physical properties to myself by means of ascriptions like, 'I am fat', or 'I am dark', the predicates 'am dark' and 'am fat' apply to the same object that 'I' refers to. But these properties that I am ascribing cannot be the properties of the self as conceived by the Brahmanical thinkers, a self that is distinct from the physical aggregates. So, if these ascriptions are indeed correct, the referent of 'I' cannot be distinct from the physical aggregates.

I don't find myself persuaded by these arguments, and neither should you. Start with the argument from self-love. We can reconstruct it as follows.

P1. The referent of 'I' serves as the object of a peculiar kind of affection or concern, what Vasubandhu and other Buddhist thinkers call self-love (*ātmasneha*).

P2. The aggregates are the object of such self-love or self-concern.

C. So, the aggregates are the referent of 'I'.

Here, the Brahmanical thinkers wouldn't deny P1: typically Nyāya and Mīmāṃsā philosophers are happy to grant that the object of self-love is in fact what 'I' refers to. However, such Brahmanical thinkers would resist P2. They could argue that if there is any object of self-love – more specifically, the kind of future-directed self-concern that underlies many of our ordinary actions – then it cannot be the momentary aggregates, but must be a unitary self that performs actions at an earlier time and later comes to experience the results of those actions.

Vasubandhu seems to reject this line of objection elsewhere. In the third chapter of his *Commentary on the Treasury of Abhidharma*, Vasubandhu considers why *bodhisattva*s (i.e., morally ideal beings that can achieve enlightenment but delay it so as to alleviate the suffering of others) undertake altruistic actions (AKBh 182.7–15 ad AK 3.94a). His opponent here is a psychological egoist, who thinks that no one acts out of any motive other than self-concern. In response, Vasubandhu offers an account of self-interested actions. Under this account, we ordinarily undertake self-interested actions because we are unfamiliar with the true characteristics of the conditioned factors that constitute us as persons. Persons are nothing over and above streams of aggregates, and these aggregates are causally conditioned. As such, they share a number of general characteristics (*sāmānyalakṣaṇa*) such as impermanence and so on. However, we ordinarily overlook these aspects of the aggregates, and wrongly conceptualize them as a unitary self that persists through time, performs actions, and then later experiences the result of those actions. This habitual misconception of ourselves, in turn, makes us think that there genuinely is a fundamentally real distinction between ourselves and others. This belief in the self-other distinction gives rise to the peculiar kind of concern – what Vasubandhu calls self-love – towards the aggregates that we falsely take to be our unitary selves. How does such self-love manifest itself? According to Vasubandhu, it motivates us to perform prudentially rational actions, like saving money, that involve making present sacrifices for the sake of our own future well-being. However, the *bodhisattva*s are not subject to this misconception about the aggregates. Since they habituate themselves to a picture of reality on which there is no strict self-other distinction, they are able to withdraw their self-love from the aggregates and increase their concern for others. This motivates them to perform altruistic actions that require them to subject themselves to suffering for the sake of the well-being of others.

This defence of the possibility of altruism might be taken to support P2. But, on reflection, it is unsatisfactory. Suppose, for the purposes of supporting P2, we were to rely on Vasubandhu's claim that our attitude of self-love is based on a misconception of the aggregates as a unitary self. That would make the argument from self-love flagrantly circular; for one of its premises would now be based on something very much like the conclusion of the argument. Thus, the argument strikes me as dubious.

So, consider the argument from self-ascriptions:

P1*. Our ordinary self-ascriptions – such as 'I am fair', 'I am dark', and so on – can correctly ascribe physical characteristics to the referent of 'I.'

P2*. They can only be correct if physical aggregates can be the referent of 'I.'

C*. So, the physical aggregates can be the referent of 'I.'

Like the previous argument, this argument would fail to convince the Brahmanical thinkers. Vasubandhu himself anticipates two objections against it.

There is a figurative ascription of selfhood to the body, even though it [merely] assists the self. For example, [in the case of the awareness], 'Whoever this is, it is just I, it is just this servant of mine', there is a figurative ascription of selfhood even to someone who assists [oneself], but there is no 'I'-awareness. And if the objective basis [i.e., the independently existing intentional object of the 'I'-awareness] is the body, why doesn't it have some other body as its objective basis? (AKBh 476.9–476.11)

There are two distinct objections here. The first objection is an *objection from figurative use*. The claim is that ascriptions of physical properties like 'I am fair', and so on, are not literally true; they are figuratively true. Sometimes, we apparently ascribe to an object a property that in fact belongs to something to which the object is related. Consider the following pairs of sentences (Nunberg, 1995):

(1a) I am parked out the back.
(1b) My car is parked out the back.
(2a) Yeats is still widely read.
(2b) Yeats' poetry is still widely read.

In at least some contexts, (1a) can express the same meaning as (1b), and (2a) can express the same meaning as (2b). One might argue that the sentences (1a) and (2a) aren't literally true. But we can infer (given the context) that they have the same meaning as (1b) and (2b) respectively, and therefore infer that the expressions 'I', and 'Yeats' in fact are being used non-literally or figuratively to refer to other things that are related to the semantic referents of these expressions: 'I' refers to the speaker's car, while 'Yeats' refers to Yeats' poetry. In the same way, as Vasubandhu notes, one can sometimes figuratively speak of one's servant as 'I' because one's servant assists oneself. The important point is that, in these cases, the speaker doesn't literally identify Yeats with his poetry, or herself with her car or servant. The same diagnosis can apply to apparent self-ascriptions of physical properties. When we say, 'I am fair', or 'I am dark', we may be figuratively using 'I' to speak of our bodies. So, these self-ascriptions needn't be taken to correctly ascribe physical characteristics to the semantic referent of 'I'. Therefore, the argument from self-ascriptions needn't be sound.

The second objection is an *objection from arbitrariness*: if our own body could be the objective basis (*ālambana*) – the independently existing intentional object – of our 'I'-awareness, then why could someone else's body not also be picked out by the first-person pronoun? Here is one way of understanding the worry. On Vasubandhu's view about the first-person pronoun, the first-person pronoun can *literally* refer to one's body, e.g., when one says:

(3a)   I am fair.

But there are other contexts where the first-person pronoun can literally refer to something that is distinct from a person's body, e.g., when a person says:

(3b)   My body is fair.

In other words, the first-person pronoun, on this view, is *doubly* context-sensitive. On the one hand, it can refer to the mental or physical aggregates associated with different persons in different contexts of utterances. On the other hand, depending on the context, it may refer to different sets of aggregates associated with the same person. This, in turn, opens up room for the following question. What are the contextual factors that determine which aggregates will be picked out by 'I' in a particular context? If the answer is simply that this is determined by the speaker's intention, then the semantics of the first-person pronoun will be too unconstrained. For, now, if a speaker intends to pick someone else's body by means the first-person pronoun 'I', she may indeed succeed in doing so. As a result, the pronoun may indeed end up referring to the physical aggregates associated with another person in that context. But, surely, that will be a misuse of the expression 'I'. A natural way of blocking this result will be to say that the first-person pronoun has a fixed referent that doesn't vary depending on the context (as Vasubandhu suggests). And the easiest way of implementing this strategy will be to say that ascriptions like (3a) are at best only figuratively or non-literally true; in such cases, the use of 'I' in such ascriptions is intended to convey the same meaning that is ordinarily conveyed by the definite description 'my body'.

It's time to take stock. In this section, we have considered two arguments for the conclusion that the first-person pronoun refers to the aggregates or a stream of aggregates. But neither of these arguments seems to succeed. There is no obvious way for Vasubandhu to defend the argument from self-love without making it flagrantly circular. And the argument from self-ascriptions of physical properties can be resisted either by appealing to the possibility of figurative uses of 'I' or by appealing to the danger that, if this argument were sound, someone else's body could also be picked out by 'I'.

5. 'I' and the Causal Theory of Reference

To see how Vasubandhu might resist these objections to his two arguments, it's best to begin with his response to the second objection from arbitrariness to the argument from self-ascriptions. He writes:

> [Vasubandhu:] Because there is no connection. For, whatever body or mental event with which this 'I'-awareness is connected, the 'I'-awareness arises with respect to that, and not with respect to anything else. The reason is that there has been a habituation of this kind in the beginningless cycle of rebirth.
> [The Brahmanical opponent:] And what is that connection?
> [Vasubandhu:] The connection between an effect and its cause.
> (AKBh 476.11–13)

The claim is that 'I'-awareness is directed at the physical or mental aggregates – the body or the mental events – that it is causally connected to (in an appropriate way), but not at anything else. For Vasubandhu, the 'I'-awareness is one mental event amongst others, embedded through certain relations of causal dependence within a causally connected stream of physical and mental aggregates. So, when we think first-personal thoughts, we can only pick out by 'I' other physical or mental aggregates that are part of the relevant stream, but not physical or mental aggregates that fail to overlap with that stream. That is why 'I' cannot refer to a body that doesn't overlap with the physical aggregates that are part of the stream of aggregates that the 'I'-awareness is part of. Why is that? This is because – as Vasubandhu says – we have formed the habit of applying the concept or the conventional designation 'I' to the physical or mental aggregates that the relevant 'I'-awareness is part of.

I wish to show that this theory of what 'I' refers to follows from a more general theory of reference that Vasubandhu subscribes to. The aim of this section is to spell out this theory and explore its consequences for the first-person pronoun.

5.1 The Causal Theory of Reference

We see this theory in action when Vasubandhu argues against certain Buddhists – the Vātsīputrīyas, sometimes known as the Personalists (*pudgalavādins*) – who reject the Abhidharma reductionist theory of persons.

The Vātsīputrīyas don't think that persons just are the aggregates connected in some way. Rather, they claim that persons – even though they ontologically and conceptually depend on the aggregates – are nevertheless irreducible to the aggregates. The Vātsīputrīyas, in effect, endorse what looks like an emergentist theory of persons:[6] persons are emergent entities that arise and are conceptualised when the aggregates enter into certain relations with each other, but nevertheless have novel properties and causal powers that cannot be explained solely in terms of the properties and the causal powers of the aggregates themselves. But, as they are represented in the ninth chapter of Vasubandhu's *Commentary*, they state this idea in a somewhat puzzling manner. They say that the relation between the aggregates and persons is indeterminable or inexplicable (*avakta-vya*): while the conventional designation 'person' is applied in dependence on the aggregates, a person can be neither determinately identical (i.e., reducible) to the aggregates, nor determinately completely distinct (i.e., independent) of them.

In response to this theory, Vasubandhu asks what exactly the Vātsīputrīyas mean when they say that the conventional designation 'person' is applied in dependence on the aggregates (AKBh 461.20–24). Either the conventional designation 'person' is applied after one has apprehended the aggregates, or its application is caused by the aggregates themselves. In either case, the conventional designation will only pick out the aggregates and nothing else. The example that Vasubandhu gives of the first kind of application is

---

[6] For discussion, see Priestley (1999), Châu and Boin-Webb (1999), and Carpenter (2015).

the application of the conventional designation 'milk'. On Vasubandhu's view, we apply the conventional designation 'milk' in our ordinary discourse by initially becoming perceptually aware of the sensible qualities of milk such as its visible form, its taste, and so on. If that is right, then, Vasubandhu claims, our conventional designation 'milk' can only pick out those qualities alone, not any substance that exists over and above them, since only the initial awareness of those qualities triggers the application of the relevant term. Similarly, if an awareness of the aggregates triggers the application of 'person', the term can only refer to the aggregates themselves, since the awareness of those aggregates alone is responsible for the application of the term. And, Vasubandhu adds, if the aggregates were to produce the application of 'person' without the mediation of any such awareness, even then the same result would follow; for we would be tracking those aggregates alone through our application of that term.

Vasubandhu later returns to the first point, again, while responding to the Vatsīputrīyas' claim that the person is neither determinately identical to the aggregates nor determinately distinct from them (AKBh 463.10–17). Vasubandhu argues that there is no room for such indeterminacy given the following principle:

The Causal Theory of Reference
A conventional designation or a concept E refers to an object of kind K if, in competent users of E, applications of E are (typically or normally) caused by an initial awareness of objects of kind K.

Take the case of milk and water. Suppose that we are competent users of the expressions 'milk' and 'water', and that we typically apply these expressions in ordinary discourse on the basis of detecting their sensible qualities like colours, tactile qualities, flavours, odours and so on. So, Vasubandhu's causal theory of reference would predict that these expressions refer to these four kinds of sensible qualities that can be detected by the four senses, and nothing else. Moreover, we shouldn't assume that the term 'milk' or 'water' is ambiguous or context-sensitive: it is not the case that, in some contexts, the term 'milk' refers to the visible form of milk; in some, it refers just to its tactile qualities; in others, just to its flavour or odour. We are not aware of any such ambiguity or context-sensitivity in our linguistic usage. Rather, the right conclusion to draw is that the term 'milk' simply refers to the collection of these qualities, i.e., to these sensible qualities arranged together in a certain way. Vasubandhu explicitly claims that, from this, it straightforwardly follows that milk and water just are these qualities themselves collected together in a certain way; there is simply no scope for any (epistemic or metaphysical) indeterminacy about whether milk and water are identical to the sensible qualities that can be detected by the four senses. The facts about our application of these expressions decisively settle the matter.

Given the *Causal Theory of Reference*, Vasubandhu would want to draw the same lesson about our use of the conventional designation 'person'. Assume that we are competent users of the term 'person'. Suppose also that we typically or normally apply this expression either on the basis of our perceptual awareness of physical aggregates like the parts of our bodies arranged in a certain way, or on the basis of our introspective awareness (*manovijñāna*) of the mental aggregates such as our conscious mental occurrences. Then, it follows from Vasubandhu's theory of reference that this conventional designation should simply refer to those objects of those kinds: the aggregates collected together. If that is so, it is determinately true that a person just is the physical and mental aggregates arranged in a way, which can be either apprehended by one's senses such as sight, or by means of introspective awareness. So, there is no room for any epistemic or metaphysical indeterminacy about whether the person is identical to those aggregates or not.

A feature of the *Causal Theory of Reference* is worth highlighting. Earlier, I said that, on Vasubandhu's view, even though language may not be a reliable guide to the structure of reality, the relationship between language and reality is not so dysfunctional that our linguistic utterances cannot indirectly (or partly) reflect the way fundamentally existent objects are. The *Causal Theory of Reference* helps us to see why that might be the case. It allows Vasubandhu to do two things at once: it allows him to give a reductionist semantics for expressions like 'pot', 'chariot', and 'person', *and* it allows him to say that we (ordinary people as well as philosophers) can be subject to massive error about what these expressions refer to. On the one hand, the *Causal Theory of Reference* will predict that these terms pick out certain collections of mental or physical tropes insofar as they are typically applied on the basis of our initial awareness of those tropes. So, using these linguistic expressions, we can indeed talk about fundamentally existent objects. On the other hand, it is compatible with the *Causal Theory of Reference* that we have lots of false beliefs about these collections of tropes. We might think that ordinary objects like pots and chariots exist over and above their parts and persist through time. Similarly, we might think that selves and persons are persisting entities that serve as subjects of mental states and perform actions, but aren't reducible to the aggregates themselves. But these false beliefs needn't prevent expressions like 'pot', 'chariot', and 'person' from referring to collections of fundamentally existent objects; for, despite having these beliefs, we may continue to apply these terms – in ordinary discourse – on the basis of our initial awareness of the relevant collections of fundamentally existent objects. Thus, the *Causal Theory of Reference* permits our uses of language to track truths about how the world fundamentally is, while leaving room for us to be massively mistaken about the structure of reality.

Notice that we can apply the *Causal Theory of Reference* to the first-person pronoun 'I'. Even though we are massively mistaken about who we are, 'I' nevertheless refers to a stream of aggregates. 'I' is applied in our first-personal thoughts, either on the basis of our sensory awareness of our body (e.g., when one thinks 'I am fair') or on the basis of our introspective awareness of our inner conscious mental occurrences (e.g., when one thinks 'I am in pain'). In either case, the application of 'I' is typically based on certain states of awareness that are directed at aggregates belonging to a particular stream. So, 'I' should refer to those aggregates. This just means that, if we accept the *Causal Theory of Reference* and Vasubandhu's general theory about how we apply the first-person pronoun, the eliminativist view about the reference of 'I' cannot be right. In the rest of this section, I will explain how this theory of reference allows Vasubandhu to respond to the objections to at least one of his arguments for the reductionist semantics of 'I'.

5.2 The Objection from Figurative Use

The *Causal Theory of Reference* enables Vasubandhu to defend his argument from the self-ascriptions of physical properties. The initial objection to that argument was the objection from figurative use: namely, that our self-ascriptions of physical properties aren't literally true. On this view, an ascription like 'I am fair', is like the statement 'I am parked outside'. The latter is figuratively or non-literally true insofar as it conveys the content that one's car is parked outside. Similarly, the self-ascription of fairness is figuratively or non-literally true insofar as it conveys the content that one's body is fair.

In response, Vasubandhu could begin by noting that 'I' is context-sensitive in two ways. First, unlike words like 'milk' or 'water', 'I' is context-sensitive because 'I' can pick out aggregates associated with different persons in different contexts. When 'I' is used by Devadatta, it will pick out the aggregates associated with Devadatta; when it is used by Yajñadatta, it will pick out the aggregates associated with Yajñadatta. But 'I' can be context-sensitive in a second way. In some contexts of utterance, Devadatta may correctly say, 'I am fair'. Yet, in other contexts of utterance, the same Devadatta may correctly say, 'My body is fair'. In contexts of the latter sort, the second ascription can only be literally correct if the referent of 'I' is something that is distinct from Devadatta's body. But, then, the first self-ascription cannot be correct in those contexts, since it entails the referent of 'I' is a bearer of Devadatta's physical properties and therefore is Devadatta's body. The best way to preserve the truth of both ascriptions is to say that 'I' is context-sensitive in a second way. In the contexts where 'I am fair' is true, 'I' refers to the body, or a stream of aggregates that includes the body. But, in the contexts where 'My body is fair' is true, 'I' doesn't refer to the body, or a stream of aggregates that includes the body, but rather to something that is separate from the body.

Vasubandhu's theory of reference can explain these shifts of reference without treating any of these uses of 'I' as non-literal or figurative. Vasubandhu has already told us that 'I' can refer to physical aggregates as long as there is the right sort of causal connection between the relevant 'I'-awareness and those physical aggregates. But, in another context, Vasubandhu notes that, at least sometimes, 'I' only refers to mental events.

> Since mental events are the basis (*saṃniśraya*) [i.e., the intentional object] of 'I'-awareness, they are figuratively described as the self. It has been said [in the *Dhammapada*]: 'For a wise person attains heaven by means of a self that is well restrained'. And, in another context, the Blessed One has spoken of the restraint of mental events [also in the *Dhammapada*]: 'The restraint of mental events is good, and mental events, when restrained, bring happiness'. (AKBh 27.6–12 ad AK 1.39a)

This suggests that, in the final analysis, the first-person pronoun can refer to different collections of aggregates in different contexts of utterance. What a certain use of 'I' refers to depends on which aggregates serve as the proximate causes of the relevant use of the pronoun. For example, if the use of 'I' is triggered by the perceptual awareness of one's body, then it may indeed refer to an embodied entity. But, when it is triggered only by one's introspective awareness of one's conscious mental life, then it needn't refer to an embodied entity. Thus, depending on the context, 'I' may pick out mental aggregates, or physical aggregates, or both. We can state the theory as follows:

Nilanjan Das

The Semantics of 'I'
In any context of thought or utterance, an application of the expression or concept 'I' refers to a contextually salient collection of (i) purely mental, or (ii) purely physical, or (iii) mental and physical aggregates, which serve (in the right way) as the proximate causes of the relevant 'I'-awareness or 'I'-thought.

Thus, Vasubandhu can block the objection from figurative use by appealing to the two kinds of context-sensitivity that affect the use of 'I'.

5.3 The Objection from Arbitrariness

Consider next the objection from arbitrariness. Given that the expression 'I' is context-sensitive on Vasubandhu's view, it can refer sometimes to both the mental and physical aggregates that are part of the stream within which the relevant 'I'-awareness occurs, sometimes only to the mental aggregates, and sometimes only to the physical aggregates. Then, why can't it refer to a body associated with another stream? Vasubandhu has told us (in the passage quoted at the beginning of this section) that this is because the appropriate kind of causal connection between another person's body and the 'I'-awareness is absent. But we might not find this response satisfying.

For instance, one could argue that our 'I'-thoughts can indeed be causally connected in some way to other people's bodies. Imagine an agent who is wired up in such a way, such that, on the basis of her perceptual awareness of other people's bodies, she thinks thoughts like 'I am fair' or 'I am thin'. Surely, if that person's own body is not fair or thin, we would want to say that the contents of her 'I'-thoughts are false. This means that this person is misapplying the expression 'I'; she is conceptually or linguistically incompetent. Yet, in this case, there is a causal connection between the other people's bodies and the agent's 'I'-awareness: just as an 'I'-awareness may arise for a person with respect to her own body through the mediation of the perceptual awareness of her own body, so too, in this case, an 'I'-awareness for the deviant user of 'I' arises from a perceptual awareness of another's body. Vasubandhu needs to say why conceptually or linguistically competent agents never use the first-person pronoun in the same way as this deviant user of 'I' uses it. What makes the causal connections that hold between the 'I'-awareness and the mental or physical aggregates that it picks out special such that 'I' cannot refer to other people's bodies?

Notice that there is no analogous challenge for the Brahmanical thinker. For a Nyāya or Vaiśeṣika thinker, any use of the concept 'I' in a thought refers to a subject who serves as the owner of that thought. Who is this subject? It's just a particular self in which various mental qualities – including states of awareness – reside. The fact that the 'I'-thought resides in that self makes that self exclusively the owner of the relevant 'I'-thought. So, on this view, 'I' refers neither to one's own body nor to someone else' body. So, a defender of this view asks Vasubandhu: 'If the self doesn't exist, whose is this 'I'-awareness?' (AKBh 476.13–14). The implicit thought seems to be that causal connections alone aren't enough to single out an owner of any 'I'-thought, which the first-person pronoun 'I' could then refer to.

In reply, Vasubandhu appeals to a theory of ownership that he develops elsewhere while discussing an analogous challenge about the ownership of memory (*smṛti*). In response to a Nyāya opponent, Vasubandhu argues that, in order to explain memory, we don't have to appeal to a self. In the absence of impediments, e.g., disease, grief, *etc.*, a memory arises from a mental event – e.g., an impression (*vāsanā*) or a memory trace – which is characterised by a mental label (*saṃjñā*), *etc.* that resembles and is causally connected to an earlier act of attending to the relevant intentional object (AKBh 472.16–22). Suppose I tasted a raspberry sorbet some years ago. When I tasted that sorbet, not only did I attend to that sorbet, but I also determined it to have a number of characteristics, e.g., a purple colour, a crunchy texture, and so on. This is what is meant by mental labelling: in determining the object to have these characteristics, I attached a bunch of mental labels (which are concept-like representational devices) to it. This determination may have left a memory trace in the stream of aggregates that constitute me. That memory trace resembles the earlier determination I made when I tasted the sorbet and is causally connected to it. This memory trace, though momentary, may be replicated over and over again, and carried down my stream of aggregates. When that memory trace is ready to give rise to a conscious memory, then (in the absence of impediments) it will give rise to that memory. This explanation of memory doesn't appeal to any self that is distinct from the stream of aggregates.

The Nyāya opponent here notices that these relations of resemblance and causation between the memory trace and the earlier experience aren't enough to explain the phenomenon of memory. Take the following case. Yajñadatta tells Devadatta about his childhood experience of blowing the candles out on his fifth birthday. As a result of that testimony, Devadatta comes to have a memory trace that later gives rise to a non-veridical awareness where he seems to remember himself blowing out the candles on his fifth birthday. Surely, we cannot say that Devadatta remembers blowing out the candle on his fifth birthday. As Nyāya philosophers would tell us, 'One person doesn't remember what another has experienced'. The only obvious way of getting around this problem to appeal to the owner of the relevant memory: a conscious memory can only belong to someone who originally served as the subject of the experience that the memory is derived from. Now, the Nyāya philosopher would have an easy time explaining who the owner of the memory is: it is the unitary self that serves as the substratum of the original experience as well as the later memory that arises from it. But Vasubandhu cannot appeal to such a self. So, the objector asks: 'If the self does not exist, whose is this memory?' (AKBh 473.2).

In response, Vasubandhu develops a theory that includes two claims. The first claim is that it is a mistake to construe the relation of ownership between a person and her own mental states in the way as we understand the relation of ownership between a person and her external possessions. The argument, in a nutshell, is this (AKBh 473.2–6). The relation of ownership between a person and her ordinary possessions (like a cow) consists in her ability to use that possession for whatever purpose she wants. Since there may be no purpose external to a mental state itself for which the mental state may be used, this relation of ownership doesn't hold between a person and her mental states. This suggests that Vasubandhu is mildly sceptical of the idea that there is anything like a relation of ownership that holds between a person and her mental states.

Vasubandhu's second claim arises from a slightly more conciliatory position. Perhaps, we can grant that a mental state is owned by a person only insofar as it can be used by that person (e.g., for the purposes of thinking or reasoning about a certain object). A mental state can be used in this way only insofar as the relevant person is causally connected to it in the right way. But, then, the ownership consists in nothing but a causal relation. This yields the second claim: the relation of ownership between a person and her mental states can be reduced to a causal relation (AKBh 473.7–10). This allows Vasubandhu to offer a reductionist account of ownership. On Vasubandhu's view, Caitra is said to be the owner of the cow insofar as the physical and mental aggregates that constitute Caitra serve as the cause of various changes in the aggregates that constitute the cow.

Furthermore, when that stream of collections of causally conditioned factors – called 'Caitra' – is said to be the owner of the stream called a 'cow', that too is done keeping in mind [Caitra's] status as a cause in relation of changes that are taking place in a different spatial region [i.e., in the cow]. However, there is no unitary object called Caitra, nor is there any cow. Therefore, even in that case, there is no status of ownership beyond the status of being a cause. (AKBh 473.10–13)

Vasubandhu will grant that streams of aggregates other than that which we call 'Caitra' can be causally connected to the stream of aggregates that is the cow. But that doesn't mean that those streams of aggregates can be treated as owners of the cow. The relation of ownership which holds between Caitra and his cow holds not in virtue of any *arbitrary* causal connection, but only certain *specific* causal connections. But, importantly, for Vasubandhu, this relation of ownership consists in *nothing but* causal connections. This idea, on his view, transfers over to the case of persons and their mental states. While other people can be causally connected to our memories, those memories cannot be said to belong to those other people. This is because, even though the relation of ownership that connects a memory to its owner consists in causal connections, not every causal connection is sufficient for ownership. However, it still remains true that the relationship between a person and her mental states consists in *nothing but* causal connections.

Let's see how this applies to the case of 'I'-awareness. Just as the owner of a conscious memory is just a collection of aggregates that are causally related to it in specific ways, so also the owner of an 'I'-awareness is a collection of aggregates that is causally connected to it in the right way.

[The opponent:] And what is that cause other than [a self]?
[Reply:] A defective mental event, which is causally conditioned by earlier states of 'I'-awareness and has its own stream as its intentional object. (AKBh 476.15–16)

This suggests a broader story about how we come to ascribe physical or mental properties to ourselves. On Vasubandhu's view, a conscious memory (which may or may not be first-personal in content) arises from an immediately preceding mental event, i.e., a memory trace which is causally connected to a past determination of a previously experienced object and which is therefore directed at that object. Similarly, a first-personal thought that takes the form 'I am fair' or 'I am in pain', arises from an immediately preceding mental event, i.e., a memory trace which is left by previous states of 'I'-awareness that were directed at the same stream of aggregates within which the memory trace occurs. Therefore, the memory trace is directed at the stream of aggregates within which it occurs. Since this memory trace is connected to the false conception of the aggregates as a unitary persisting self, it is said to be a 'defective mental event'.

This analogy between conscious memories and 'I'-thoughts helps us to see how Vasubandhu might be able to respond to the objection from arbitrariness satisfactorily. On Vasubandhu's view, our competence with the concept or expression 'I' isn't something that we acquire through our exposure to the linguistic behaviour of other competent users of the relevant concept or expression. Rather, it is inherited from past lives in virtue of memory traces that are left behind by our previous 'I'-thoughts. These memory traces – as Vasubandhu notes – involve the disposition to conceptualize the momentary aggregates as a unitary self that persists through time. Thus, we are born with an innate disposition to use the word 'I' to pick out a certain stream of mental or physical aggregates while, at the same time, remaining unaware of certain key characteristics of those aggregates (such as their impermanence). This innate disposition is part of our beginningless ignorance (*avidyā*) regarding who we are: it forces upon us the view that we are unitary selves. Importantly, the memory traces – which underlie our uses of 'I' – are only directed at the stream of aggregates within it occurs, but not at other streams of aggregates. That explains why we (as competent users of 'I') cannot use 'I' to pick out other people's bodies. So, there is no arbitrariness in the way we use 'I'.

6. Conclusion

We are now in a position to see how this account allows Vasubandhu to reconcile the *'No Self' Thesis* with the view that 'I' is a referring expression. On this view, 'I' refers to a stream of aggregates. Thus, the view can explain how our ascriptions of mental states and actions to ourselves can be conventionally true (or false). Consider self-ascriptions of mental states like:

(4)   I am pleased.
(5)   I am in pain.

The Nyāya philosophers assume that (4) and (5) ascribe mental states of pleasure and pain to a substratum or basis (*āśraya*) in which they reside: a distinct substance called the self. By contrast, for Vasubandhu, these self-ascriptions are like:

(6)   The forest has borne fruit.

He explains the point as follows:

[The Brahmanical opponent:] If the self doesn't exist, who is this being that is pleased or in pain?
[Vasubandhu:] It is that basis in which pleasure or pain arises, just as in the case of the ascriptions 'The tree has blossomed', 'The forest has borne fruit', and so on.
[The Brahmanical thinker:] Still, what is the basis of these two mental events?
[Vasubandhu:] The six sense-bases [i.e., the senses]. (AKBh 476.16–18)

In (6), the expression 'the forest' refers to a collection of trees while the ascription of the predicate 'has borne fruit' conveys that some fruit has arisen having as its causal basis one or more of the trees in that collection. Similarly, in self-ascriptions of mental states like (4) and (5), the expression 'I' refers to a stream of physical aggregates (e.g., the sense-bases) in dependence on which these mental events of pleasure and pain can arise, while 'am pleased' or 'am in pain' conveys that one or more those aggregates have given rise to a state of pleasure or pain. But note that ascriptions like (4)–(6) cannot be ultimately true: they presuppose or entail the existence of ultimately non-existent objects like forests and streams of aggregates. However, they can still be conventionally true or false, since they indirectly track or reflect certain facts about fundamentally real entities such as the material *dharma*s that constitute the forest, or the physical and mental aggregates that are picked out by 'I'.

This account would allow Vasubandhu to explain how inferences of the following kind can be truth-preserving: 'I am in pain. I am Nilanjan. Therefore, Nilanjan is in pain'. In this case, both 'I' and 'Nilanjan' are expressions that pick out streams of mental and physical aggregates. So, if a hedonic state of pain occurs in the stream of aggregates that is referred to by 'I', and that stream is identical to the stream of aggregates picked out by 'Nilanjan', then the conclusion that this state of pain occurs in the stream of aggregates picked out by 'Nilanjan' will necessarily be true. Thus, Vasubandhu's reductionist semantics for 'I' can explain the truth-aptness of our ordinary ascriptions of mental and physical properties to ourselves as well as the validity of our ordinary inferences about ourselves.[7]

[7]   I would like to thank Joachim Aufderheide, Julian Baggini, Sophia Connell, Davey Tomlinson, Shaul Tor, and the audiences at the Ancient

Nilanjan Das

References

Primary Texts and Abbreviations

AK   Vasubandhu's   *Abhidharmakośakārikā*   in *Abhidharmakośabhāṣyam of Vasubandhu*, edited by Prahlad Pradhan and Aruna Haldar, second edition, (Patna: K.P. Jayaswal Institute, 1975).

AKBh   Vasubandhu's   *Abhidharmakośabhāṣya*   in *Abhidharmakośabhāṣyam of Vasubandhu*, edited by Prahlad Pradhan and Aruna Haldar, second edition, (Patna: K.P. Jayaswal Institute, 1975).

AKBh$_D$ Vasubandhu's *Abhidharmakośabhāṣya* in *Abhidharmakośa and Bhāṣya of Ācārya Vasubandhu with Sputārthā Commentary of Ācārya Yaśomitra*, edited by Svāmī Dvārikādāsa Śāstrī, (Varanasi: Bauddha Bhāratī, 1987).

Sphu   Yaśomitra's *Sputārthā* in Svāmī Dvārikādāsa Śāstrī (ed.), *Abhidharmakośa and Bhāṣya of Ācārya Vasubandhu with Sputārthā Commentary of Ācārya Yaśomitra* (Varanasi: Bauddha Bhāratī, 1987).

Secondary Literature and Other Sources

Amber D. Carpenter, '*Persons Keeping Their Karma Together*', in Koji Tanaka, Yasuo Deguchi, Jay L. Garfield, and Graham Priest (eds.), *The Moon Points Back* (New York: Oxford University Press, 2015), 1–44.

K.L. Dhammajoti, *Sarvāstivāda Abhidharma*, third edition, (Hong Kong: Centre for Buddhist Studies, University of Hong Kong, 2007).

James Duerlinger, *Indian Buddhist Theories of Persons: Vasubandhu's 'Refutation of the Theory of a Self'* (London: Routledge, 2003).

Jonardon Ganeri, *Philosophy in Classical India: An Introduction and Analysis* (London: Routledge, 2001).

Jonardon Ganeri, 'Subjectivity, Selfhood and the Use of the Word 'I'', in Mark Siderits, Evan Thompson, and Dan Zahavi (eds.), *Self, No Self?: Perspectives From Analytical, Phenomenological, and Indian Traditions* (Oxford: Oxford University Press, 2010).

Philosophy Seminar at the Institute of Classical Studies, London, and at the Royal Institute of Philosophy London Lectures for their helpful comments.

Jonardon Ganeri, *The Self: Naturalism, Consciousness, and the First-Person Stance* (Oxford: Oxford University Press, 2012).

Charles Goodman, 'The Treasury of Metaphysics and the Physical World', *The Philosophical Quarterly*, 54:216 (2004), 389–401.

Jonathan Gold, *Paving the Great Way: Vasubandhu's Unifying Buddhist Philosophy* (New York: Columbia University Press, 2014).

Matthew Kapstein, *Reason's Traces: Identity and Interpretation in Indian Tibetan Buddhist Thought* (Somerville, MA: Wisdom Publications, 2003).

Geoffrey Nunberg, 'Transfers of Meaning', *The Journal of Semantics*, 12 (1995), 109–132.

Mark Siderits, *Buddhism as Philosophy: An Introduction* (London: Ashgate, 2007).

Leonard Priestley, *Pudgalavāda Buddhism: The Reality of the Indeterminate Self* (Toronto: Centre for South Asian Studies, University of Toronto, 1999).

Thích Thiện Châu and Sara Boin-Webb, *The Literature of the Personalists of Early Buddhism* (Delhi: Motilal Banarsidass, 1999).

Japanese Philosophers on Plato's Ideas[1]

NOBURU NOTOMI

Abstract
Although Plato studies occupy an important place in academia, the empiricist stance in considering reality, the modern epistemology of the self-identical *ego*, the devaluation of the image and imagination, and the restrictions on philosophy within academic research sometimes cause us to lose sight of the essence of Plato's texts and thought when analysing them. Discussing Plato from a Japanese perspective, this paper will introduce three Japanese thinkers, Sakabe Megumi, Izutsu Toshihiko, and Ino-ue Tadashi, who have critically examined modern Western philosophy from their own philosophical backgrounds and provided valuable suggestions. Taking into account the arguments of these Japanese thinkers, this paper emphasizes the notions of separation, purification, and transcendence as core concepts of Plato's philosophy.

1. Reading Plato in the Twenty-First Century

Plato (427–347 BC) has long been one of the most important philosophers, and is even regarded as the greatest philosopher in Western Europe and North America. He has also been a major figure in Eastern Europe, Latin America, the Near East and Middle East, and East Asia. In this paper, I will discuss Plato from a Japanese perspective. My discussion will show that, although Platonic studies are an important part of philosophical activities in the academic world, modern readers miss some essential elements in analysing Plato's texts and thoughts.

What I believe we are missing is the correct understanding of his central thesis. People acknowledge the theory of Ideas (transcendent Forms)[2] as a major contribution to the history of philosophy. In the

[1] This paper was presented online for *The London Lectures 2021: Expanding Horizons*, the Royal Institute of Philosophy, 25 November 2021. I thank Julian Baggini for the kind invitation and valuable discussion. The names of the Japanese authors are given in the order of family name first and then given name.

[2] In the history of philosophy, the term 'idea' is ambiguous. While modern philosophers use it as an innate concept in our minds, Plato, the inventor of this philosophical concept, thought of it as a separate entity that

doi:10.1017/S1358246123000085

middle dialogues,[3] Plato suggested that the real entities, such as the beautiful itself and the just itself, which he called the 'Idea of Beauty' and 'Idea of Justice', exist beyond the world we experience and that they are causes of beautiful things and just states and people in this world. This theory has had much influence on the history of Western philosophy, but only a few philosophers ascribe to it any actual role in contemporary philosophy. It appears to be considered simply as a bizarre doctrine that ignores our reality. What is called Platonic 'transcendence' or 'dualism' is regarded as a negative heritage to be overcome in modern philosophy.[4] If it is only of historical interest, the relevance of Plato to our philosophy today is clearly greatly diminished. However, I hope that my Japanese background will help to shed some light on how to read Plato today.[5] In this paper, I'll first examine some preconceptions of modern philosophy that prevent us from correctly understanding the theory of Ideas.

The theory of Ideas has long been a target of severe criticism by many philosophers, from Aristotle to Nietzsche and postmodernism.[6] Of several types of criticisms, the most important and regularly recurring one is that the Ideas are redundant metaphysical entities, unnecessarily added to this world; therefore, the theory is mistaken. The first critic, Aristotle (384–322 BC), raised twenty-three points against the theory of Ideas in the *Metaphysics*.[7] He argued that Plato added extra entities to the things in our world by positing 'one Idea over many things'. This corresponds, for example, to the hypotheses of Ideas stated in the *Phaedo*. The speaker Socrates first hypothesizes that the 'beautiful itself by itself', that is, the Idea of

---

exists beyond our sensible world. The Greek 'idea' (*idea*) and 'form' (*eidos*) were ordinary words for shape and appearance. Plato used these words almost synonymously, but Aristotle distinguished 'idea' (transcendent entity) from 'form' (immanent entity).

[3]   The dialogues that are supposed to have been written in the middle period of Plato's life, i.e. between 386 and 367 BC, include the *Symposium, Phaedo, Republic, Phaedrus* and *Cratylus*. The characteristic feature of these dialogues is their discussion of transcendental Ideas.

[4]   In particular, many twentieth-century philosophers, influenced by Friedrich Nietzsche, have criticised Plato as an idealist and mind-body dualist. Karl Popper also criticised him as a totalitarian.

[5]   I also discuss the reception of Plato in modern Japan in Notomi (2015, 2017, and 2021).

[6]   Notomi (2015) examines the criticisms of Aristotle, Nietzsche, and Karl Popper, and offers answers on behalf of Plato.

[7]   Aristotle, *Metaphysics* A9 990a34–b8, M4 1078b34–1079a4.

Beauty, exists, and that 'if anything else is beautiful besides the beautiful itself, it is beautiful for no reason at all other than that it participates in that beautiful'.[8] Here Socrates appears to add an extra entity to things already existent in our world. According to the principle of the economy of thought or Ockham's razor, the hypothesis of Ideas as separate entities is philosophically weak and mistaken. In this way, the *separation* of Ideas from sensible things became a focus of Aristotle's criticism.

Modern philosophers raise similar questions to Plato. For example, Gail Fine, scholar of ancient philosophy, in examining the theory of Ideas, says that, 'if, as Aristotle and I believe, forms are universals, then to say that they are separate is to say they can exist uninstantiated by sensible particulars' (Fine, 2003, p. 32).[9] However, I believe that such a question as 'are there universals, independently of sensible objects?' fails to grasp the core of Plato's philosophy. But before judging the validity of this criticism, we should note on what assumptions the criticism is based. I examine the four main background assumptions, which I will outline in turn: first, the empiricist stance in considering reality; second, the modern epistemology of the self-identical *ego*; third, the devaluation of the image and imagination; and fourth, the restrictions on philosophy within academic research.

First, we find Aristotle, whom Fine mentions, firmly promoting the empiricist stance in considering reality. The philosophical position called empiricism assumes that reality is what we perceive and experience and nothing else. Aristotle argues that 'this particular man' or 'this particular horse' is a primary being, while kinds like 'man', 'horse', and 'animal' are secondary.[10] Accordingly, he criticised the theory of Ideas, and regarded mathematical objects as mere abstractions from concrete things, in contrast to Plato, who placed them at a higher level than sensible things. Generally speaking, the empiricist position, which includes modern Anglo-analytic philosophy, is reluctant to admit anything other than what we experience and perceive in this world with our senses.

Second, modern philosophers are inclined to accept this criticism because of another assumption. After Descartes separated the *ego* or *res cogitans* from external things, called *res extensa*, the former

---

[8] Plato, *Phaedo* 100B–C.
[9] Cf. Fine (2003, pp. 252–300).
[10] In his *Categories*, Aristotle distinguished between substances (e.g. horse, man) and attributes (e.g. white, one meter long), and between the individual (*kath' hekaston*) and the universal (*katholou*). He considered the Platonic Ideas as universal.

became the fixed viewpoint from which the world is perceived. The *ego* is a non-corporeal 'I' and thus a pure subject detached from the outer world. In this way, modern philosophy posits the cognitive subject 'I' which perceives objects and experiences the world. This was typically presented in Kant's notion of 'Apperzeption' or 'Ich selbst' and Husserl's 'transzendentale Subjektivität'. These modern conceptions assume that the 'I' subject is self-identical, absolute, yet plays a cognitive role, like the viewpoint in perspective.

These background assumptions together raise a severe criticism of Platonic Ideas. If the cognitive subject is fixed as self-identical, and if reality is what we experience in this world, then the Ideas are nothing but abstract objects postulated in vain. They are redundant, and the theory is erroneous. Seen from this modern empiricist point of view, Plato's dualism is simply doubling realities. However, what is missing in modern epistemology (theory of knowledge) is a consideration of the possibility of change or a transformation of the 'I', whereas Plato believed that the subject 'I' will change in doing philosophy and see the world differently. He also believed that under different states of cognition, the world may also change. It should be noted that continental philosophers such as Hegel, Nietzsche, and Heidegger also considered this possibility.

The third modern assumption that prevents us from understanding the theory of Ideas is the devaluation of the image and imagination:[11] that is, to regard the image as meaningless in relation to reality, and to treat imagination as an inferior capacity. Although we know that Plato has been criticised as an 'iconoclastic' philosopher in the history of Western philosophy, since, in addition to the notorious criticism of poets in *Republic* Book X, he located the power of imagining at the lowest level of the four stages of our knowledge and cognition in Book VI, it is not Plato but we, modern readers who are deeply involved in sustaining this negative view of the image, assuming that it derives from Plato's metaphysics. To approach Plato's Ideas, however, we need to reform our conception of the image and imagination.

Fourth, the notion of 'philosophy' is different between Plato and our contemporary world. Modern universities across the world have departments of philosophy in which professional philosophers and students engage in academic research on philosophical problems and the history of philosophy. However, in antiquity, philosophy was

---

[11]   'Image' is a copy or a likeness of the original: e.g. a picture, a sculpture, a shadow, and a mental image. 'Imagination' is the capacity of making images.

not so much academic research as a way of life.[12] So while the theory of Ideas was not just a pure theory but a practice of living well, we can scarcely find any philosopher reading it in this way in contemporary universities.

By reconsidering these four background assumptions of modern philosophy, we may be able to understand Plato's Ideas more adequately. To this end, Japanese philosophers who have critically examined modern Western philosophy from their philosophical backgrounds can provide valuable insights.

2. Plato's Philosophy as Shaking our Conception of Reality

Sakabe Megumi (坂部恵, 1936–2009) taught at the Department of Philosophy at the University of Tokyo and re-evaluated Japanese traditional thought to reconsider modern Western philosophy. His main academic subject was Immanuel Kant, but he was one of the academic scholars who first introduced postmodern philosophers into Japan and took their attempts seriously. From this postmodern perspective, he was naturally critical towards Platonism, which he sought to overturn. But instead of replacing the traditional Platonic thinking with a new trend, Sakabe tried to shake its foundations by recalling the deep unconscious cultural resources that are common in Europe, especially in ancient Greece, and the East. He also pursued the philosophical potentiality of the Japanese language, including *Yamato-kotoba*, namely, native Japanese words, to reconsider or relativize Western philosophy.

In the collection of essays, *Hermeneutics of the Mask* (仮面の解釈学), published in 1976, Sakabe argued that modern Western philosophers assume the self-identical *ego* and take the world as 're-presentation' to the subject (what is called 'metaphysics of presence'). This modern obsession misses the important sense of *metamorphosis* (transformation) in philosophy. He presented our current situation as follows:

> It is not simple for us today to awaken and recollect such experiences or feelings that shake our ordinary flat sense of 'real thing' and its 'shadow' in a deeper phase; experiences where we suffer some mixed feelings of awe and fear in recognising the higher revelation of reality in one's 'avatar', 'other', and 'shadow', which are most deeply related to one's own self; and situations

---

[12]   Pierre Hadot discussed and demonstrated this point.

where our ordinary flat sense of reality is reversed between light and dark (*yin-yang* 陰陽), and where a part of 'shadow' which is passed unnoticed in everyday life starts to speak with a vivid sense of reality. (Sakabe, 1976, p. 25, 'A Sketch on *Kage*', my translation)

To put forward an alternative, Sakabe examined the Japanese word '*kage*' (shadow 影、陰、蔭). We may sometimes recognise in *kage* an appearance of a higher reality, as one may see there a part and the 'other' of our own self (*alter ego*). He then reminded us of Plato's Simile of the Cave along with the 'material imagination' of Gaston Bachelard's *L'eau et les rêves* (Sakabe, 1976, pp. 26–40, 'A Sketch on *Kage*'). Sakabe suggested a fusion or interchange between *kage* and reality. *Kage* is not just an inferior appearance of the real object but contains the potential power of fundamentally shaking our consciousness and ordinary sense of reality; it awakens us and may lead us back to our origin.

The Japanese *kage* means 'shadow' or 'image', but also 'light'. On the surface of water, it reflects (*utsu-su*) the world. Sakabe discussed the etymological connotation of '*utsu-shi*', which comes from '*utsu-ru*' (to transfer 写、映、移、遷、憑) (Sakabe, 1976, p. 191, '*Utsushi-mi*'). *Utsu-ru* basically means something emerging at another place with the same form and content. Therefore, its basic meaning is, first, a projection of the very form or shape on another place, second, a colour or scent transfers to another thing, and third, an evil spirit possesses something. In the last sense, *utsu-ru* may imply an emergence of the divine or a soul through divination, and a mysterious experience that someone becomes another. Its derivative word '*utsu-tsu* (現)' means reality, but Sakabe noted that it does not correspond to 'presence' in Western traditional metaphysics. Rather, it signifies a transition or interaction between absence and presence, life and death, the invisible or formless and the visible and form. Between these, we see no absolute hierarchy since they reflect each other and transform between themselves to maintain an identity of *utsu-tsu*. Therefore, *utsu-tsu* occasionally overlaps with, or changes into, *yume* (夢, dream), as in the phrase '*yume utsu-tsu*' (half asleep, half awake, or trance). This dynamic relation and balance constitute a reality, and therefore, transfer or metaphor (*metaphora*) is an essential factor of our world.

For Sakabe, although Plato is still the origin of Western metaphysics, he is at the same time a rich source of alternatives, just as Sakabe saw in old Japanese thoughts. His criticism of Western philosophy sheds light on Plato as its origin. With reference to the Simile of the Cave, Sakabe pursued the interaction and transfer (*metaphora*) between thing and shadow, and self and object. The 'self' is not self-identical, as modern Western philosophers assume. This dynamic and flexible view on reality and the 'self' points to a philosophical motivation of Plato: that is, to shake our ordinary sense of reality, to reveal another phase, and to intimate another possibility of 'I'. This dynamism is what Sakabe believed philosophy should consider.

On the other hand, he tried to avoid hierarchical structuring of beings and rejected any idea of fixing the different stages, in particular Platonism as traditionally understood. So he went so far as to suggest radical interpenetration or fusion between thing and shadow, self and other, and reality and dream, which represents a typically Japanese way of thinking, as we see in Noh plays (能楽). The Noh mask is at once a face to cover reality and to reveal reality, or the mask itself is the reality that changes (Sakabe, 1976, pp. 3–23, 'An Essay on Hermeneutics of *Omote*'). Mask is '*omote*', which means front, surface, and face.

3. Plato's Philosophy as Experiencing the Ideas

Izutsu Toshihiko (井筒俊彦, 1914–1993) taught at Keio University in Tokyo, the Iranian Research Institute of Philosophy in Tehran, and McGill University in Montreal. As an active participant in Eranus (an intellectual discussion group meeting held in Switzerland sine 1933) from Japan, he obtained a global reputation as a specialist in Sufism and Eastern Philosophy. In his first monograph *Mystic Philosophy: A Study on Greek Philosophy* (神秘哲学 ギリシアの部), published in 1949,[13] he tried to interpret Greek thought in terms of mysticism. This original approach illuminates one important aspect of Plato that has been neglected in Western scholarship: namely, Idea-experience as transformation of our soul.

Izutsu was born and brought up in the strong familial atmosphere of the 'East (東洋)'. In his youth, he discovered in Greek philosophy the crucial hints for transferring religious experiences into words (*logos*). In Eastern philosophy, especially Zen Buddhism, words or speech tend to be disbelieved and avoided; they say *Gonsen-fukyu* (言詮不及), that truth cannot be reached through words and

---

[13]   This book was first published in 1949 by Hikari-no-shobo. A later revised edition by Izutsu into two volumes was published by Jinbun-shoin in 1978. The two versions have been reprinted four times. I use the first version reprinted by Iwanami in 2019.

speech, and *Furyu-monji* (不立文字), that Spiritual enlightenment cannot be attained with words and letters. However, Izutsu believed that Greek thinkers had similar spiritual experiences as Eastern mystics, but unlike the latter, they succeeded in making their experiences 'philosophy' by means of *logos* (Izutsu, 2019, pp. 3–13). Therefore, he called the fusion of the conflicting elements of mysticism and philosophy 'mystic philosophy (神秘哲学)'.

Izutsu treated Plato as the first culmination of Greek mystic philosophy. Plato's philosophy completed the Orphic and Pythagorean mysticism of salvation of the soul. Taking the theory of Ideas as realisation of mystic philosophy, Izutsu claimed that 'Plato's dialecticians are nothing other than mystics' (Izutsu, 2019, p. 108), and that 'Idea-experiences must precede the theory of Ideas' (Izutsu, 2019, p. 119).

Studying the mystical tradition in both the West and the East, Izutsu rehabilitated the philosophical role of the image. In his masterpiece *Consciousness and Essence* (意識と本質), published in 1983, he classified and examined three types of 'Oriental', of which the second is the symbolist philosophy that includes different forms of mysticism. He argued that this tradition takes the archetypal images in the subconscious domain to be the universal essence of reality, to be evoked through poetic or mythopoetic imagination. Izutsu first pointed out that human consciousness (意識) as a whole is image-productive and full of images.

The mystic tradition of Oriental philosophy sees the image experience as a kind of reality experience: for example, Shamanism experiences the real world as appearing as the world of images. Izutsu introduced the notion of the 'imaginal world',[14] which is *more real* than what we ordinarily see as the 'real world', as a core in the mystic and Platonist philosophy of Suhrawardi (1154–1191). Izutsu discussed the image as follows:

> For men of common sense who see things from the empirical basis, the 'metaphor' which lacks the material basis is nothing but the 'likeness', i.e. a shadowy thing. But from another viewpoint, this shadowy entity turns out to have far denser existence than real things in our empirical world. For Suhrawardi – and thinkers of Shamanism, Gnosticism, Tantrism – the things in what we call the 'real world' are nothing but literally 'shadowy

[14] This word '*mundus imaginalis*' was coined by Henry Corbin in explaining Suhrawardi, the twelfth-century Persian Sufi philosopher, as opposed to the common adjective 'imaginary', which has always been treated negatively, i.e. as something *unreal*, in Western philosophy.

entities', or shadows of shadow. The true weight of reality lies in the 'metaphor'. Otherwise, how can we explain the overwhelming *reality*, for example, of the Tantric Mandala Space, which consists only of images? (Izutsu, 1991, pp. 203–204, section VIII, my translation)

In the hierarchy of realities, Suhrawardi posited the independent intermediary world that is governed by the cognitive power of imagination but which is nevertheless *more real* than the sensible world. From this, Izutsu took inspiration to rehabilitate the notion of images for understanding our deep consciousness. He pointed out the interesting fact that several philosophers of Islamic mysticism, namely Suhrawardi, Ibun Arabi, and Molla Sadra, regarded themselves as followers of Plato's philosophy and as interpreting his theory of Ideas in a new way.

By examining different stages or levels of reality and the self, based on Eastern philosophies, Izutsu aimed to return to a deeper phase of the undifferentiated state of our unconsciousness (無意識), far below our ordinary consciousness. He showed another extreme direction of Platonism, which ends in mystic unification with the Absolute.

4. Plato's Philosophy as Encounter with Ideas

Ino-ue Tadashi (井上忠, 1926–2014) lectured at Komaba Campus of the University of Tokyo and engaged with Plato and Aristotle in philosophically challenging ways. Unlike Sakabe and Izutsu, Ino-ue was a specialist in Greek Philosophy. He first studied Plato's later dialogues intensively, and his main research articles on these dialogues are included in his first book *Challenge from Konkyo* (根拠よりの挑戦), published in 1974.

Ino-ue's attitude towards the philosophy of Plato is clearly stated in one of his essays:

Of course, I seek a way to understand the Ideas (イデア理解の途). But the approach to it is not to discuss what the 'Ideas' are in the history of philosophy. That is only a reference and a point to consider. What counts is that we should truly *encounter* them '*ide-a-u* (出て遭う)', and that we clearly see what we encounter in the way of doing philosophy. (Ino-ue, 1985, p. 90, 'Revival of the Dead', my translation)

He identified the true philosophy with '*ide-ai* (出て遭い)', namely encounter with the Ideas. The Ideas are what grounds our reality and are therefore called *Konkyo* (根拠, *archē*, ground or origin).[15] Our reality is based or grounded on *that thing* behind, and we are grasped by that *Konkyo*. Ino-ue argued that philosophers, therefore, must recognise that we ourselves are a part of it.

The world of facts in which we live is *different* from what we seek in philosophy, i.e. *Konkyo*. This is how Ino-ue interpreted Plato's theory of Ideas. Plato suggested that we should separate ourselves from the confusing world of generation, and encounter another horizon of reality, namely Ideas. Ino-ue understood that 'separation' and 'participation' – the two key concepts of Platonic philosophy – indicate the relation between our factual world (a part) and the grounding *Konkyo* (the whole). He proposed that participation (*meta-echein*) means 'being grasped from behind (背後)' (Ino-ue, 1974, p. 141, 'Practice for *Ideai*').

> We must recognise that 'separated-ness (離存性)', and '*koto-nari* (異なり)' (difference, *heteron, thateron*) from our horizon lie in the Ideas (*ideai*), which *are not* on our side, being separated from us. (Ino-ue, 1974, p. 143, 'Practice for *Ideai*', my translation)

Ino-ue devised many puns in the Japanese language and '*ide-a-i* (出て遭い)' is one of them: the plural of the Greek word 'Idea' and the Japanese word 'to encounter'. He took our philosophical mission as to respond to the challenge from *Konkyo* and to create ourselves as a work of the *Konkyo*. In other words, we must expose ourselves to *Konkyo* and carve ourselves to become his son '*ko-to-nari* (子となり)'.[16] Although he emphasized the special experience of encounter, his stance was different from Izutsu, in so far as he avoided the label 'mysticism (神秘主義)'.[17] In this way, Ino-ue understood philosophy not as mere theoretical enquiry or systematic research, but as a challenging way of living our own life in this world.

Although Ino-ue reached this position in the 1960s, he later became a harsh critic of Plato's philosophy. He considered Plato to

---

[15] The term '*konkyo*' (German 'Grund') seems to show the deep influence of German mysticism on modern Japanese thoughts. Meister Eckhardt and other thinkers discussed God as the 'Grund' of all beings and emphasized '*unio mystica*'.

[16] Ino-ue appealed to the etymological connection of *Yamato-kotoba*: '*koto*/*goto* (事, 言, 如, 同, 殊, 別, 異), in Ino-ue (1974, p. 161, 'Practice for *Ideai*'). This use of etymological association is shared with his former colleague, Sakabe Megumi.

[17] Ino-ue criticised 'mysticism' as empty secrecy (Ino-ue, 1974, p. 216, '*Ideai*').

resort to an intuitive search for truth in the soul.[18] He argued that, even if Plato encountered the Ideas and saw the truth (as Plato believed), this turned out to be another belief. Insofar as Plato heavily relied on his own conviction of the encounter experience, he can never come out of the closed, 'private' world of the soul. This, Ino-ue believed, was blind faith as opposed to philosophy.

I think that we should face his criticism of Plato, since it shows us how mystic understandings of Plato's philosophy reach an impasse. Ino-ue showed both a provocative but straightforward way for approaching the Platonic Ideas and its fundamental drawbacks.

5. The Theory of Ideas Reconsidered

Studying Plato first at the University of Tokyo in Japan and next in Cambridge (UK), I gradually realised that the essence of Plato's theory of Ideas may be missing in current philosophical studies. In my recent papers, both in English and Japanese, I emphasize the aspects of separation (離在), purification (浄化), and transcendence (超越) as the core concepts of Plato's philosophy.

We know that Aristotle identified 'separation' of intelligible things from sensible things as the essential aspect of Plato's theory of Ideas. This aspect was fully examined by Matsunaga Yuji (松永雄二, 1929–2021), a Plato scholar at Kyushu University and close friend of Ino-ue Tadashi. Matsunaga analysed the dynamism of 'separation' in the following way (Matsunaga, 1993, 'On the Separation and Participation of the Forms'). The Ideas are *separated* from many changing and conflicting *states of affairs*. We should stand away from the so-called conflicting appearances (for example, that something is both just and unjust, or beautiful and ugly) to realise the absolute being of the just or the beautiful. The Idea of the beautiful is beautiful *itself by itself*. Here 'separation' is twofold: it is separated from many beautiful things, on the one hand, and from the other Ideas, such as Ugliness and Justice, on the other. Matsunaga stressed the significance of correctly understanding 'separation' rather than 'participation' in Plato's theory of Ideas.

Following Matsunaga's interpretation, I suggest that Plato also used the concept of 'separation' in another way in the *Phaedo*: it

---

[18] Ino-ue stayed abroad in the USA from 1967 to 1968. During this time he met G.E.L. Owen at Harvard University and was greatly influenced by Owen's analytic reading of Aristotle. This caused his radical shift from Plato to Aristotle.

also signifies the separation of the soul from the body, in the definition of death. Socrates says that the philosopher 'does not concern himself with the body, but in so far as he can, *separates* himself from it, and concentrates upon the soul'.[19] This separation enables the soul to reach the higher cognitive state called 'wisdom' (*phronesis*), concerning the Ideas. When Socrates characterises the soul in terms of 'separation', he connects it with the ontological 'separation' of the Ideas from sensible things. Thus, the double use of the word 'separation' for the soul and the Idea clarifies the close relationship between the soul and Ideas. The soul's being alone by itself and the Ideas' being themselves by themselves stand or fall together. They are correlative and make a pair.

We come to know the Ideas when the soul gets separated from the body to be alone by itself. This separating process is called 'purification'. Here, the two 'separations' coincide to make an experience of transcendence:

Experience of transcendence

Soul itself = intellect --- <wisdom> --- Idea: always being the same

⇧ ⟋ ⇧

separation or purification   conversion   separation

⇧ ⟋ ⇧

I: soul & body   ---   <sensation> --- Sensible things: 'are and are not'

Transformation of subject   **Revelation of reality**

In this diagram, our initial state is at the bottom: the embodied soul perceives sensible objects which both *are* and *are not* so and so.[20] Then, as the soul becomes aware of something beyond these, it is separated and eventually becomes the true soul, that is, the intellect. Then it observes and knows purely the Ideas, which always *are*. This shift from the bottom to the upper stage is the double change of the subject and the reality. This experience can be traditionally called 'transcendence (超越)'.[21]

---

[19] Plato, *Phaedo*, 64E. For 'separation' in the *Phaedo*, see Notomi (2018).

[20] This confusing state is called 'conflicting appearances' in modern commentaries.

[21] For the diagram, see Notomi (2018, p. 292).

The theory of Ideas indicates not only the transcendence of the objects but also a transcending experience of the subject, namely our-*selves*. Therefore, although the Ideas may appear to be unnecessary and a mistake to the embodied soul in the corporeal world, once it gets separated, the intelligible world of Ideas is revealed as its proper object. In other words, at the lower stage, we live everyday life with bodily sensations and opinions, but we can proceed to the higher stage where we contemplate the Ideas with knowledge and wisdom.

I take transcendence and transformation of the subject as a response to 'care for the soul' in Plato's *Apology of Socrates* since it means to convert from the bodily concerns to our true self. The 'practice of death' in the *Phaedo* signifies the same conversion of the soul from various earthly things, such as property, honour, appearance, desire, and body, to the true *self*.[22] In the transcendence experience, the transformation of our soul into its original form, namely intellect, undergoes a complete change of view of reality, from grasping confusing and conflicting sensibles to absolute and eternal Ideas. When the soul is awakened, the world appears totally different, and only then does the sensible experience seem like a dream. The philosophy of Plato awakens our soul from the dreaming state and helps us go up to contemplation of the Ideas and transform our*selves*. If this interpretation is correct, the theory of Ideas is not just a theory about metaphysical entities, but an ethical practice of the soul.

This is my present reading of Plato's theory of Ideas, which in certain ways has been strongly influenced by my Japanese predecessors. Plato is a major philosopher who has had a great influence on Japanese thinking and society since the mid-nineteenth century. Since then, we have developed a new approach and proper reading for doing and living philosophy through philosophical dialogue with Plato.

References

Gail Fine, *Plato on Knowledge and Forms: Selected Essays* (Oxford: Oxford University Press, 2003).

Tadashi Ino-ue, *Challenge from Konkyo* (根拠よりの挑戦), (Tokyo: University of Tokyo Press, 1974).

Tadashi Ino-ue, *Carving of Philosophy 1: Beyond Sex and Death* (哲学の刻み 1, 性と死を超えるもの), (Kyoto: Hozo-kan, 1985).

---

[22] In Notomi (2013) I examine the continuity from the *Apology of Socrates* to the *Phaedo*.

Noburu Notomi

Toshihiko Izutsu, *Mystic Philosophy: A Study on Greek Philosophy* (神秘哲学 ギリシアの部), (Tokyo: Hikari-no-shobo, 1949; reprinted, Tokyo: Iwanami, 2019).

Toshihiko Izutsu, *Consciousness and Essence: Toward the Spiritual Orient* (意識と本質 精神的東洋を索めて), (Tokyo: Iwanami, 1983; reprinted, 1991).

Yuji Matsunaga, *Knowing and Not-Knowing: Prelude to the Study of Plato's Philosophy* (知と不知—プラトン哲学研究序説) (Tokyo: University of Tokyo Press, 1993).

Noburu Notomi, 'Socrates in the *Phaedo*', in George Boys-Stones, Dimitri El Murr, and Christopher Gill (eds.), *The Platonic Art of Philosophy* (Cambridge: Cambridge University Press, 2013), 51–69.

Noburu Notomi, 'The Platonic Idea of Ideal and its Reception in East Asia', in Konstantine Boudouris, Costas Dimitracopoulos, and Evangelos Protopapadakis (eds.), *Selected Papers from the XXIII World Congress of Philosophy: Philosophy as Inquiry and Way of Life* (Charlottesville, Virginia: Philosophy Documentation Center, 2015), 137–147.

Noburu Notomi, 'Freedom and the State in Plato's *Politeia* (*Republic*): Reconsidering the Concept of '*Politeia*'', *Japan Studies in Classical Antiquity*, 3 (2017), 57–68.

Noburu Notomi, 'The Soul and Forms in Plato's *Phaedo*', in Gabriele Cornelli, Thomas M. Robinson, and Francisco Bravo (eds.), *Plato's* Phaedo*: Selected Papers from the Eleventh Symposium Platonicum* (Sankt Augustin: Academia Verlag, 2018), 288–293.

Noburu Notomi, 'How Modern Japanese People Read Plato's *Politeia*', in Yosef Z. Liebersohn, John Glucker, and Ivor Ludlam (eds.), *Plato and His Legacy* (Cambridge: Cambridge Scholars Publishing, 2021), 219–232.

Megumi Sakabe, *Hermeneutics of the Mask* (仮面の解釈学) (Tokyo: University of Tokyo Press, 1976).

How to Change Your Mind: The Contemplative Practices of Philosophy

LEAH KALMANSON

Abstract
The methods of philosophy may be associated with practices such as rational dialogue, logical analysis, argumentation, and intellectual inquiry. However, many philosophical traditions in Asia, as well as in the ancient Greek world, consider an array of embodied contemplative practices as central to the work of philosophy and as philosophical methods in themselves. Here we will survey a few such practices, including those of the ancient Greeks as well as examples from East Asian traditions. Revisiting the contemplative practices of philosophy can help us to rethink the boundaries of the discipline, the nature and scope of scholarly methods, and the role of philosophy in everyday life.

1. Introduction

In 2021, two new books were released with the same title: *Philosophy as a Way of Life*. The first, co-authored by Matthew Sharpe and Michael Ure, inaugurates a new book series at Bloomsbury on the topic 're-inventing' philosophy as a way of life. The second, an edited volume by James M. Ambury, Tushar Irani, and Kathleen Wallace, is a contribution to Wiley's series in metaphilosophy. All such publications hearken back to the 1995 book *Philosophy as a Way of Life*, an English-language collection of the writings of Pierre Hadot, whose French-language publications in the 1980s introduced the notion of 'philosophy as a way of life' and the 'spiritual exercises' associated with it. As evidenced by the spate of new publications and the book series, the topic undoubtedly remains popular.

Hadot's work, and the work that follows in his wake, focuses on the various practices of the ancient Greek philosophers, such as the Stoics and Epicureans, many of which can be described as meditations or structured contemplative methodologies aimed at self-betterment and self-cultivation. Such 'spiritual exercises' convey practitioners toward a way of living that is more rational, more reasonable, and, we might say, more existentially content. As Sharpe and Ure trace in their impressive history of the idea, the approach to philosophy

doi:10.1017/S1358246123000024

Leah Kalmanson

as a 'way of life' is repeatedly revived by various thinkers throughout European history such as the Italian Renaissance humanists and French Enlightenment literati. However, such revivals are ultimately unable to stem the tide that carries us to where we are today, where philosophy has become, we might say, somewhat pedantic, focused often exclusively on logical analysis and argumentation, and perhaps overly concerned with thought experiments that are, by design, abstractions. Without casting judgement on the contemporary approach to academic philosophy as a discipline, we may nonetheless note that it is not invested, at least not explicitly, in the kind of holistic project of self-formation and transformation that marked earlier Greek models.

Sharpe and Ure note that the central, founding premise of any approach to philosophy as a 'way of life' is the claim that 'philosophical discourse, through teaching and intellectual exercises, can change people's deep-set beliefs' (Sharpe and Ure, 2021, p. 15). At stake, they say, is the philosopher's contention that human beings are rational animals and hence that rational contemplation is meaningfully transformative. Nonetheless, there has been sobering data recently on what has been called the 'backfire effect', which documents our tendency to double down on our deeply held beliefs *especially* when we are presented with facts, evidence, or good argumentation to the contrary (see Nyhan and Reifler, 2010). In other words, when confronted with good reasons that we might be wrong about something, we tend to believe even more strongly that we are right.

Here, I want to pursue this issue cross-culturally. In response to the recent renewal of interest in philosophical contemplative practices, I explore examples from the schools of ancient Greek philosophy as well as the scholarly academies of Song-dynasty China (960–1279). This rich period in Chinese intellectual history has much to contribute to the ongoing discussion of 'philosophy as a way of life'. In what follows, we will see many similarities in the Greek and Chinese practices themselves but some fundamental differences in the understanding of why those practices are effective. If we dig down into these differences, we will find divergent assumptions about the world, the mind, how the mind works, and what happens when we change it.

2. Philosophical Practices of the Greeks

We begin with perhaps the most familiar philosophical practice of the Greeks – i.e., dialogue, as in the famous Socratic dialogues written by

Plato. When I teach these in my undergraduate classes, I often have students compose their own philosophical argument in dialogue form. Plato uses a set of tools that I want students to use – I want them to identify the unstated or hidden premises in a partner's proposed claim; I want them to identify gaps or mistakes in another's deductive reasoning; and I want them to understand the role of counterexamples and thought experiments in philosophical argumentation. The dialogue activity communicates to students what many philosophers today might consider the core values of philosophy as a discipline – namely, that philosophy is a *joint venture* of people in *conversation* seeking the *truth*.

Dialogue as a philosophical methodology was not special to Socrates because Socrates never wrote anything down, nor was it special to Plato because Plato was a playwright. As Pierre Hadot discusses, the question-and-answer style of self-examination is rooted in various 'spiritual exercises' that predate Socrates himself (Hadot, 1995, p. 89). Such a process brings a person to confront her own uncertainties and unearth the contradictions in her own beliefs, so as to develop the properly humble orientation toward truth – or, better to say, *the* truth – that transcends the finite human condition. In this way, the Socratic dialogue, when pursued to its end, results in a spiritual conversion on a path that aims at wisdom.

In addition to this practice of dialogue, which does remain recognizably philosophical today, there were other practices that we do not routinely use in the discipline any longer. These include types of meditations, memorization practices, and other contemplative exercises. For example, the Epicureans recommend various meditations to dispel the fear of death: we should contemplate for ourselves the time before we were born; we should feel, for ourselves, that our own non-existence prior to birth does not provoke any feelings of anxiety; and from there we should work to transfer this calm experience of our previous non-existence to our anticipation of a future non-existence after death (Sharpe and Ure, 2021, pp. 67–68).

Some such meditation exercises were linked to practices of memorization. In these, a practitioner aims to commit to memory certain philosophical doctrines, so as to be able to recall them to the mind in a contemplative mode. The contemplative mode itself is a kind of training for everyday life. By setting aside dedicated time to internalize philosophical doctrines, intentionally and calmly, the practitioner is able to face everyday stresses, anxieties, tragedies, and sorrows, and to apply her learning on the spot. For the Stoics and Neoplatonists, such memorized doctrines might be reminders to practice detachment from the vicissitudes of mortal life and align instead with the true and unchanging nature of ultimate reality. For the Neoplatonists, this ultimate reality is the eternal cosmic unity on which our world of diversity depends. For the Stoics, ultimate nature referred to a material conception of 'god' or a god-principle as the animating intelligence that structures the cosmic body of which we all are a part. As I stated earlier, if we dig down into the philosophical practices of the Greeks, we eventually find that these are rooted in beliefs about the world, the mind, how the mind works, and what happens when we change it.

Let us return to our earlier definition of philosophy as a *joint venture* of people in *conversation* seeking the *truth*. This gives us a picture of philosophy that is, perhaps, somewhat static and purpose driven. It is static in the sense that this kind of philosophy leads to the analytical breakdown of arguments and assertions – philosophy is not an open-ended process but an exercise with a stopping point. This notion of philosophy is purpose driven, then, for that same reason – i.e., we are progressing toward a fixed goal that is, in most cases, a judgment of truth. We can now see that the static and goal-oriented nature of such spiritual exercises are in line with foundational beliefs regarding the unchanging nature of truth and reality in the ancient Greek sense.

We can also see that, obviously, there can be winners and losers. Some of us may take the dialogical journey of philosophy only to find out at some point along the way that we are wrong about something. The issue we face concerns how to admit mistakes and correct our course without provoking the backfire effect I mentioned earlier, which reveals our tendencies to double down on what we believe, especially in the face of good argumentation and evidence to the contrary. My point is that we have to practice taming those emotions that cause us to become defensive; we have to cultivate that reverence for truth, or at least for truth-seeking, that humbles us and coaxes us when needed to concede when we are wrong. This, I think, is a fuller picture of why philosophy *has* to be a way of life – it has to be a full set of physical, psychical, and spiritual practices, because rationality alone is not effective if we are not constitutionally and emotionally prepared for the truth-driven process of argumentation.

Perhaps the above picture takes us beyond the Greek approach to philosophy as a way of life, since the Greeks did seem to believe that contradiction was its own pain and that we naturally do not abide it. As Epictetus says, 'Socrates knew that, if a rational soul be moved by anything [...] [s]how the governing faculty of reason a contradiction, and it will renounce it' (quoted in Sharpe and Ure, 2021, p. 77). My concern, however, is that we actually do need a bit more priming before we are so sensitive to the so-called pain of contradiction. This is why we turn now to a cultural context that is different, but which offers a set of practices with a similar goal – namely, helping us become the kinds of people who can change our minds.

3. Philosophical Practices in Song-Dynasty China

Our setting is Song-dynasty China and the scholarly culture of the academies associated with the tradition we often call 'Confucianism'. This is a somewhat misleading translation for the tradition known as *rujia* (儒家), because it suggests that the historical figure of 'Confucius' (Kongzi 孔子, 551–479 BCE) is the founder of a school. In fact, he was a member of the 'lineage' or 'family' (*jia* 家) of the *ru* (儒), a term better translated as 'scholar' or 'literati'. The *ru*, whose lineage predates the life of Kongzi, were members of China's educated elite: they were often employed as educators or government officials, they were versed in the classic scholarly and literary texts, and they were qualified to preside over various state rites and civic ceremonies as well as the rituals performed at ancestral shrines. In what follows, I use an alternative English word 'Ruism' instead of 'Confucianism' to talk about this rich heritage of what we might call, after Hadot, 'scholarship as a way of life'.

Scholarship in this context is understood as 'investigating things' (*gewu* 格物) and 'extending knowledge' (*zhizhi* 致知), two terms taken from the chapter on 'Great Learning' (*Daxue* 大學) in the Chinese classic *Liji* (禮記) or *Book of Rites*. The investigation of things did have connotations of empirical inquiry into the natural world, but it was most closely associated with reading, reflection, and scholarly study. Practitioners would read the classics, the histories, and all the many commentaries on them in order to perceive certain patterns or tendencies (*li* 理). These might be seasonal cycles, for example, and their effects on agriculture, but most often the focus would be on political, social, and moral affairs. Observing tendencies in human aspirations and endeavours, both in relation to our successes and failures, can help us understand optimal ways of flourishing together in the world and also analyse the causes of mistakes and disasters. All such patterns were seen as interconnected, in that understanding imbalances in an agricultural context might be seen to help us understand imbalances in a social context, regarding strife, or in a medical context, regarding bodily health, and so on.

Leah Kalmanson

In other words, grasping patterns and tendencies in one area can be extended or applied to others. This is the extension of knowledge.

However, before we can do any of this – before we can observe anything, or read anything, or extend what we know – we have to prepare the mind to learn. The famous Song-dynasty philosopher Zhu Xi 朱熹 (1130–1200) says, 'Now, when you want to read books, you must first settle the mind to make it like still water or a clear mirror' (今且要讀書, 須先定其心, 使之 如止水, 如明鏡) (Zhu Xi, *Zhuzi yulei*).[1] One would do this usually by a brief period of quiet sitting and calm breathing before even opening a book. At that point, reading itself is not so much an endeavour aimed at intellectual understanding – although intellectual understanding is one outcome – but rather, reading is an active and audible practice of recitation. As Zhu Xi says, 'The value of a book is in reciting it. By reciting it often, we naturally come to an understanding' (書只貴讀, 讀多自然曉) (*ibid.*).[2] Here, Zhu suggests that there is a kind of inevitability to intellectual insight. That is, the brain will respond to the words of a text according to certain predictable patterns and tendencies. Readers need only to let the process play out.

Zhu Xi describes this process via reference to dynamics such as vibration, resonance, and harmonization. He advises that we open our minds to the way a text itself resonates, even suggesting that we might sit still and hum as a way to calm the mind and perhaps better 'tune in' to a text's meaning: 'Scholars, when reading books, must collect themselves, sit up straight, relax their gaze, hum softly, empty the mind [of forms], and fully immerse themselves [in the texts]' (學者讀書, 須要斂身正坐, 緩視微吟, 虛心涵泳) (*ibid.*).[3] We can see here that in making the mind still like water or clear like a mirror, we are not rendering it simply passive or receptive; rather, we are making it actively responsive so as to better sensitize it to the dynamics of the content that we are studying as it passes through our lips in recitation.

I have said twice now that if we dig down into certain philosophical practices, we will eventually find assumptions about the nature of the world and the mind which help undergird the understanding of *why* these practices are thought to be effective. Here, these quotes from

---

[1] See passage 12 at https://ctext.org/zhuzi-yulei/10/zh. I consulted Daniel K. Gardner (trans.) (1990, p.145).
[2] See passage 65 at https://ctext.org/zhuzi-yulei/10/zh. See also Gardner (1990, p. 137).
[3] See passage 21 at https://ctext.org/zhuzi-yulei/10/zh. See also Gardner (1990, p. 147).

Zhu Xi reflect his own assumptions about what the mind is and how it operates. To take us back to the Greeks for a moment, the important assumptions we saw there included the idea that human beings are uniquely rational, that rationality is at the core of what it means to be human, and that proceeding via reasoning takes us toward the true and unchanging reality at the foundation of all existence. In the Chinese context, we also find the assumption that human beings are rational but not uniquely rational. In different sources, animals are described as having some capacity for rational understanding, in that they can reason their way through tasks, or out of dilemmas, or toward their intended aims. Without digressing too far on this point, we may at least safely say that what the human mind accomplishes via investigating things and extending knowledge is not completely explainable simply by our capacity for rational thought. Moreover, in the Chinese context, we will see a different understanding of the nature of what is ultimately real and what that means for human life. To better understand this, we look next into relevant Chinese theories regarding the nature and origins of the cosmos, all of which play a special role in the philosophical practices of the Song.

4. Cosmological Assumptions in Song-Dynasty Thought

Common cosmogonies in Chinese sources often make reference to a primal state described variously as a great unity (*taiyi* 太一), as the unsurpassable supreme (*taiji* 太極), as limitless (*wuji* 無極), or as chaotic (*hundun* 混沌). Daoist sources may use terms that suggest a void, absence, or emptiness (*xu* 虛, *wu* 無, *kong* 空). In Ruist context, such terms most clearly function as descriptors of a primal state that has not yet been differentiated into any one thing or another – i.e., it is void of form, absent of distinctions, and empty of things.[4] This can be understood as 'primordial *qi*' (*yuanqi* 元氣), where *qi* refers to the basic 'stuff' – i.e., both matter and energy, both physical and psychical – that constitutes the existence of anything that exists at all. *Qi* is an important term which, in the Song dynasty, takes on an especially philosophical usage. The contemporary philosopher JeeLoo Liu refers to this as 'qi-realism': '1) *Qi* is permanent and ubiquitous in the world of nature. There is nothing over and above the realm of *qi*. 2) *Qi* is real in virtue of its causal power. It constitutes everything and is responsible for all changes' (Liu, 2011, p. 61).

[4]   For more on this, see Liu (2014).

Leah Kalmanson

English-language translations of *qi* include 'psychophysical stuff' (Gardner, 1990), 'vital stuff' (Angle and Tiwald, 2017), and 'lively material' (Ivanhoe, 2016). Such terms attempt to capture the sense in which *qi* can refer to material and physical things as well as intangible things, such as thoughts and emotions, or spiritual things, including what the Ruists thought to be the spiritual aspects of people both living and dead. The primal *qi* at our cosmological origin, as an undifferentiated matter-energy matrix not yet divided into either matter, energy, or anything at all, is hence a kind of pure potency.

Then, out of this initial phase comes the spontaneous differentiation into the polar aspects of *yin* (陰) and *yang* (楊), which can refer to differences such as heavy versus light, condensed versus dispersed, or coarse versus refined. This initial distinction allows for recursive interactions, in layers of escalating complexity, to produce more and more complex manifestations of 'stuff'. Eventually, the distinctions result in the earth and the cosmos as we know them, with all the 'myriad things' (*wanwu* 萬物) of our everyday lives.

Here, we are finally coming back around to what the Ruists intend to accomplish when they sit and clear their minds before reading texts or studying. The primal formless *qi* is not only a feature of our cosmological origins, but it is a force that remains with us in the present. In other words, all existing stuff emerges from undifferentiated *qi*, whether we are talking about the first stuff at the inception of the cosmos or all the myriad things around us now that continue to live out, in the present, ongoing processes of materialization, persistence, and eventual disintegration. Meditation is that practice that allows the mind to relax into its primal formless state, a process that is believed to be healthy, refreshing, and invigorating. From this exercise in relaxation, or in settling the mind, we draw down on that primal potency that is the ever-present source of new forms and new ideas, enabling us to call forth those more refined thoughts and emotions that mark the wisdom of the sage (*shengren* 聖人).

Let me be clear that this is not a wilful or ego-driven creativity. By that I mean that the goal of Ruist meditation is to get our own egos out of the way, as it were, and to stay ahead of our ordinary thoughts and emotions so that we are not overtaken by them. Through philosophical practice, we can provide the right conditions in our own mental ecologies through which the power of formless *qi*, or the raw power of reality itself, can express, through us, its own natural tendency to manifest form. This, if anything, distinguishes the human from the animal in the Chinese context: we are a partner in the cosmic project of reality. Or, in the words of the classic text the *Book of Rites* (*Liji* 禮記):

> In the world only people of utmost integrity [*cheng* 誠] are able to make the most of themselves. Those who can make the most of themselves are then able to make the most of others. Those who can make the most of others are then able to make the most of things. Those who can make the most of things are then able to assist the Cosmos and Earth in their transforming [*hua* 化] and creating [*yu* 育]. Those who can assist the Cosmos and Earth in their transforming and creating can then join with them as a triad. (Johnston and Wang (trans.), 2012, p. 325)

In Ruist thought, it is the one who pursues scholarship as a way of life that attains this uniquely human capacity to be a partner in shaping the continued flux of reality.

Earlier we mentioned a Greek understanding of philosophy as a progression toward that eternal unchanging reality that underlies the world of temporary things we ordinarily inhabit. Accordingly, we mentioned the contemplative practices of the Greeks that help orient our minds along this path. In contrast, the Chinese tradition gives us a picture of philosophy that is, perhaps, more dynamic, creative, and open ended. It is dynamic in the sense that we mean the active conditioning of the mind to prime it for learning. Here, critical thinking is not absent but is a baseline minimum needed to avoid certain basic errors in reasoning. Beyond this baseline, philosophy is about conditioning and transforming the mind through scholarly discipline. For that same reason, it is open ended. The goal of philosophical learning is good living, framed in terms of a heightened state of flexibility or as a capacity for appropriate responsiveness in unfamiliar situations.

In other words, whereas we might understand rationality in the Greek context as putting us in touch with a pre-given true *reality*, here we see that our own dynamic creativity is part of the ongoing process of *realizing* what exists, moment to moment. Like with the Greeks, this philosophical process is thought to cultivate in us the kind of humbleness that makes changing our minds possible. This is not a humbleness born of awe before that eternal truth that transcends our understanding, as we might say for the Greeks. Rather, it is a humbleness born of an acceptance of the flux of things, or an acceptance that we must be ready to let go of what we think we know, at a moment's notice, because rapidly changing conditions often do not wait for us to catch up.

Leah Kalmanson

Now, at the outset, I promised two different accounts of what it means to change our minds, and I would not be surprised if readers feel, at the end, that both options are overly optimistic and maybe even a little naïve. Is it naïve to think that there is a greater, truer reality out there, other than the one we are currently experiencing? Is it naïve to think that contradiction is all that painful for people? Or, if we pose these questions from the Ruist perspective, is it naïve to think that reading a book has the power over the mind to bring about understanding naturally? Is it naïve to think that a meditation practice can actually put us in touch with primal cosmic forces? Some days, I do feel far from optimistic on these matters. That said, I have been inspired by the Ruist approach to learning and changing, which does not appeal to our capacity for intellectual deliberation so much as it bypasses our tendency to over-intellectualize according to our own agendas. It purports to give us the tools to train our minds well, despite our own tendencies toward what the Chinese tradition might call 'pettiness' or 'small-mindedness' (*xiaoren* 小人). At the end of his essay *Spiritual Exercises*, Pierre Hadot notes that 'we have forgotten how to read: how to pause, liberate ourselves from our worries, return into ourselves, and leave aside our search for subtlety and originality, in order to meditate calmly, ruminate, and let the texts speak to us' (Hadot, 1995, p. 109). He hopes at most that his work encourages us to appreciate a few 'old truths' and the necessity of reading for ourselves the old books that contain them. That is undoubtedly a satisfying goal for this brief essay, as well.

References

James M. Ambury, Tushar Irani, Kathleen Wallace (eds.), *Philosophy as a Way of Life: Historica, Contemporary, and Pedagogical Perspectives* (Malden, MA: Wiley, 2021).

Stephen C. Angle and Justin Tiwald, *Neo-Confucianism: A Philosophical Introduction* (Cambridge: Polity Press, 2017).

Gao Panlong, *Ru Meditation: Gao Panlong* (1562–1626), Bin Song (trans.), (Boston: Ru Media Company, 2018).

Daniel K. Gardner (trans.), *Learning to Be a Sage: Selection from the Conversations of Master Chu, Arranged Topically*, by Chu Hsi [Zhu Xi], (Berkeley: University of California Press, 1990).

Pierre Hadot, *Philosophy as a Way of Life* (Oxford: Wiley-Blackwell, 1995).

Philip J. Ivanhoe, *Three Streams: Confucian Reflections on Learning and the Moral Heart-Mind in China, Korea, and Japan* (Oxford: Oxford University Press, 2016).

Ian Johnston and Wang Ping (trans.), *Daxue and Zhongyong* (Hong Kong: Chinese University of Hong Kong Press, 2012).

JeeLoo Liu, 'The Is-Ought Correlation in Neo-Confucian *Qi*-Realism: How Normative Facts Exist in Natural States of *Qi*', *Contemporary Chinese Thought* 42:1 (2011), 60–77.

JeeLoo Liu, 'Was There Something in Nothingness? The Debate on the Primordial State between Daoism and Neo-Confucianism', in JeeLoo Liu and Douglas L. Berger (eds.), *Nothingness in Asian Philosophy*, (New York: Routledge, 2014), 181–196.

Brendan Nyhan and Jason Reifler, 'When Corrections Fail: The Persistence of Political Misperceptions', *Political Behavior* 32:2 (June 2010), 303–330.

Matthew Sharpe and Michael Ure, *Philosophy as a Way of Life* (London: Bloomsbury, 2021).

Zhu Xi 朱熹, *Zhuzi yulei* 朱子語類, in Donald Sturgeon (ed.), *Chinese Text Project* (2011), http://ctext.org/zhuzi-yulei/zh.

'Zoetology': A New Name for an Old Way of Thinking[1]

ROGER T. AMES

Abstract

The classical Greeks give us a substance ontology grounded in 'being *qua* being' or 'being *per se*' (*to on he on*) that guarantees a permanent and unchanging subject as the substratum for the human experience. With the combination of *eidos* and *telos* as the formal and final cause of independent things such as persons, this 'substance' necessarily persists through change. This substratum or essence includes its purpose for being, and is defining of the 'what-it-means-to-be-a-thing-of-this-kind' of any particular thing in setting a closed, exclusive boundary and the strict identity necessary for it to be this, and not that.

In the *Yijing* 易經 or *Book of Changes* we find a vocabulary that makes explicit cosmological assumptions that are a stark alternative to this substance ontology, and provides the interpretive context for the Confucian canons by locating them within a holistic, organic, and ecological worldview. To provide a meaningful contrast with this fundamental assumption of *on* or 'being' we might borrow the Greek notion of *zoe* or 'life' and create the neologism '*zoe*-tology' as 'the art of living'. This cosmology begins from 'living' (*sheng* 生) itself as the motive force behind change, and gives us a world of boundless 'becomings': not 'things' that *are*, but 'events' that are *happening,* a contrast between an ontological conception of the human 'being' and a process conception of what I will call human 'becomings'.

1. Taking Advantage of our Gadamerian Prejudices

A familiar way of thinking about 'methodologies' that we associate with rational, systematic philosophies are the formal principles or theoretical procedures of inquiry employed in a particular field or discipline. For example, in philosophy, we might speak of Socratic dialectics or Cartesian rational skepticism as methodologies, and of analytic, logical, and phenomenological methodologies among many others. The term 'methodology' itself suggests the familiar theory and practice dichotomy by

---

[1]   This essay is excerpted from a draft of a book-length manuscript presently in progress tentatively entitled *Zoetology: A New Name for an Old Way of Thinking.*

doi:10.1017/S1358246123000012   © The Royal Institute of Philosophy and the contributors 2023

formalizing the method and making the principles of explanation prior to their application.

In looking for a starting point in formulating my own method (rather than methodology) for doing comparative philosophy, I appeal to John Dewey's postulate of 'immediate empiricism' (the notion that our immediate experience is our reality) and the primacy he gives to practice. As a philosophical method, Dewey's radical empiricism requires that since all human problems arise within the 'hadness' of immediate experience as it is had by specific persons in the world, the resolution to these problems must be sought through theorizing this same experience in our best efforts to make its outcomes more productive and intelligent. 'Hadness' for Dewey is not some claim to 'pure' or 'primordial' experience, but simply what experience *is* as it is *had* by those persons experiencing it. In formulating this method, Dewey begins by asserting that

> Immediate empiricism postulates that things – anything, everything, in the ordinary or non-technical use of the term 'thing' – are what they are experienced as. [...] If you wish to find out what subjective, objective, physical, mental, cosmic, psychic, cause, substance, purpose, activity, evil, being, quality – any philosophic term, in short – means, go to experience and see what the thing is experienced *as*. (Dewey, 1977, Vol. 3, pp. 158, 165)

As Dewey's alternative to starting from abstract philosophical concepts and theories, he is arguing that all such terms of art must be understood as the 'thats' of specifically experienced meanings. Dewey's method provides us with a way of ascertaining what the language we use actually means, and precludes the dualisms that usually follow in the wake of deploying abstract and thus decontextualizing terms such as reality, rationality, objectivity, justice, and indeed, methodology itself.

Corollary to Dewey's immediate empiricism is recognition of the fact that experience itself is always a continuous, a collaborative, and an unbounded affair. Thus, his 'hadness', far from precluding a robust subjective aspect, insists upon it. Before Dewey formulated his postulate of immediate empiricism, William James had earlier offered his own version of a similar idea that probably inspired Dewey, referring to it as a 'radical empiricism':

> To be radical, an empiricism must neither admit into its constructions any element that is not directly experienced, nor exclude from them any element that is directly experienced. For such a philosophy, *the relations that connect experiences*

must themselves be experienced relations, and any kind of relation experienced must be accounted as 'real' as anything else in the system. (James, 1976, p. 22, italics in original)

And more recently, yet another advocate of a pragmatic approach to philosophy, Hilary Putnam, brings additional clarity to this postulate of immediate empiricism by not only rejecting 'view-from-nowhere' objectivism, but by further insisting that the subjective dimension of experience is always integral to what the world really is. Putnam insists that

[...] elements of what we call "language" or "mind" *penetrate so deeply into what we call "reality" that the very project of represent-ing ourselves as being "mapper's" of something "language-independ-ent" is fatally compromised from the start.* Like Relativism, but in a different way, Realism is an impossible attempt to view the world from Nowhere. (Putnam, 1990, p. 28, italics in original)

Putnam will not admit of any understanding of the real world that cleaves it off from its human participation and that does not accept our experience of it as what the world *really* is. He is making this same point regarding the holistic and inclusive nature of experience when he insists that

[...] the heart of pragmatism, it seems to me – of James's and Dewey's pragmatism if not of Peirce's – was the supremacy of the agent point of view. If we find that we must take a certain point of view, use a certain 'conceptual system', when engaged in a practical activity, in the widest sense of practical activity, then we must not simultaneously advance the claim that it is not really 'the way things are in themselves'. (Putnam, 1987, p. 83)

When we carry Dewey's postulate of immediate empiricism over to the task of interpreting another philosophical tradition, if we are to resist cultural reductionism and to allow the other culture to speak on its own terms, we do best to employ a comparative cultural hermeneutics as our method of inquiry. The starting point of hermeneutics, the branch of philosophy that has to do with the theory and practice of interpretation, is an acknowledgment of the interpretive interdependence of the structures of meaning within the experience from which understanding is to be gained. Hans-Georg Gadamer insists that

[...] understanding is not a method which the inquiring consciousness applies to an object it chooses and so turns it into objective knowledge; rather, being situated within an event of tradition, a process of handing down, is a prior condition of understanding. *Understanding proves to be an event.* (Gadamer, 1997, p. 309, italics in original)

It is in this spirit of understanding as an event that Gadamer uses the term 'prejudices' (*Vorurteil*) not as blind biases, but on the contrary, as acknowledging that a deliberate cognizance of our own prejudgments facilitates rather than obstructs our access and insight into something we do not know. These prejudgments are not only our presuppositions, but also our projective interests and concerns. For Gadamer, the hermeneutical circle (that is, locating a text within its interpretive context) within which understanding is always situated requires of us that we continually strive to be aware of what we carry over into our new experience, since critical attention to our own assumptions and purposes can serve to positively condition the depth and quality of our interpretation of what we encounter.[2] To be clear, the claim is that a comparative cultural hermeneutics has the potential to inspire a greater degree of insight than simply working within either tradition separately, because the analogical associations and contrasts that emerge in the process are productive of additional meaning. Even fundamental differences when used properly can be activated to serve the interests of clearer understanding. J.L. Austin remarks that

[...] the world must exhibit (we must observe) similarities and dissimilarities (there could not be one without the other): if everything were either absolutely indistinguishable from anything else or completely unlike anything else, there would be nothing to say. (Austin, 1961, pp. 89–90)

Such analogical correlations that appeal to either similarities or differences between cultural traditions can be productive or otherwise to the extent that they are a source of increased meaning; that is, to the extent that they provide us with something to say.

2. Comparative Cultural Hermeneutics as Analogical Thinking

It can be argued that all meaningful interpretation of experience, with 'interpretation' itself literally meaning 'a go-between negotiation', emerges analogically through establishing and aggregating a pattern of truly productive correlations between what we already know and what we would know. Of course, since analogize we must, at the

---

[2] See Malpas (2018).

same time we might also want to allow that not all analogies are equally apposite. As has become apparent in the troubled history of having translated and thus 'carried over' Chinese philosophy into the Western academy, poorly chosen comparisons can be a persisting source of distortion and of cultural condescension. A heavy-handed and impositional 'Christian', 'Heideggerian', and yes, a 'Pragmatic' or 'Whiteheadian' reading of Chinese philosophy as well, betrays the reader by distorting both the Chinese tradition and the Western analogue in the comparison. As inescapably correlative thinkers, we need to be analogically retail and piecemeal rather than working in whole cloth.

Again, analogies can be productive of both associations and contrasts, and we can learn much from both. To take one example, the *Focusing the Familiar* (*Zhongyong* 中庸) has been hugely influential as one of the Confucian *Four Books*. In this canonical text, it argues that the best of human beings have both the capacity and the responsibility to be co-creators with the heavens and the earth. In seeking to interpret this text, we might find an associative analogy with the process philosophy of A.N. Whitehead in his attempt to reinstate 'creativity' within the evolving life process as an important human value. For Whitehead, claims about the 'aseity' – that is, the self-sufficiency and perfection – of God in traditional theology precludes any interesting or coherent sense of human creativity. Following the sustained challenge Whitehead directs at conventional ways of thinking about creativity, the word 'creativity' itself becomes an individual entry in a 1971 supplement to the *Oxford English Dictionary* with two of the three references being made to Whitehead's own *Religion in the Making*. At the same time, however, we might be keenly aware that when the same Whitehead invokes the primordial nature of God and the Eternal Objects that are sustained in His thinking, the long shadow of Aristotelian metaphysics and the Unmoved Mover sets a real limit on the relevance for classical Chinese process cosmology of these aspects of Whitehead's philosophy.

Aristotle's teleology (his doctrine of design and purpose), his substance ontology (his doctrine that all things are defined by an unchanging essence), and his reliance upon logic as *the* demonstrable method that will secure us truth, might serve as contrastive analogies with a Chinese process cosmology that abjures fixed beginnings and ends, that precludes any strict formal identity, and that will not yield up the principle of non-contradiction as enabling of erstwhile apodictic or unconditional knowledge. On the other hand, Aristotle's resistance to Platonic abstraction in promoting an aggregating practical wisdom correlates rather productively with one of the central issues in classical Confucian moral philosophy. That is, Aristotelian *phron-esis* (practical wisdom) with its commitment to the cultivation of excellent habits (*hexis*) in the practical affairs of everyday living has some immediate resonance with the ubiquitous Confucian assumption that knowing and doing are inseparable and mutually entailing (*zhixingheyi* 知行合一).

In our project of cultural interpretation, whether they be associative or contrastive analogies, we have no choice but to identify productive correlations that, with effort and imagination, can be qualified and refined in such a way as to introduce culturally novel ideas into our own world as a source of enrichment for our own ways of thinking and living. In this cultural translation, we certainly must be deliberate in the picking and choosing of our analogies – but at the end of the day, pick and choose we must.

3. Classical Greek Ontology and Chinese Zoetology: 'A Small Stock of Ideas'[3]

As a self-confessed philosopher of culture, I take it as my task to identify, excavate, and articulate generalizations that distinguish different cultural narratives. It is only in being cognizant of these uncommon cultural assumptions that, in some degree at least, we are able to respect fundamental differences and locate the philosophical discussion somewhere between the alternative worldviews. Just as with the watershed of the Western cultural narrative we would identify with Plato and Aristotle and Hellenistic culture, certain enduring commitments were made explicit in the formative period of Chinese philosophy that are more persistent than others, and that allow us to make useful generalizations about the evolution of this continuing tradition. In the language of the *Yijing* 易經 or *Book of Changes*, we must anticipate 'continuities in change' (*biantong* 變通).

Again if we, as what Charles Taylor has called 'language animals', acknowledge the power that entrenched linguistic propensities might have in shaping the philosophy of grammar of a given population, it might occasion a reconsideration of our usual way of thinking about

---

[3] Ontology too is 'a new term for an old way of thinking' that can be traced back to the classical Greek sources and their philosophical problematics. The oldest extant record of the term 'ontology' as Gk. *onto-* 'being' or 'that which is', and *-logia* discourse', is in its Latin form *ontologia* and appears in the writings of two German philosophers, Jacob Lorhard's *Ogdoas Scholastica* (1606) and Rudolf Gockel's *Lexicon Philosophicum* (1613).

the originality of our own great philosophers. Without slighting their defining influence on their respective traditions, we might ask to what extent in the 'history of thought' are a Plato and an Aristotle and indeed a Confucius constructing their philosophical oeuvres out of whole cloth, and to what extent are they – with penetrating insight, certainly – making explicit what is already implicated in the structure and function of the languages they have inherited from their predecessors? In what degree are they cultural archaeologists in the business of 'recovering' and laying bare the legacy of 'common sense' bequeathed to them by their progenitors?

While the meticulous scholar Nathan Sivin is adamant in exhorting us to resist 'either-or' simplicity in our cultural comparisons, at the same time he has also observed that 'man's prodigious creativity seems to be based on the permutations and recastings of a rather small stock of ideas' (Sivin, 1974, p. xi). If such is the case, how do we then get to this 'rather small stock of ideas' that might allow for the mapping out of their subsequent permutations and recastings? What in our ways of thinking grounded in the classical Greek and Chinese worldviews are the underlying similarities and dissimilarities; what are their respective prejudices? Where in their deepest cultural strata are the uncommon assumptions, the prejudgments that have their beginnings in the self-understanding of the always situated human experience as these cultural habits have been sedimented into their persistent yet ever evolving common sense?

One prejudice of the first order that emerges early in the Western philosophical narrative is the commitment to substance ontology with all of its far-reaching implications. Ontology is the branch of metaphysics that seeks to classify and explain the things that exist, and its underlying assumption is that there are substances or essences internal to things that are available to us to classify them as this and not that. Ontology privileges 'being *per se*' and a categorical language with its 'essence' and 'attribute' dualism, giving us substances as property-bearers, and properties that are borne, respectively. Such ontological thinking animates Plato's pursuit of formal, 'real' definitions in his quest for certainty (that is, definitions not of words but of what really *is*), and underlies Aristotle's taxonomical science of knowing 'what *is* what'. For these classical Greek philosophers, only what is real and thus true can be the proper object of knowledge, giving us a logic of the changeless. Indeed, such ontological assumptions produce a decidedly categorical way of thinking captured in the principle of non-contradiction that claims something cannot be 'A' and 'not-A' at the same time.

Roger T. Ames

G.W.F. Hegel in his Introduction to the *Encyclopaedia Logic* reflects at great length upon the question: where does philosophy begin and the inquiry start? And in this reverie, he concludes that because philosophy 'does not have a beginning in the sense of the other sciences', it must be the case that 'the beginning only has a relation to the subject who takes the decision to philosophise' (Hegel, 1991, p. 41).[4] I want to embrace Hegel's concern about the importance of understanding the starting point of our philosophical inquiry, and I also want to heed his injunction to begin from the subjects who take the decision to philosophize. As my starting point, I will posit a contrast between a classical Greek ontological conception of human 'beings' and a classical *Book of Changes* process conception of what I will call human 'becomings', a contrast between a discrete human being as a noun and interdependent human becomings as gerunds.

The ontological intuition that 'only Being is' is at the core of Parmenides' treatise *The Way of Truth* and is the basis of the ontology that follows from it. The classical Greeks give us a substance ontology grounded in 'being *qua* (or 'as') being' or 'being *per se*' (that is, the self-sufficiency of being in itself as it defines any particular thing) that guarantees a permanent and unchanging subject as the substratum for the human experience. With the combination of *eidos* (the essential characteristic that makes something this and not that) and *telos* (the design and purpose of a thing) as the formal and final causes of independent things such as persons, this 'sub-stance' necessarily persists through change. In this ontology, 'to exist' and 'to be' are implicated in one term. The same copula verb 'is' (or L. *esse*) answers the two-fold questions of first *why* something exists, that is, its origins and its goal, and then *what* it is, its substance. This substratum or essence includes its purpose for being, and is defining of the 'what-it-means-to-be-a-thing-of-this-kind' of any particular thing in setting a closed, exclusive boundary and the strict identity necessary for it to be this, and not that.

---

[4]   For Hegel himself, it is the ultimate project of such philosophizing to bring this person – the finite spirit, the single intellect, the philosopher – into identity with God as the object of pure thinking. And for Hegel like Confucianism and unlike the Greeks, persons are not facts (like legs) but achievements (like walking) that could not do what they do and become what they are without the structures of the human community. For Hegel, the person as an abstract fact does not do justice to the process of becoming a person. Personhood is an irreducibly social achievement in the sense that identities emerge in and through difference, being at once affirmed by oneself and conferred on one by others.

The question of *why* something exists is answered by an appeal to determinative, originative, and indemonstrable first principles (Gk. *arche*, L. *principium*), and provides the metaphysical separation between creator and creature. The question of *what* something is, is answered by its limitation and definition, and provides the onto-logical distinction between substance and incidental qualities, between real essence and its contingent attributes. In expressing the necessity, self-sufficiency, and independence of things, this substance or essence as the subject of predication is the object of knowledge. It tells us, as a matter of logical necessity, what is what, and is the source of truth in revealing to us with certainty, what is real and what is not. As the contemporary philosopher Zhao Tingyang 趙汀陽 avers, this kind of substance ontology defining the real things that constitute the content of an orderly and structured cosmos

> [...] provides a 'dictionary' kind of explanation of the world, seeking to set up an accurate understanding of the limits of all things. In simple terms, it determines 'what is what' and all concepts are footnotes to 'being' or 'is'.[5] (Zhao, 2016, p. 147)

This kind of causal thinking is precisely what John Dewey is refer-encing in his concern about what he calls *the* philosophical fallacy. Dewey alerts us to our inveterate habit of decontextualizing and essentializing one element within the continuity of experience, and then in our best efforts to overcome this post hoc distinction, of then construing this same element as foundational and causal. As a concrete example of this habit, in achieving our personal identities in the process of our ongoing narratives, we abstract something called 'being' or 'human nature' out of the complexity of this continu-ing experience, and then make this abstraction antecedent to and causal of the process itself. For Dewey,

> [...] the reality is the growth-process itself. [...] The real exist-ence is the history in its entirety, the history just as what it is. The operations of splitting it up into two parts and then having to unite them again by appeal to causative power are equally arbitrary and gratuitous. (Dewey, 1985, Vol. 1, p. 210)

---

[5] [...] 是对世界的"字典式"解释，试图建立界定万物的决定理解，简单的说，就是断定"什么是什么，"一切观念皆为"在／是"(being/is) 的注脚。I am using with minor changes the translation of this book by Edmund Ryden that is forthcoming from the University of California Press.

Roger T. Ames

In the *Book of Changes*, we find a vocabulary that makes explicit cosmological assumptions that stand in stark alternative to this substance ontology, and provides the interpretive context for the Confucian canons by locating them within a holistic, organic, and ecological worldview. In this essay, I have taken it upon myself to create the neologism 'zoetology' with Gk. *zoe-* 'life' and *-logia* 'discourse' as a new term for an old way of thinking that has deep roots in classical Chinese cosmology. It gives us a contrast between '*on*-tology' as 'the science of being *per se*' and '*zoe*-tology' that we might translate as *shengshenglun* 生生論: 'the art of living'. This cosmology begins from 'living' (*sheng* 生) itself as the motive force behind change, and gives us a world of boundless 'becomings'; it gives us not 'things' that *are*, but 'events' that are *happening*. And it is the nature of life itself that it seeks to optimize the available conditions for its continuing growth.

The starting point in this zoetological cosmology then is that nothing does anything by itself; association is a fact. Since the very nature of life is associative and transactional, the vocabulary appealed to in defining Confucian cosmology is irreducibly collateral: always multiple, never one. Everything is at once what it is for itself, for its specific context, and for the unsummed totality. Thus there are always correlative *yinyang* 陰陽 aspects within any process of change, describing the focal identity that makes something uniquely what it is, and by virtue of its vital relations, what it is becoming. Important to an understanding of this vocabulary is the gestalt shift (that is, a paradigm shift in one's perception of something) from the Greek noun-dominated thinking with its world of human 'beings' and essential 'things', to the Confucian gerundive assumptions about the always eventful nature of human 'becomings' living their lives within their unbounded natural, social, and cultural ecologies. It is the difference between a leg and walking, between a lung and breathing.

Turning to the human experience specifically, persons are not defined in terms of limitation, self-sufficiency, and independence, but ecologically by the growth they experience in their intercourse with other persons and their worlds. Given the primacy of vital relations that give persons their focal identities, any particular person is holographic in existing at the pleasure of everything else. Holography – literally, the whole as it is implicated in each thing – is that way of understanding things that begins from the notion that everything is constituted by its particular relations with everything else. The question of why such persons exist is explained by how they exist and what they mean for each other. And the necessity in ontology of defining what is what is replaced by the zoetological possibilities each thing affords everything else for growth, revision, and redefinition. Zhao Tingyang suggests that in contrast to the 'dictionary' definition afforded by Greek ontology, the Confucian cosmology provides

> [...] an explanation of the 'grammar' of the world, striving for a coordinated understanding of the relationships – between heaven and humankind, humankind and things, and humans and humans – by which all doings are generated, with a special emphasis on the mutuality of relationships, and the compatibility of all things.[6] (Zhao, 2016, pp. 147–148)

'Things' as constituted by their relations are continually being redefined by the growth they experience in their intercourse with other things. Like words in a sentence, relational meaning begins from the conventional grammar that provides the basic ordering of these words necessary for them to be intelligible. And in the composition, it is the productive association the words come to have with each other that is the basic source of their meanings. The rhetorical effectiveness of a sentence is achieved as the relations among the words are cultivated and are thus grown to become increasingly eloquent in their expression. And the sentence rises to the level of poetry through the artistry of optimizing the contribution each inimitable word makes to its specific others as it draws upon its own history of associations.

4. Zoetology and its Far-Reaching Implications

In contrast with Greek 'ontology', there is an alternative, equally engrained prejudice in classical Chinese cosmology made explicit in the *Book of Changes* that we might call '*zoetology*' (*shengshenglun* 生生論). The *Changes* is the first among the Chinese classics, and as a text is itself an object lesson in the ecological worldview it attempts to present. That is, when we reflect on the nature of 'events' rather than 'things' within this process worldview, the relationship of these particular foci to their fields lends itself to a holographic understanding of world systems. The totality or field is both implicated in and construed from the unique perspective of each particular focus; in this case, the *Book of Changes* itself. The 'Great Commentary'

---

[6] [...]是对世界的 "语法式" 解释，力求对万事所生成的关系 (天与人，人与物，人与人) 的协调理解，尤其重视关系的互 相性或万事的合宜性.

Roger T. Ames

(*Dazhuan* 大傳) on the *Changes* makes just such a claim in announcing the importance of this canonical text:

《易》之為書也，廣大悉備。有天道焉，有人道焉，有地道焉。

As a document, the *Changes* is vast and far ranging, and has everything complete within it. It contains the way of the heavens, the way of human beings, and the way of the earth.

Indeed, it is this open-ended *Book of Changes* with its centuries of accruing commentaries that has set the terms of art for a persistent yet evolving cosmology and for its cultural common sense. As such, it provides a shared interpretive context for the evolving Confucian, Daoist, and Buddhist traditions, and most recently, for their engagement with the Western philosophical narrative.

The *Changes*, taking 'change' (*yi* 易) as its title, defines the motive force within way-making or world-making (*dao* 道) itself specifically and denotatively as 'ceaseless procreating':

富有之謂大業，日新之謂盛德。生生之謂易 . . . 通變之謂事，陰陽不測之謂神。

It is because of its sheer abundance we call it 'the grand workings'; it is because of its daily renewal we call it 'copious virtuosity'; it is because of its ceaseless procreating we call it 'the changes' (*yi*). [...] The continuity in flux we call events. And what cannot be fathomed by appeal to *yinyang* thinking is what we call the truly mysterious (*shen*).[7]

Each phrase in this passage isolates one specific way of looking at our continuing life experience, and then gives it a denotative name.[8] In the language of the text, each name references one aspect of *dao* 'way-making', or perhaps less metaphorically, the unfolding of the cosmic order. The last phrase in this passage then takes us back to where we began, reminding us of the open-endedness of those processes of change expressed through *yinyang* 陰陽 correlations. Whatever 'things' in this cosmos might be, their ever-changing identities must ultimately be understood as uniquely centered foci constituted by a manifold of vital relations within a boundless ecological field. It recalls a related description in this same text

[7]   All translations are my own unless otherwise noted.

[8]   There is an important grammatical distinction we find throughout the text. Sometimes the text uses the denotative 'is what is meant by' (*zhiwei* 之謂) and sometimes the conative 'is called or termed' (*weizhi* 謂之). The former expression defines its antecedent explicitly, while the latter connotes or references what is only one 'aspect' of some greater whole.

wherein the sages, like the heavens and the earth, 神无方而易无體 'in their mystery [...] remain undefined, and in their changes have no set structure'.

Sheng 生 as 'life, growth, and the kind of birthing that occurs within this vital process' is real and will not be denied. This *Book of Changes* cosmology gives privilege to events as irreducibly relational 'becomings', and provides the correlative *yinyang* categories needed to 'speak' process and its eventful content. A popular mantra often invoked to capture the spirit of the *Changes* is 生生不已，創造不息 'procreative living is without end; creativity never ceases'. In this processual cosmology, the growth that attends such generative living is not only ceaseless and boundless, but is further elevated to be celebrated as the most vigorous potency and highest value of the cosmos itself:

> 天地之大德曰生，聖人之大寶曰位。何以守位曰仁，何以聚人-曰財，理財正辭、禁民為非曰義。
>
> The greatest capacity (*dade* 大德) of the cosmos is life itself. The greatest treasure of the sages is the attainment of standing (*wei* 位). The means of maintaining standing is aspiring to become consummate in one's conduct (*ren* 仁). The means of attracting and mobilizing others is the use of all available resources. Regulating these resources effectively, insuring that language is used properly, and preventing the common people from doing what is undesirable is what is optimally appropriate and most meaningful (*yi* 義).

Life as growth in relations is the magic of a fundamentally moral cosmos. A full complement of the Confucian values is expressed here as nothing more than assiduous cultivation of growth in the various dimensions of the human experience, from the achieved stature of the sages to best practices in the use of resources and in the effecting of social and political order. In this human world, such effective living is the substance of morality and education, and as the continuing source of meaning, is expressed through the boundless creativity and beauty that is its greatest treasure. Meaning is not available to us from putative metaphysical foundations – what David Keightley has described as 'a Platonic metaphysics of certainties, ideal forms, and right answers' (Keightley, 1988, p. 376). Instead, guidance for leading the most meaningful lives must be formulated and passed on within the historical narrative by the most sagacious of our progenitors as they have coordinated the human experience with the changing cosmic processes. Confucian morality itself is a cosmic phenomenon emerging out of the symbiotic and synergistic transactions that take place between the operations of nature and our concerted human efforts.

The *Book of Changes* has been compiled from a sagacious awareness of the nature of the world around us, and thus provides access to the mysteries and wonders of the human experience in all of its parts:

《易》與天地準，故能彌綸天地之道。仰以觀於天文，俯以察於地理，是故知幽明之故。原始反終，故知死生之說。精氣為物，遊魂為變，是故知鬼神之情狀。

It is because the *Changes* is modelled on the heavens and earth that it is able to cover the full complement of their operations (*dao*). Looking upward, we avail ourselves of the *Changes* to observe the constellations in the heavens, and looking downward, we avail of it to discern the topography of the earth. It is thus that we come to understand the source of both what is apparent and what is obscure. In tracing things back to their origins and then following them to their end, we come to understand what can be said about living and dying. Things are formed through the condensing of *qi*, and change occurs in them through the wanderings of their life-force. It is thus that we come to understand the actual circumstances of the gods and spirits.

There is a cluster of key philosophical terms around which this 'Great Commentary' on the *Changes* is constructed that reveals the world as it is immediately experienced, providing us with a proliferation of correlated dyadic or 'paired' terms: the high and the low, the moving and the still, the hard and the soft, the full and the empty, the large and the small, the bright and the dark, the hot and the cold, and so on. Rather than appealing to an Unmoved Mover or some other external source of change, it is the correlative, bipolar, and dynamic tensions inherent in a *yinyang* life-world so defined, that produce the energy of transformation. These same tensions between the determinate and the indeterminate are the source from which the novelty that always attends these processes continually emerges. Important here is a description of how things and events, from the most ordinary and everyday to the noncorporeal world of gods and spirits, are formed and eventually dissipate, animated by motive life-forces and taking shape through perturbations in the psychophysical *qi*. The correlative relationship of the dyadic pairs such as 'living and dying' (*sisheng* 死生) and 'gods and spirits' (*guishen* 鬼神) in which each is implicated in the other, reflects the porousness of such classifications and the absence of the categorical thinking that would set any final and exclusive limits on them.

The way in which this canonical text has been compiled by the sages and how it appeals to imagistic thinking in the production of meaning is described specifically in terms of change and transformation:

聖人設卦觀象，繫辭焉而明吉凶。剛柔相推而生變化。是故吉凶者、失得之象也，悔吝者、憂虞之象也，變化者、進退之象也，剛柔者、晝夜之象也。六爻之動、三極之道也。

The sages set out the hexagrams and observed the images. Attaching their commentaries to them, they made clear what is auspicious and inauspicious. The firm and the yielding lines displacing each other produces the changes and transformations. It is thus that auspiciousness and inauspiciousness are the image of gaining and losing, that regret and care are the image of anxiety and concern, that change and transformation are the image of advancing and withdrawing, that firm and yielding are the image of day and night. The movement of the six lines is progress along the way-making (*dao*) of the three ultimates: the heavens, the earth, and humankind.

The sages have created a dynamic, imagistic discourse drawn from their understanding of the generative procreativity of the cosmos to communicate their insights into how we might guide the human experience deliberately, enabling it to unfold within the context of the heavens and the earth in the most auspicious way.

5. Zoetology, Imagistic Thinking, and Identity Construction

Contemporary philosophers such as Mark Johnson and John Dewey before him are making an argument that resonates with the one we find here in the *Changes*. The imagistic discourse of the sages is not only descriptive of the physical operations of the cosmos, but through promoting benign growth it also provides a resource for the human being to create the higher-order values and concepts that make the human experience increasingly moral and intelligent. The subtitle of Johnson's *The Body in the Mind* is *The Bodily Basis of Meaning, Imagination, and Reason*.[9] In this work, Johnson has done much to argue for the bodily basis of human meaning-formation, and also for what is ultimately the aesthetic ground of human flourishing. He maps the way in which the barest of physical

---

[9]   In many ways Johnson is following John Dewey's pioneering work *Experience and Nature*.

images such as 'balanced' or 'centre and periphery' are extended through the metaphorical projections and elaborations of our imagination to generate complex cognitive and affective patterns of meaning:

> Our world radiates out from our bodies as perceptual centers from which we see, hear, touch, taste, and smell our world. (Johnson, 1987, p. 124)

For Johnson, the formal, logical structures of human understanding are a direct extension of the activities of our lived bodies with such higher-order intelligence emerging through the exercise of our seemingly boundless imagination. Such is the human capacity to produce complex culture. Johnson identifies his own basic image-schemata as 'containment', 'force', 'balance', 'cycles', 'scales', 'links', and 'center-periphery'. In his reflection on what is 'learning to become human', Johnson has urged the view

> [...] that understanding is never merely a matter of holding beliefs, either consciously or unconsciously. More basically, one's understanding is one's way of being in, or having, a world. This is very much a matter of one's embodiment, that is, of perceptual mechanisms, patterns of discrimination, motor programs, and various bodily skills. And it is equally a matter of our embeddedness within culture, language, institutions, and historical traditions. (Johnson, 1987, p. 137)

In appreciating this emergent process of the structures of human understanding, we have to be wary of simple epiphenomenal language that would separate root from tree as cause and effect, making the tree a secondary by-product of the root with itself having no causal effect. Rather, root and tree are a holistic, symbiotic process where they grow together or not at all. Similarly, lived bodies and our embodied living are two aspectual ways of looking at the same process of growth.

The image-schemata we find in the *Changes* is captured in the correlative images as the early sages have described them, and are reflective of the primacy given to vital relationality in the classical Chinese process cosmology. That is, these always situated images are understood in fundamentally and irreducibly relational terms with agency being a second-order consideration. Such images describe the transactional relationships that locate the activities of organisms within their human and natural ecologies. To give just one example of how higher-order thinking might be the extension of bodily actions, it is not difficult to conceive of how recurrent, habituated physical patterns such as giving and getting, rising and falling, agitation and equilibrium could be transformed and metaphorically extended to produce higher-order economic and political concepts defining of a mature culture such as 'relational equity' and 'social justice'. Again, such higher-order but still zoetological 'forms of life' in turn are internalized to become integral to our body consciousness.

Turning to the human experience specifically, zoetological persons are not defined in terms of limitation, self-sufficiency, and independence, but ecologically by the growth they experience in their intercourse with other persons and their worlds. Since any one thing exists at the pleasure of everything else, the question of why things exist is explained by how they exist and what they mean for each other. And the cognitive necessity that emerges in defining what is what is superseded by the possibilities each thing affords everything else for growth, revision, and redefinition. Just as human flourishing arises from positive growth in the relations of family and community, the symbiotic, co-terminous, and mutually entailing cosmic flourishing is an extension of this same kind of transactional growth but on a more expansive scale. Indeed, human values and a moral cosmic order are both grounded in life and its productive growth, and are thus continuous with each other as interpenetrating complementarities. In canonical texts such as *Focusing the Familiar* (*Zhongyong* 中庸) and the *Classic of Family Reverence* (*Xiaojing* 孝經), human moral imperatives such as 'sincerity, resolution' (*cheng* 誠) and 'family reverence' *(xiao* 孝) respectively, are discerned in the natural order of things and thus elevated beyond the human experience as cosmic values, giving the best among human beings the stature of co-creators with the heavens and the earth. At the same time the terms that describes erstwhile cosmic forces such as 'way-making' (*dao* 道), 'imaging' (*xiang* 象), and 'patterning' (*li* 理) are also used to express the human capacity to be meaning-makers.

Appealing to this concrete example of identity formation, a person's own potentialities, far from being front-loaded by locating their latent qualities or abilities as some inherent nature that is then available to them for actualization, is inclusive of and a collaboration with their evolving processual contexts. It is thus that such persons, rather than being self-standing human 'beings', can best be characterized in the language of human 'becomings' who are constantly internalizing their environing conditions as their identities emerge in the world. Such human 'becomings' are vital, interpenetrating, and irreducibly social 'events' that create meaning through the continuing cultivation of their relations with others, and transform ordinary experience into poetry through the elevation and refinement of the hours shared together as their lives become increasingly significant.

Roger T. Ames

References

J.L. Austin, *Philosophical Papers* (Oxford: Oxford University Press, 1961).

John Dewey, *The Later Works of John Dewey* (1925–53), Jo Ann Boydston (ed.), (Carbondale: Southern Illinois University Press, 1985).

John Dewey, *The Middle Works of John Dewey* (1899–1924), Jo Ann Boydston (ed.), (Carbondale: Southern Illinois University Press, 1977).

Hans-Georg Gadamer, *Truth and Method*, 2nd ed. (New York: The Crossroad Publishing Corporation, 1997).

G.W.F. Hegel, *The Encyclopedia Logic* (Indianapolis/Cambridge: Hackett Publishing Company, 1991).

William James, *Essays in Radical Pragmatism* (Cambridge MA: Harvard University Press, 1976).

Mark Johnson, *The Body in the Mind: The Bodily Basis of Meaning, Imagination, and Reason* (Chicago: University of Chicago Press, 1987).

David N. Keightley, 'Shang Divination and Metaphysics', *Philosophy East and West* 38:4 (October 1988).

Jeff Malpas, 'Hans-Georg Gadamer', *The Stanford Encyclopedia of Philosophy* (Fall 2018 Edition), Edward N. Zalta (ed.), URL = <https://plato.stanford.edu/archives/fall2018/entries/gadamer/>.

Hilary Putnam, *Realism with a Human Face* (Cambridge, MA: Harvard University Press, 1990).

Hilary Putnam, *The Many Faces of Realism*, (La Salle, Ill: Open Court, 1987).

Nathan Sivin, 'Forward' to Manfred Porkert, *The Theoretical Foundations of Chinese Medicine* (Cambridge, MA: MIT Press, 1974).

Zhao Tingyang 趙汀陽, 惠此中國 (*The Making and Becoming of China: Its Way of Historicity*) (Beijing: CITIC Press, 2016).

What Counts as a Collective Gift? Culture and Value in Du Bois' *The Gift of Black Folk*

CHIKE JEFFERS

Abstract

In *The Conservation of Races*, Du Bois advocates that African Americans hold on to their distinctiveness as members of the black race because this enables them to participate in a cosmopolitan process of cultural exchange in which different races collectively advance human civilization by means of different contributions. Kwame Anthony Appiah and Tommie Shelby have criticized the position that Du Bois expresses in that essay as a problematic form of racial essentialism. This article investigates how Du Bois' 1924 book *The Gift of Black Folk* escapes or fails to escape that criticism. It is easy to worry that the diversity of what Du Bois in this book is willing to treat as a black contribution to the development of America pushes us from the problem of essentialism to the other extreme: a lack of any conceptual constraints whatsoever on what can count as a black gift. I will argue that recognizing the cultivation of historical memory as a form of cultural activity is key to understanding the concept's unity.

1. Introduction

W.E.B. Du Bois, long known as an African American intellectual and activist of towering importance, has in recent times become increasingly recognized as a philosopher of uncommon depth and historical significance. In order to appreciate him as such, there are certain essays and books that one must read. Most notable among the essays is 'The Conservation of Races', an 1897 work that did much to stimulate and shape the concerns of philosophy of race as an area of professional research as it developed over the course of the last few decades of the twentieth century and the first couple of decades of the present one. I will say more in the first section of this article about why that essay has been so influential. Among his books, I would single out three as essential: *The Souls of Black Folk* (1903), his most famous work; *Darkwater* (1920), a politically charged collection of essays, short stories, and poems; and *Dusk of Dawn* (1940), an autobiography that is also a study of the complexities of conceptualizing race.

doi:10.1017/S1358246123000115   © The Royal Institute of Philosophy and the contributors 2023

Chike Jeffers

In what follows, I will not be delving into the significance of any of those three books but rather shining a light on a book that has thus far received much less attention: *The Gift of Black Folk*, published in 1924 as part of a book series commissioned by the Knights of Columbus on the contributions of various ethnic minorities to the United States. The other two books that appeared in the series were titled *The Jews in the Making of America* and *The Germans in the Making of America*, and thus, accordingly, the subtitle of Du Bois' book is *The Negroes in the Making of America*. While I do not count it as one of the works that one simply must read in order to appreciate Du Bois as a philosopher, I nevertheless view *The Gift of Black Folk* as indispensably important for puzzling through some questions of fundamental importance raised by his general theoretical approach to the fight against racism.

Du Bois was, to use a term that first rose to prominence in Canadian politics not long after his death, a proponent of *multiculturalism*. He believed in the productive and progressive power of cultural diversity and, directly related to that belief, he was also a black cultural nationalist, a proponent of the pursuit of autonomy for black people through the preservation and cultivation of black cultural difference. When we encounter cultural nationalism, there are critical questions we ought to ask concerning what might be involved in the collective task of valuing and maintaining distinctive cultural practices. What demands upon individuals within the group are being made here? Does this approach to culture wrongfully constrain the freedom of individuals to construct their own identities in ways that ought to worry us? These questions become tougher still when what we are talking about is a racial form of cultural nationalism. Might the black cultural nationalist be leading us toward a model of cultural identity rooted in problematic notions of heritable racial essences?

My claim about *The Gift of Black Folk* is that it is helpful and, indeed, necessary for figuring out what we can or cannot say on Du Bois' behalf in answer to such pointed questions. In the first section, I will rehearse the expressions of multiculturalism and black cultural nationalism in 'Conservation' and the criticisms of his position in that essay by the philosophers Kwame Anthony Appiah and Tommie Shelby. In the second section, I will explain why it makes sense to turn to *The Gift of Black Folk* to think about how applicable Appiah and Shelby's criticisms are to Du Bois once we move beyond 'Conservation'. We will see that the diversity of things that Du Bois is willing to call a gift in this book raises the question of whether, far from pegging him as too much of an essentialist, we might rather see him as so permissive in what he will treat as a special black contribution that there are no limits on the concept whatsoever. Finally, in the third section, I will focus on the blatantly paradoxical idea of an involuntary gift, which comes up multiple times in *The Gift of Black Folk*. We should worry about the ethical implications of viewing history the way Du Bois encourages when he invokes this idea. Still, noticing the freedom we have to revise our attitudes toward the past is key, I will claim, to recognizing the idea as meaningful, and this furthermore allows me to identify the self-conscious practice of remembering the past as a cultural activity able to bring unity to the concept of the black gift.

2. 'Conservation' and its Critics

On March 5, 1897, in Washington, D.C., Du Bois delivered 'Conservation' at the very first meeting of the American Negro Academy, a learned society founded by his mentor, Alexander Crummell. At what we might call the climax of the essay, Du Bois envisions the Academy helping to generate and standing at the centre of an organized invigoration and proliferation of African American cultural institutions: 'Negro colleges, Negro newspapers, Negro business organizations, a Negro school of literature and art, and an intellectual clearing house, for all these products of the Negro mind, which we may call a Negro Academy' (Du Bois, 1996, p. 44). Preceding this climactic point, however, and thus forming the bulk of the essay, is the theoretical background justifying this practical stance. The question that Du Bois sets out to investigate is 'the real meaning of race' (Du Bois, 1996, p. 39). He suggests that African Americans in his time often worry when encountering discussions of the nature of race because it is so common for these discussions to end up having disturbing implications concerning their status as human beings. There is a temptation, as a result, to 'deprecate and minimize race distinctions' (Du Bois, 1996, p. 38). Du Bois also suggests that, in addition to emphasizing the unity of humanity, African Americans discussing race tend to focus on the wrongs of discrimination. He announces his intention, by contrast, to look at race from a broader perspective: 'It is necessary in planning our movements, in guiding our future development, that at times we rise above the pressing, but smaller questions of separate schools and cars, wage-discrimination and lynch law, to survey the whole question of race in human philosophy and to lay, on a basis of broad knowledge and careful insight, those large lines of policy and higher ideals which may form our guiding lines and boundaries in the practical difficulties of everyday' (Du Bois, 1996, p. 39).

Du Bois then makes the move that has made the essay seem so prophetic to many philosophers of race in the present: he denies that research in the natural sciences has been able to illuminate the significance of racial difference and claims we must instead take up the perspective of 'the historian and sociologist' (Du Bois, 1996, p. 40). From that perspective, a race may be defined, according to him, as 'a vast family of human beings, generally of common blood and language, always of common history, traditions and impulses, who are both voluntarily and involuntarily striving together for the accomplishment of certain more or less vividly conceived ideals of life' (Du Bois, 1996, p. 40). Given this talk of shared traditions, impulses, and ideals, the sociohistorical account of race that Du Bois offers us here is an account of races as sharing cultures.

Note, further, that this definition of races as cultural groups is directly connected to his multiculturalism. Modern civilization, as Du Bois understands it, is the ongoing result of strivings for ideals by different groups that he considers to be races in the sociohistorical sense of the term: 'The English nation stood for constitutional liberty and commercial freedom; the German nation for science and philosophy; the Romance nations stood for literature and art, and the other race groups are striving, each in its own way, to develop for civilization its particular message, its particular ideal, which shall help to guide the world nearer and nearer that perfection of human life for which we all long, that 'one far-off Divine event'' (Du Bois, 1996, p. 42).

Given this understanding of race, Du Bois suggests that, if black people fail to value their racial identity, they do a disservice not only to themselves but to the world as a whole. They rob themselves and the world of the valuable cultural contributions that their particularity enables them to develop. Du Bois acknowledges, however, that it can be tempting for African Americans to see the cessation of any perception of them as racially different as the only hope for the coming to an end of the oppression they experience in the United States. He considers as an objection to his imperative of embracing black identity the idea that 'our sole hope of salvation lies in being able to lose our race identity in the commingled blood of the nation' (Du Bois, 1996, p. 43).

In response to this objection, Du Bois provides a remarkable affirmation of the reality and value of cultural hybridity. He says of his people, on the one hand: 'We are Americans, not only by birth and by citizenship, but by our political ideals, our language, our religion' (Du Bois, 1996, p. 44). On the other hand, he claims:

'Farther than that, our Americanism does not go. At that point, we are Negroes, members of a vast historic race' (Du Bois, 1996, p. 44). As a distinct black African-descended people, they can credit themselves, in his view, with having already greatly contributed a number of distinctive cultural contributions to America: 'We are that people whose subtle sense of song has given America its only American music, its only American fairy tales, its only touch of pathos and humor amid its mad money-getting plutocracy' (Du Bois, 1996, p. 44). This evidence of the ability to contribute further justifies the practical conclusion that African Americans must avoid downplaying racial difference and instead hold on to their distinctive group identity as members of the black race. In doing so, they will not replace the goal of ending anti-black discrimination with the goal of making more cultural contributions but rather they will combine these goals: 'it is our duty to conserve our physical powers, our intellectual endowments, our spiritual ideals; as a race we must strive by race organization, by race solidarity, by race unity to the realization of that broader humanity which freely recognizes differences in men, but sternly deprecates inequality in their opportunities of development' (Du Bois, 1996, p. 44).

Kwame Anthony Appiah's 1985 article, 'The Uncompleted Argument: Du Bois and the Illusion of Race', sparked a vigorous debate on what to make of 'Conservation' and of race in general in ways that have shaped philosophy of race as an area of study ever since. For one thing, Appiah's piece established anti-realism about race as an important position in philosophy, requiring a sophisticated response from those who disagree. It begins with discussion of how little genetic difference there is among humans and thus how little reason to think that any significant biological differences between humans may be captured by talk of racial difference. Toward the end, Appiah quips: 'The truth is that there are no races: there is nothing in the world that can do all we ask 'race' to do for us' (Appiah, 1985, p. 35).

Before that conclusion, however, he performs a famous and controversial critical analysis of Du Bois' definition of a race. (It should be noted that Appiah has in recent years abandoned the critique of 'Conservation' expressed in 'The Uncompleted Argument', but it remains worth revisiting for its powerful attack on the possibility of a sociohistorical account of race.) Appiah investigates how each of the components of Du Bois' definition could help us distinguish between races on a non-biological basis and finds that none of them do the job. Most notably, he argues that Du Bois' appeal to the notion of a 'common history' is circular: 'sharing a common group

Chike Jeffers

history cannot be a criterion for being members of the same group, for we would have to be able to identify the group in order to identify *its* history' (Appiah, 1985, p. 27). Appiah furthermore claims that what Du Bois implicitly relies on to distinguish his idiosyncratic list of races (which, as we have seen, includes black people alongside groups such as the English, the Germans, and the Romance nations) is really a geographic criterion: 'people are members of the same race if they share features in virtue of being descended largely from people of the same region' (Appiah, 1985, p. 29). But while the shared feature may be cultural in certain cases, as far as Appiah can see, the only thing that can plausibly be seen as uniting the diverse members of the black race is a broad physical resemblance. His critique, then, is that 'Conservation' does not really move beyond the traditional notion of race as a matter of biologically inherited characteristics, both physical and behavioural: 'Du Bois elected, in effect, to admit that color was a sign of a racial essence but to deny that the cultural capacities of the black-skinned, curly-haired members of humankind were inferior to those of the white-skinned, straighter-haired ones' (Appiah, 1985, p. 30).

Tommie Shelby, in his 2005 book *We Who Are Dark: The Philosophical Foundations of Black Solidarity*, also takes a critical stance on 'Conservation' but there is a big difference between his critique and Appiah's. If Appiah's main concern was that Du Bois misrepresents human reality with a biologically essentialist *description* of racial difference, then Shelby leads us to worry about how racial essentialism can be a source of unjustified *prescriptions*, even when the racial essence is supposedly non-biological. Shelby's target is thus not the definition of race in 'Conservation' but rather what he takes to be the essay's main moral and political principle: 'Du Bois was convinced that a collective black identity – based primarily on a shared history and culture, and only secondarily, if at all, on a common biological inheritance – is a necessary component of an emancipatory black solidarity' (Shelby, 2005, pp. 205–206).

Shelby believes this requirement of a sense of shared cultural identity is, first of all, unnecessary for cultivating unity among black people for the purpose of fighting racism. Secondly, he believes it is not just unnecessary but actively hurtful. He claims that pushing for allegiance to a common cultural identity is counterproductive to black solidarity because doing so constrains individual freedom in a way that discourages unity: 'If there is group pressure to conform to some prototype of blackness, which collective identity theory would seem to require, this would likely create 'core' and 'fringe' subgroups, thus alienating those on the fringe and providing them with an incentive to defect from the collective effort' (Shelby, 2005, p. 229). Racial essentialism, on this account, ostracizes those who feel unable to identify with the chosen set image of blackness. It is therefore self-defeating in a call for black solidarity in the face of oppression.

Appiah and Shelby's critiques of 'Conservation' force us to question what we ought to see as the ultimate legacy of this influential essay. There should be no doubt that it is a philosophical classic, even if only for the way it seeks to create space for what we today call social constructionism about race. The tougher question is how plausible and attractive we should find its vision of black cultural unity. Should we find it laudable to encourage a sense of pride in racial difference among African Americans and other black people, based on a self-understanding as members of a culturally distinct group whose cultural difference is beneficial not only to themselves but to the world as a whole? Or is this a way in which Du Bois leads us astray? I believe engaging with *The Gift of Black Folk* can help us wrestle with this question.

3. Introducing *The Gift of Black Folk*

Near the end of the first chapter of *The Souls of Black Folk*, which is a revised version of an essay that Du Bois published in the same year as the year in which he presented 'Conservation', we find Du Bois once again claiming that the goals of achieving equality and of preserving and cultivating the distinctiveness of black culture are not at odds but must be pursued simultaneously. He writes of 'striving toward that vaster ideal that swims before the Negro people, the ideal of human brotherhood, gained through the unifying ideal of Race; the ideal of fostering and developing the traits and talents of the Negro, not in opposition to or contempt for other races, but rather in large conformity to the greater ideals of the American Republic, in order that some day on American soil two world-races may give each to each those characteristics both so sadly lack' (Du Bois, 1903, p. 11). As in 'Conservation', he also claims that there is a history of black cultural contributions to America preparing the way for future giving: 'We the darker ones come even now not altogether empty-handed: there are to-day no truer exponents of the pure human spirit of the Declaration of Independence than the American Negroes; there is no true American music but the wild sweet melodies of the Negro slave; the American fairy tales and folklore are Indian and African; and, all in all, we black men seem the sole oasis of simple faith and

Chike Jeffers

reverence in a dusty desert of dollars and smartness' (Du Bois, 1903, pp. 11–12).

These words from *Souls* require us to ask the same questions inspired by 'Conservation': should we be led by Appiah to view the traits and talents of black people that Du Bois talks about here as naturally inherited – passed down in the blood, so to speak – and, if not, how else should we understand them? Does the goal of fostering and developing these traits and talents place a burden on black individuals to live up to cultural standards of blackness in the way that Shelby argues is counterproductive? Given the fame of this book, *The Souls of Black Folk*, it is perhaps curious that so few read and discuss *The Gift of Black Folk*, since the title evidently makes it sound like something of a sequel.

So what do we find, when we look for answers to the questions we have raised, in *The Gift* (as I'll now call it)? Well, there is at least one passage in the book that seems to confirm rather clearly that Appiah was right – that is, that Du Bois understands the cultural uniqueness of black people in a straightforwardly biologically essentialist way. Chapter 8 of *The Gift*, entitled 'Negro Art and Literature', begins with this paragraph: 'The Negro is primarily an artist. The usual way of putting this is to speak disdainfully of his 'sensuous' nature. This means that the only race which has held at bay the life destroying forces of the tropics, has gained therefrom in some slight compensation a sense of beauty, particularly for sound and color, which characterizes the race. The Negro blood which flowed in the veins of many of the mightiest of the Pharaohs accounts for much of Egyptian art, and indeed Egyptian civilization owes much in its origin to the development of the large strain of Negro blood which manifested itself in every grade of Egyptian society' (Du Bois, 1924, p. 287). Note how Du Bois protests the disdain with which people talk of the alleged sensuousness of black people, but not because he wants to reject the stereotype thus labeled. It is the disdain that constitutes the problem. The concern here with revaluing what has been denigrated fits well with Appiah's description of what is going on in 'Conservation'. And then, of course, the final sentence of the paragraph confronts us with a direct appeal to the power of black blood flowing through veins.

So maybe we should say 'case closed' and simply accept that what Du Bois has to say about black culture is rooted in an outdated understanding of racial belonging, making his work of no less historical interest but much less practical relevance. Or, perhaps, we should not be so hasty. Consider how, later in the same chapter, Du Bois begins to talk about the black contribution to literature. If you know something about the history of African American literature, you might suspect that he would begin with Phillis Wheatley. He does, in fact, go on to call her 'easily the pioneer', but before that, he has pages on what he calls 'the influence which the Negro has had on American literature', by which he means literature by white Americans (Du Bois, 1924, pp. 292, 298). You might wonder whether this influence is a matter of how the special black sense of beauty has had effects beyond that which is produced by black people themselves. What we find, though, is that he is talking simply about the presence of black people and the problems surrounding them as a theme in the writing and oratory of white Americans. He tells a story that reaches all the way back to Shakespeare, for whom he says (presumably speaking of Othello) 'the black man of fiction was a man, a brave, fine, if withal overtrustful and impulsive, hero' (Du Bois, 1924, p. 293). In the context of American slavery, by contrast, 'he emerged slowly beginning about 1830 as a dull, stupid but contented slave, capable of doglike devotion, superstitious and incapable of education' (Du Bois, 1924, p. 294). Controversy over abolition made him 'a victim, a man of sorrows, a fugitive chased by bloodhounds, a beautiful raped octoroon, a crucified Uncle Tom, but a lay figure, objectively pitiable but seldom subjectively conceived' (Du Bois, 1924, p. 294). After the era of Reconstruction following the Civil War, 'the black man was either a faithful old 'Before de wah' darky worshipping lordly white folk, or a frolicking ape, or a villain, a sullen scoundrel, a violator of womanhood, a low thief and misbirthed monster' (Du Bois, 1924, p. 294). At the time Du Bois is writing, he says the black character in literature is 'slowly but tentatively, almost apologetically rising – a somewhat deserving, often poignant, but hopeless figure; a man whose only proper end is dramatic suicide physically or morally' (Du Bois, 1924, p. 294).

This is a fascinating overview of how black people have been depicted in literature by white authors and, given that Du Bois was a Harvard-trained historian, it is not surprising to see him offering us such a perspective. What is curious, however, is that we are being offered this account of how black people have influenced American literature simply by being depicted within it as an example of how black people have contributed to America. If we are to call this a contribution, it seems fair at least to say that it is not a very active kind of contributing. All that needs to be done by black people to contribute in this way is to simply exist and, by virtue of existing, within this American context, they are able to be depicted. Du Bois acknowledges precisely this concern when he writes: 'It may be said that the influence of the Negro here is a passive influence and yet one must remember that it would be inconceivable to have an American literature, even that written by white men, and not have the Negro as a subject. He has been the lay figure, but after all, the figure has been alive, it has moved, it has talked, felt and influenced' (Du Bois, 1924, p. 293). As a reply to an objection, this is intriguing, but not very clear. I take him to be saying, at least in part, that the kind of presence black people have had in American literature is by itself evidence of the active part they have played in American life, even if to be written about is a passive experience.

Part of what seems paradoxical about treating being written about as a contribution, however, is the emphasis Du Bois places on how black people have been depicted in literature so often as caricatures. They have been not merely depicted but distorted and dehumanized. Du Bois writes: 'As a normal human being reacting humanly to human problems the Negro has never appeared in the fiction or the science of white writers, with a bare half dozen exceptions; while to the white southerner who 'knows him best' he is always an idiot or a monster, and he sees him as such, no matter what is before his very eyes' (Du Bois, 1924, p. 295). If it is already strange to think of being depicted as a contribution, then it seems even stranger to think of being distorted and misrepresented as a contribution. After all, we can imagine situations in which allowing ourselves to be depicted – say, by serving as the model for an aspiring painter – might be a gift of sorts, but it is difficult to imagine knowingly consenting to being represented in false and damaging ways.

Du Bois continues: 'And yet, with all this, the Negro has held the stage. In the South he is everything. You cannot discuss religion, morals, politics, social life, science, earth or sky, God or devil without touching the Negro. It is a perennial and continuous and continual subject of books, editorials, sermons, lectures and smoking car confabs. In the north and west while seldom in the center, the Negro is always in the wings waiting to appear or screaming shrill lines off stage. What would intellectual America do if she woke some fine morning to find no 'Negro' Problem?' (Du Bois, 1924, p. 295). Again, understood as a defence of taking the fact of being misrepresented as a contribution to American culture, this is not quite clear. What we can most certainly take from it is a major theme of the book – namely, that America is not America without black people, that to imagine America without black people is to come up with a fiction so vastly different from what America is that it would be misleading to think of it as in any way an envisioning of America, given how central black people have been to American life, history, and culture. This is a powerful, insightful sentiment. What it leaves unresolved, however, is how acknowledgement of this centrality relates to promoting the goal of black people preserving their cultural difference in order to enrich America and the rest of the world with their distinctive cultural contributions.

This is why I say we should not be hasty, as it is inaccurate to see *The Gift* as simply providing a clearly essentialist answer to the question of how black people can and should view themselves as having contributed and as able to contribute further. Nowhere beyond that opening portion of Chapter 8 is there so blatant an appeal to the idea of special powers in racial blood. What we get instead is a bewildering variety of activities, experiences, and characteristics, sometimes active but sometimes seemingly passive, sometimes complimentary to black people but sometimes degrading. One helpful feature of the book given the task of summarizing this variety is that each chapter has a kind of subtitle encapsulating its content, and so I will now delve further into the book by quoting and commenting upon these subtitles.

Chapter 1, 'The Black Explorers', is summarized this way: 'How the Negro helped in the discovery of America and gave his ancient customs to the land' (Du Bois, 1924, p. 35). Central to the chapter is the story of Estevanico, the enslaved black Moroccan who ended up becoming the first black person to visit various parts of what is now the United States in the 1530s. His story is an important one but notice the difference between telling that story and speaking of the gift of black music, or even of the gifted poetry of Phillis Wheatley. It is not clear what, if anything, we might see as culturally distinct about this black man's role in the Spanish exploration of North America. The part of the summary about giving ancient customs to the land seems to refer not to anything Estevanico did but rather to Du Bois' discussion of the hypothesis that Africans visited the Americas before 1492, a hypothesis partly supported by reference to artistic forms and agricultural practices among the indigenous peoples of the Americas. Even if accurate (and it should be noted that the hypothesis is viewed by most historians today as exceedingly doubtful), there are critical questions we should ask about how contributions to indigenous cultures preceding the European colonization of the Americas relate or do not relate to culturally contributing to the United States.

Let us move on, nevertheless, to Chapter 2, 'Black Labor', which is summarized as follows: 'How the Negro gave his brawn and brain to fell the forests, till the soil and make America a rich and prosperous land' (Du Bois, 1924, p. 52). The language here is active, suitable to how we would think of a gift, even if not a culturally distinctive one. And yet, central to this chapter is the experience of slavery, which we obviously have much reason to think of as the very opposite of the idea of a gift. I will say more about this in the next and final section of this article. Chapter 3, 'Black Soldiers', is summarized: 'How the Negro fought in every American war for a cause that was not his and to gain for others a freedom which was not his own' (Du Bois, 1924, p. 80). Here again, we have active language, suitable to gift-giving, and yet once again reason to worry that compelled service will be misidentified as a gift. Even if we are talking about service freely and voluntarily performed, the question remains of how we value this as a gift given the basic unfairness that this summary evokes.

Chapter 4, 'The Emancipation of Democracy', is summarized: 'How the black slave by his incessant struggle to be free has broadened the basis of democracy in America and in the world' (Du Bois, 1924, p. 135). It is usefully combined with Chapter 5, 'The Reconstruction of Freedom', which is summarized: 'How the black fugitive, soldier, and Freedman after the Civil War helped to restore the Union, establish public schools, enfranchise the poor white and initiate industrial democracy in America' (Du Bois, 1924, p. 184). It is in Chapter 5 that Du Bois specifies what he takes to be the 'greatest gift' of black people to America, an evidently important point to which we will return (Du Bois, 1924, p. 212).

Chapter 6, 'The Freedom of Womanhood', is summarized: 'How the black woman from her low estate not only united two great human races, but helped lift herself and all women to economic independence and self-expression' (Du Bois, 1924, p. 259). You might wonder how it is possible to talk of the black and white races as united, before even wondering how this accomplishment of unity might be attributed to black women. On the other hand, you might be the kind of quick-witted person who realizes immediately that Du Bois is talking about the way that the systemic problem of rape under slavery biologically united the two races and, if so, you might also be duly horrified at the idea of this as a gift.

Chapter 7, 'The American Folk Song', is summarized: 'How black folk sang their sorrow songs in the land of their bondage and made this music the only American folk music' (Du Bois, 1924, p. 274). This chapter is, in one way, relatively uncontroversial for our purposes, as it fits well with the idea of a distinctive cultural gift that we get in 'Conservation', but it is thus also questionable how much it advances our understanding of the nature of black gift-giving. Chapter 8, which I have already discussed at length, is summarized:

'How the tragic story of the black slave has become a central theme of the story of America and has inspired literature and created art' (Du Bois, 1924, p. 287). Lastly, Chapter 9, 'The Gift of the Spirit,' is summarized: 'How the fine, sweet spirit of black folk, despite superstition and passion, has breathed the soul of humility and forgiveness into the formalism and cant of American religion' (Du Bois, 1924, p. 320).

The opening paragraphs of this final chapter of the book are relevant to how we judge the seemingly blatant essentialism we found in Chapter 8, and so are very much worth discussing. Du Bois writes: 'Above and beyond all that we have mentioned, perhaps least tangible but just as true, is the peculiar spiritual quality which the Negro has injected into American life and civilization. It is hard to define or characterize it – a certain spiritual joyousness; a sensuous, tropical love of life, in vivid contrast to the cool and cautious New England reason; a slow and dreamful conception of the universe, a drawling and slurring of speech, an intense sensitiveness to spiritual values – all these things and others like them, tell of the imprint of Africa on Europe in America' (Du Bois, 1924, p. 320). The admission that he is dealing with something real but hard to define, hard to characterize, and barely tangible, is interesting as a reflection upon the difficulty of precision when dealing with aspects of culture like general style, common mannerisms, and so on. How is this influence transmitted, according to Du Bois? He writes: 'One way this influence has been brought to bear is through the actual mingling of blood. But this is the smaller cause of Negro influence. Heredity is always stronger through the influence of acts and deeds and imitations than through actual blood descent; and the presence of the Negro in the United States quite apart from the mingling of blood has always strongly influenced the land' (Du Bois, 1924, pp. 320–321). We see here that, for Du Bois, it is indeed possible for biological reproduction to pass on cultural characteristics, but that is not the primary way in which black cultural influence should be measured. This stance is reminiscent of his claim in 'Conservation' that race is more social and historical than natural because, while racial difference *generally* involves 'common blood', it does not *always* involve it.

In any case, if Du Bois was concerned primarily with the power of blood, one would expect the greatest gift of black people in his eyes to be some characteristic behavioural tendency that he isolates and praises. By contrast, what Du Bois actually identifies as the greatest gift of black people is the way that they used what political power they had during the exceptional period of post-Civil War

Chike Jeffers

Reconstruction. Chapter 5, 'The Reconstruction of Freedom', was something of a trial run for his masterpiece of historical writing, published a little over a decade later: *Black Reconstruction in America* (1935). In the part of the chapter where he uses the term 'greatest gift', he has just been discussing the passing of the Fifteenth Amendment, which gave the vote to black men. Du Bois describes the passing of the amendment as a necessity in the face of the determination of former secessionists to re-enslave and re-subjugate black people as best they could. Du Bois writes: 'Thus, Negro suffrage was forced to the front, not as a method of humiliating the South; not as a theoretical and dangerous gift to the Freedmen; not according to any preconcerted plan but simply because of the grim necessities of the situation. The North must either give up the fruits of war, keep a Freedmen's Bureau for a generation or use the Negro vote to reconstruct the Southern states and to insure such legislation as would at least begin the economic emancipation of the slave. *In other words the North being unable to free the slave, let him try to free himself. And he did, and this was his greatest gift to this nation*' (Du Bois, 1924, pp. 211–212).

How was this the greatest gift? Note, first, the framing: unlike moments where he seems to call passive experiences gifts, this gift is all about black agency. Du Bois describes the Fifteenth Amendment as if it were a form of moving out of the way by the federal government. The African American is described as responding by freeing himself through the vote, which does not sound like beneficence to others, as we would expect from a great gift, but rather caring for oneself. Black people caring for themselves, in this case, though, meant effectively advancing modern civilization, or so Du Bois argues. He provides evidence that state constitutions after the participation of black people in Southern state governments during Reconstruction were more democratic in ways that remained the case even after black people were pushed out of the political process in the wake of the end of Reconstruction and the rise of Jim Crow segregationist law. Property qualifications that excluded poor white people were removed by legislatures that included black people and depended upon black votes. The public school system that benefited coming generations of white Southerners was also pioneered during Reconstruction. Advances of these sorts represent to Du Bois the proof that freedom for black people ultimately means greater freedom for all people. Clearly, this is a gift and clearly it is great.

Still, we must ask, once again: what does it mean for thinking about black cultural difference? Reading *The Gift* may lead you to conclude that just about anything can be called a gift, resulting in the worry that it is not essentialism that should cause us concern with respect to Du Bois but rather vacuity. Let me explain by returning to Shelby's critique of black cultural nationalism. Having argued that it is an unhelpful restriction on the freedom of black individuals to require embracing a black cultural identity for participation in black solidarity against racism, Shelby considers the objection that the problem can be solved by acknowledging the diversity of black cultures: 'One could of course mean to include under 'black identity' *all* of the cultural traits that are embraced and reproduced by blacks. This, however, would have the effect of rendering collective identity theory vacuous, because blacks cannot help taking on cultural traits of one sort or another, and therefore the imperative to 'conserve black-ness' would have no prescriptive force – it would not require blacks to do anything but literally 'be themselves'' (Shelby, 2005, p. 232). Applied to *The Gift*, one might argue that Du Bois makes gift-giving not only everything black people do but everything that they experience, and this makes both the idea of progress through black cultural contribution and the associated imperative to preserve the distinctiveness of black culture rather meaningless.

But maybe we are simply reading *The Gift* wrong. Maybe we are supposed to understand it as only incidentally concerned with black cultural difference and rather as providing, first and foremost, a general account of the centrality of black people to American life, history, and culture. Maybe the word 'gift' in the title is nothing but a rhetorical flourish that should not be taken so seriously, allowing us to find it unsurprising that he discusses activities like voting and legislating during Reconstruction and experiences like being de-picted and caricatured in the literature of white American authors. Such activities and experiences are undoubtedly relevant to the claim that black people have been central to the development of America.

4. The Paradox of the Involuntary Gift

It seems to me, however, that Du Bois directly blocks this reading of the gift idea as a mere rhetorical flourish by repeatedly flaunting the paradoxical nature of some of his references to gift-giving. In Chapter 2, he refers to black labour as 'the gift of labor, one of the greatest that the Negro has made to American nationality. It was in part involun-tary, but whether given willingly or not, it was given and America profited by the gift' (Du Bois, 1924, p. 76). What are we to make of this talk of an involuntary gift? Let us first acknowledge what is so clearly distasteful about referring to the forced labour of slavery as a gift. Slavery involved violent coercion and it is quite reasonable to hold that there is no such thing as a gift that has been given through the violent coercion of the gift-giver by the gift's recipient. It is plausible to read Du Bois as suggesting that America's profit allows us to speak of a gift – that is, that where someone has benefited from the labour of another, especially in cases where this labour has not been performed for the sake of remuneration, we can focus on that unpurchased benefit and call the labour a kind of gift.

But we should reject this. We can and should insist, against Du Bois, that we move decisively away from talking about gifts whenever we move away from talking about goods or services that one offers to another by choice, with the conscious intention of providing some benefit. Labour performed without remuneration, when performed voluntarily to benefit others, can reasonably be called a gift. Labour performed without remuneration, where that labour has been extracted from the labourer by the threat of force, is a kind of dehumanizing exploitation that we should never refer to as a gift. We ought not to condone playing with words in such a way that we lose this vital distinction, because to do so dishonours those who are victimized by practices of forced labour and, correspondingly, overlooks the virtue to be honoured in cases where it is appropriate to speak of gift-giving.

But where does this leave us? Must we view Du Bois as having presented us with a picture of gift-giving so controversial as to be little better than gibberish? I think not. I have argued that we should criticize, on a moral basis, his characterization of slavery as a gift, but I also think there is a way of reconstructing what he is up to that makes the characterization richly meaningful, despite being inadvisable. Consider this striking sentence from the concluding part of Frantz Fanon's classic work of existentialism, *Black Skin White Masks*: 'I am a man, and I have to rework the world's past from the very beginning. I am not just responsible for the slave revolt in Saint Domingue. Every time a man has brought victory to the dignity of the spirit, every time a man has said no to an attempt to enslave his fellow man, I have felt a sense of solidarity with his act' (Fanon, 2008, p. 201).

Fanon is pushing us here in a direction that is, in one sense, diametrically opposed to Du Bois' orientation. Fanon recommends here a refusal to take any special pride in black accomplishments and a vow to celebrate instead any moment where human beings managed to surmount oppression. This is a repudiation of black cultural nationalism and thus a contradiction of Du Bois' position. What is nevertheless instructive about the passage for our purposes is the way that Fanon speaks of this shift in thinking – a shift from previously seeing the appeal of black pride to embracing the option of solidarity with all humans – as a matter of reworking the past. This too is purposefully paradoxical, as it sounds like making the choice to change the past, when the past cannot change.

What Fanon is bringing up with this paradoxical formulation is the freedom we have to revise our subjective relationship with the past. We cannot choose what the past is in any radical sense that would imply the ability to move backward rather than forward in time, but we can and often do choose what we want the past to mean to us. Understood in this way, what Du Bois suggests in *The Gift* is that, when we look back at the past and see the pain of slavery, there is something empowering about refusing to see it solely as a story of victimization and choosing instead to see how its part in the growth of American wealth might be understood as a benefit for which black people ought to be thanked. Du Bois implies, in other words, that black shame over enslavement ought to be replaced with white gratitude through a collective revision of the meaning of slavery. I have already claimed that we should not follow him in this, but it is a meaningful sentiment.

This key to understanding what sense it makes to speak of involuntary gifts also delivers us the key to understanding how the diversity of gifts in *The Gift* can be related to the project of preserving black culture. The decision to revise the meaning of the past is the decision to actively remember something, where part of what is active about this process of remembering is the choice of what to value in the past and how. Consider this poetic bit of the book's preface, which Du Bois calls the 'Prescript': 'We who know may not forget but must forever spread the splendid sordid truth that out of the most lowly and persecuted of men, Man made America' (Du Bois, 1924, p. 33). There are splendid things like music in the story of black people in America as well as sordid things like slavery, rape, and war, and since the splendid stuff emerges out of such a sordid context, the sordid in an important sense provides the condition for the splendid. To see value in the various parts of the African American experience is thus a complicated affair, but what is uncomplicatedly valuable for Du Bois is the choice to remember it all. The 'we' in the phrase just quoted, while not necessarily exclusively black, can plausibly be taken to refer primarily to black people. The collective remembering that Du Bois is promoting can therefore be understood as an important kind of black cultural practice.

Chike Jeffers

To promote the cultivation of collective memory is to promote a sociohistorical process that cannot be confused with any biologically essentialist rendering of black cultural activity. Indeed, given the wide variety of things to be remembered (to which future historians will constantly be adding), the promotion of this cultural practice cannot be confused in the slightest with the promotion of any constraining 'prototype of blackness'. And yet there is nothing vacuous about the demand that Du Bois makes of black people here either. This is because to remember just anything will not do. Remembering the specific story of black people is the point and, in doing so, black people do engage in gift-giving of a vital kind. Despite his questionable rhetorical use of the idea of involuntary gifts in suggesting how we revise our understanding of the African American experience, I share Du Bois' fundamental faith that the black cultural practice of telling and retelling the various stories that comprise the larger story of black life in modernity contributes profoundly to enlightening and enriching not only the minds and lives of black people but the minds and lives of all.

References

Anthony Appiah, 'The Uncompleted Argument: Du Bois and the Illusion of Race', *Critical Inquiry*, 12 (1985), 21–37.

W.E.B. Du Bois, *The Souls of Black Folk. Essays and Sketches* (Chicago: A.C. McClurg & Co., 1903).

W.E.B. Du Bois, *The Gift of Black Folk. The Negroes in the Making of America* (Boston: The Stratford Co., 1924).

W.E.B. Du Bois, 'The Conservation of Races', in Eric J. Sundquist (ed.), *The Oxford W.E.B. Du Bois Reader* (New York: Oxford University Press, 1996), 38–47.

Frantz Fanon, *Black Skin, White Masks*, Richard Philcox (trans.), (New York: Grove Press, 2008).

Tommie Shelby, *We Who Are Dark. The Philosophical Foundations of Black Solidarity* (Cambridge, MA: Belknap Press, 2005).

What Does It Mean to Colonise and Decolonise Philosophy?

LEWIS R. GORDON

Abstract

What does it mean for philosophy to be 'colonised' and what are some of the challenges involved in 'decolonising' it in philosophical and political terms? After distinguishing between philosophy and its practice as a professional enterprise, I explore six ways in which philosophy, at least as understood in its Euromodern form, could be interpreted as colonised: (1) Eurocentrism and its asserted racial and ethnic origins/misrepresentations of philosophy's history, (2) coloniality of its norms, (3) market commodification of the discipline, (4) disciplinary decadence, (5) solipsism, and (6) appeals to redemptive narratives of colonial practice. The remainder of the article examines conditions for decolonising philosophy, which include unlocking its potential as a liberatory practice, identifying its humanistic dimensions, rethinking metaphysical assumptions, and embracing political responsibility wrought from the production of knowledge.

1. Introduction

The task at hand is to examine what it means for philosophy to be 'colonised' and what some of the challenges are in 'decolonising' it in philosophical and political terms.

To begin, let us distinguish between 'philosophy' and 'professional philosophy'. Philosophy is an ancient endeavour spanning back thousands of years. Professional philosophy is an activity carried out primarily in academic institutions, although in obvious terms it is the work of people whose expertise in philosophical matters or the discipline is their job. Thus, professional philosophers also work for think tanks, publishing companies, and a variety of labour-oriented intellectual enterprises. The consequence is that professional philosophy ironically need not produce philosophy. Scholars of philosophy, for example, earn their legitimacy through publishing in journals, producing monographs, and teaching at institutions often without producing a single original philosophical thought. Philosophy, on the other hand, is an activity that could be practiced by non-professional philosophers. It could encompass ideas produced by anyone ranging from the artist to the politician, the poet to the scientist, and, yes, even the professional philosopher. This activity, whose

doi:10.1017/S1358246123000103   © The Royal Institute of Philosophy and the contributors 2023

Royal Institute of Philosophy Supplement **93** 2023

etymology is the conjunction of a Greek word and another whose origins lie in the East African language of Mdw Ntr, is popularly known as one marked by the love of wisdom.

Before addressing decolonisation specifically, the reader would no doubt like me to elaborate on my remark on 'philosophy' as a hybrid of Greek and Mdw Ntr. The latter is the language spoken by the people of Kmt, a vast, ancient East African country that was eventually colonised by Hellenic and Persian peoples and renamed Egypt. As the logic of colonisation goes, the divide between coloniser and colonised is never complete – at least in cultural terms – which means that both affect each other. A process of creolisation often ensues as, despite enmity and violence, intimacy and learning are features of human communication. We should also bear in mind that initial contact is not always a colonial one. It would be far-fetched to claim that people on the African shores of the Mediterranean and those on its Asiatic side ('Europe, after all, was just the western side of Asia) were never in contact with one another until moments of conquest. That humanity evolved in Africa and spread in many directions entailed constant flows back and forth of information and cultural knowledge. These flows naturally included language. That said, the word 'philosophy' marks the intersection of the Greek word *philia* (fondness or devotional love instead of erotic love) with the transformed word *sophia* (wisdom), whose origin lies in the more ancient Mdw Ntr word '*Sbyt*' ('wise teachings'). The word '*Sba*' ('to teach' or 'to be wise') was transformed in the Greek-speaking context in which there was a tendency to change the Mdw Ntr 'b' to '*ph*', where it was pronounced in a hardened version similar to the sound of the English letter 'f' (for elaboration see Gordon, 2021). Reflections on *Sba* and *Sbyt* precede those in Classical Greece (500 BCE) by a few thousand years. Observe, for example:

> Philosophers [lovers and seekers of wisdom] are those whose heart is informed about these things which would be otherwise ignored, those who are clear-sighted when they are deep into a problem, those moderate in their actions, who penetrate ancient writings, whose advice is [sought] to unravel complications, who are really wise, who instructed their own heart, who stay awake at night as they look for the right paths, who surpass what they accomplished yesterday, who are wiser than a sage, who brought themselves to wisdom, who ask for advice and see to it that they are asked advice. (Inscription of Antef, 2004, 12th Dynasty, Kmt/Ancient Egypt, 1991–1782 BCE, my own translation)

What Does It Mean to Colonise and Decolonise Philosophy?

I usually begin my introduction to philosophy courses with asking my students to reflect on each line of this ancient passage. They observe qualities such as attentiveness, criticality, clarity and distinction, commitments to learning, growth, and some are struck by gems such as Antef referring to 'ancient writings', which makes them wonder how ancient philosophy may actually be, and the idea of being 'wiser than a sage', which alludes to the complexity and radicality of philosophical endeavours. The questions they pose guide them on a journey to Plato's *Symposium*, to Confucius' *Analects*, to *The Treatise of Zera Yacob* and Descartes' *Meditations on First Philosophy*, to contemporary debates. From that point onward, I don't need to inform them that philosophy didn't begin in Classical Greece. The evidence speaks for itself.

Questions of colonisation and decolonisation, although not formulated explicitly as such, have been part of philosophy since ancient times. An enduring example is the Allegory of the Cave from Plato's *Republic*. As is well known, the allegory involves a group of prisoners in a cave with a bright flame behind them. The light produced shadows on the wall which the prisoners took for reality. One of them escaped from his chains, went out of the cave, and then, after adjusting to the light, realized that what he had experienced below were shadows and that what stood above were the actual representations of reality, which eventually led to a cognition of reality itself, which for Plato consisted in the forms. Plato understood that there was a profound responsibility when one acquires knowledge. Thus, this escapee returned to the cave and tried to persuade the fellow prisoners – women, men, and people with perhaps other gender designations from that time – to escape from the cave. As one could imagine, this was a difficult battle to wage.

There are many commentaries on this beautiful allegory, including its wonderful meta-structure of an allegory of allegories. The word 'allegory', after all, also means to speak openly or come out into the open. From the Greek *allos* ('another', 'something else', and 'beyond') it is conjoined with *agora* (think of the agora or open meeting place in Athens) and thus linked to *agoreuein* (to speak openly). In short, it is the appeal to something else to lead us into the open. Plato's Allegory of the Cave is thus, beautifully, an allegory also of allegories, and it is so not only in its reference but also in its performance. Among philosophers today, Alain Badiou points out that this back-and-forth debate of whether to exit or remain in the cave is the activity of 'politics' (see Kalyan and Kalyan, 2018). For our purposes, the main point is the enduring image of what it means to be imprisoned in ignorance and misinformation or –

crucially today – *disinformation* and the importance of being freed and liberated from that. Additionally, as my remarks about much of professional philosophy suggests, there are unfortunately those who, facing the mouth of the cave, roll a boulder in front of it, turn back, and report, 'Nothing to see there'.

'Nothing to see there' takes many forms. It is, of course, a lie. And in that regard, it exemplifies a feature of colonisation, wherein lies take hold and pose as truth or reality. It could be as subtle as some of the prejudices of philosophical gangs. For example, anti-phenomenologists often miss an important aspect of Edmund Husserl's demonstration of a path to what he called 'the transcendental ego' (Husserl, 1960). Some critics ignore him under the slur of 'continental philosophy'. Others within continental philosophy do so under the slur of 'Cartesianism'. His effort, however, was to achieve the following. Building from the argument that consciousness must always be of something (whether a specific object or an experience of a sound or feeling or an awareness – notice the use of 'of'), he conducted what is called a transcendental investigation of this structure. Transcendental arguments and investigations examine the conditions that make a concept meaningful or an experience or thing possible. The structure Husserl was examining was the form of intentionality, where consciousness of something takes the form '→x' (consciousness of x). His investigation led him to the point where one asks, 'What am I left with if I were to eliminate everything of which I could be conscious?' The answer – 'nothing' – is a moment ironically with the *form* – '→x' – of that idea. A step further would be to eliminate even that and, thus, all consciousness of reality.

We have already begun our own journey in these reflections on decolonisation of philosophy, since to talk about philosophy is already a meta-philosophical matter, and the announcement of colonisation as a lying practice raises a special problem for philosophy, especially when there are philosophers who have a vested interest in reporting that there is nothing to see, hear, learn, or understand in going beyond the mouth of the cave. The boulder, of course, is a metaphor for the many obstacles cultivated to maintain such lies. That there are philosophers who lie – or at least lie to themselves in practices of disinformation and misinformation – generates crises for philosophy. Think, for example, about when the boulder is enslavement or Euromodern colonialism. The reports take many (misleading) forms. They could be the formalism of analytical approaches and those of Eurocentric reductionism and the textualism of the Eurocontinental approach. All three point to a problem of philosophical practices that are cultural effects of the normative centring of thought as embodied in people or subjects that are supposedly intrinsically 'reasonable' – often spoken of as 'ideal'. 'Normative' refers to valued norms (standards or a set of principles of right actions or beliefs). As this observation concerns practices of misrepresentation that affect those who misrepresent too, we arrive at talking about decolonising philosophy through addressing what it means to colonise philosophy in the first place.

Colonisation involves not only the physical subjugation of a country or a nation but also the subjugation of what they know, think, and understand. Maintaining physical control is not cost efficient and sustainable. Having people controlling themselves meets challenges of cost and efficiency. Bear in mind, however, that focusing on controlling others inevitably leads to stratifying oneself in the process. Put succinctly, self-controlling mechanisms affect the controller as well as the controlled with the result of a society of control. In the decolonial literature, this development is called 'coloniality' (see, for example, Maldonado-Torres, 2008, and Mignolo and Walsh, 2018).

There are at least six ways in which philosophy has been colonised in the Euromodern world: (1) misrepresentations of its racial and ethnic origins, including its history, (2) coloniality of its norms, (3) market commodification, (4) disciplinary decadence, (5) solipsism, and (6) problematic redemptive narratives or notions of legitimation.

2. Racial and Ethnic Origins

The discussion of Antef already raises problems for hegemonic histories of philosophy. Received histories already presuppose a form of naivety and at times laziness in our relationship with the past when we fail to ask why we accept some portrayals that make no sense. The idea that a 300,000-year-old species remained dumbfounded until a 'miracle' happened 2,500 years ago on the soil of what would eventually be called 'Europe' is pretty ridiculous, but, as we know, this bag of goods has been sold to us for centuries. It is a function of what a certain line of practitioners of philosophy aver it *must be*. This 'must-be' logic projected onto the past has affected many areas and subjects of study, including history and notions of 'civilization'. It tends to be rooted in mythological and religious narratives – notice the old timeframe of civilization and history mapping on well to biblical history, whether in the form of the Torah or in that of the Christian Bible – and in a variety of other notions such as birth in the Northern East and 'maturation' in the Northern West as found in the Hegelian historical paradigm. The South is a place of dreaded nonbeing, nonrationality, and unreason. The bad logic became so pervasive in the Western North that the species' birth in the north was presumed to the point of another erroneous presumption of an original white or light-skin species that 'deviated' into dark-skin people who strayed to southern climates suitable for their needs. The folly here is that much is easily addressed empirically. Evidence proves otherwise. Evidence, after all, must be made evidential; it must appear. Thus, in order to see the errors, the conditions of seeing, hearing, and understanding must be met.

Made less abstract, the history of non-seeing and misrepresentation is governed by notions such as women being undeveloped men (as found in Aristotle's *De Anima*, for example), the meeting of such ideas in medieval Christendom in the Iberian Peninsula in a theonaturalism that produced the concept *raza* from which emerged 'race', a variety of other notions such as a theodicy in which evil and injustice met in a theological anthropology of degraded difference, and, although not exhaustively, conquest in which the theodicy took the form of might makes right, which resulted in genocide for some and permanent subjugation for those who survived. Along the way were the rationalizers, which included, among the most revered, philosophers (see Park, 2013). This is not to say that there were no philosophers who objected or argued otherwise (see Nelson, 2019, and Misch, 1951), but as should be familiar, it is very difficult to see a rose in a blizzard.

The racial and ethnic colonisation of philosophy became Eurocentrism. Europe, after all, was simply a presumed continent east of what became the islands of Britain. The mainland was referred to as a continent (from Latin *terra continens*, continuous tract of land) without a proper understanding that it kept going to Korea. That rude awakening led to an absurd notion of two continents in which racialisation offers a white one to the west and a non-white one to the east. There is, of course, more to this story, but the main point is that the one to the west was centred as point-zero of intelligibility. This logic was tacked onto conceptual reality with the presumption of origins moving outward. Thus, the 'must-be' logic was not only placed onto philosophy's origins in Europe but also its concomitant normative concepts ranging from good to justice, knowledge to understanding, reality to truth, and many more. Even a term such as 'modern' is still to this day treated as isomorphic with Europe, even though from the Latin *modo*, meaning 'now', it simply refers to the present. As an idea, the present is always connected to the anticipated, which means there is a link to where one is going. Thus, for modern to be reduced to being Europe or European is another way of saying the way in which humanity is going – indeed, has always been heading – is to become only European or, in racial language, white. We should bear in mind here my earlier point about lies and misrepresentation. Was western Asia ever exclusively what we call 'white'?

This white-washing element of Euromodern colonialism is part of the colonisation of philosophy. I use 'Euromodern' because it encourages one to ask about other kinds of modern. If one could belong to the direction in which humanity is heading without being reduced to being white or European, then the conflation of 'modern' with 'European' is also the colonisation of 'modern'. Embedded here is a philosophical anthropology of colonisation as Euromodern colonisation.

That there are *moderns* and *modernities*, freed from the reductionism of the birth of thought and history as European, means that the past can be visited, through investigation, in ways that could facilitate learning about not only Antef but also Imhotep (27th century BCE) through to Hor-Djed-Ef (between 2600 and 2500 BCE), Ptah-Hotep (between 2500 and 2400 BCE), Lady Peseshet (between 2500 and 2400 BCE), Kagemni (between 2300 and 2100 BCE), all the way through to Hypatia (somewhere between 350 and 370 to 415 CE), and so many others, ranging from Maitreyi (8th century BCE) and Gārgī Vāchaknavī (between 9th and 7th century BCE) to Laozi (6th century BCE) and Kongzi, most known as Confucius (c. 551–c.479 BCE), in what is today known as the East, as well as so many contributions from peoples across the globe over the past few thousand years. In short, philosophy seems to have been, as it continues to be, a global phenomenon.

3. Coloniality of Philosophical Norms

Implicit in the colonisation of philosophy is the idea that philosophy is not, in and of itself, colonial. This understanding, or at least aspiration, is already offered not only in Plato's Allegory of the Cave but also the reflections from Antef that preceded it. When philosophy is colonised, however, there is the problem of colonisation at the heart of normative practice. Coloniality, as we have seen, refers to the ongoing practices and norms by which colonialism is rationalised. I write about these issues in *Freedom, Justice, and Decolonization* (2021), but the short version is this.

First, there is the unfortunate, prevailing norm of treating philosophising as warfare to the point of it looking at times like a secondary school debate. The problem with treating philosophising as war ('attacking', 'defending' arguments, 'winning', and so forth) is that it ignores that 'winners' of arguments could be wrong. A lot of wasted time was spent (and continues to be spent) in philosophy on bad arguments and forms of argumentation that steer us away from reality. Of course, it's not the case that the fighting model is *never* necessary – especially when, as is evident these days, truth and reality are under attack – but instead it should not be the defining criterion of philosophical practice. What is often thrown to the wayside is that philosophy can also be a practice of *demonstration*, wherein evidence can appear through social practices of communication and normative practices of accountability in which communities see what they failed to see, hear what they failed to hear, understand what they failed to understand.

Second, the concepts informing normative philosophical practice are at times colonial. For example, a conception of language, sociality, and communication that is closed relies on notions of the practitioner as a being by itself or onto-itself, which undermines the creative capacity of human reality as communicative and productive of meaning. Put differently: no human being is a god. As philosophers are, as far as we know, human beings, this renders the reverential or godlike model of philosophical practice problematic.

Third, related to the second, the colonisation of philosophy derides philosophy as a public practice. There is a rich history of philosophical critique of anti-public philosophy, yet the isolated philosopher philosophising has currency. It is often gauche – think of some of the norms in professional philosophy – among some groups of philosophers for their members to engage or, even worse, be *understood* by the public. The public, however, takes many forms, including a philosophical one, since the idea of a philosophical concept being private undermines the notion of philosophy as a communicative practice. This is already weird where philosophy is written, but as most philosophy isn't written at all but conducted in real-time exchanges and reflection, it is so all the way through to the performative contradiction of being thought by the self to the self as being incapable of transcending the initial self. A paradox of communication and thought is that even giving an account to oneself transcends oneself since it must, in principle, be communicable beyond the present. Such communicability is, in other words, subjunctive as it entails what could or would be.

The public to which I am referring at this point is clearly not the popular public (although it could include that) but to what is not hidden (what, as we know, is *alethia* – disclosure, revealing, unconcealedness – in the Greek language). This idea is connected to 'truth' (from the Anglo Saxon *treowð* – faithfulness, fidelity, in short, what is, relatedly, worth placing one's faith in), which is in turn related to a variety of terms in other ancient languages such as Latin *veritas* (from *verus*, connected to, yes, the same ancient roots in trustworthiness or faithfulness). Curiously, Mdw Ntr's *mAa*, which is often translated as 'truth', also means 'reality' in addition to trustworthy. I'm focusing on these terms as they converge in the Mediterranean, but we should remember that there are so many languages in which there are words for talking about faith in reality. The main consideration here is that the idea is *relational* and saturated with accountability, which makes metaphysical notions of things-onto-themselves or substance complicit with the logic of coloniality. Those-onto-themselves are godlike, and the rest, relational, become deviations. In effect, this is a turning away from reality, which brings us back to the observation of colonialism as an effort to live lies.

A fourth consideration is similar to the discussion of 'modern' and 'European' in which each is reduced to the other. In Euromodern philosophy, there is a peculiar effort to yoke 'reason' to 'rationality'. A feature of rationality is consistency. As is well known, consistency requires no contradiction, which requires its being so even when referring to itself and beyond itself. This expands consistency into maximum-consistency. We could call this a movement from principles into laws. A law has no exception. Philosophy, as is well known, is not a practice of concluding with 'maybe', yet philosophical work depends on possibility. If the possible is presupposed as constrained to the maximally consistent, then there is no, proverbial, room for change. The problem is, however, worse. A feature of colonising philosophy is to, in effect, make philosophy behave or constrain it to maximal consistency. Philosophy, however, is guided by reason, which raises the question of what would happen if a commitment to rational constraints succeeds in making reason behave. This poses a problem in the norms of philosophy if they become colonial. Put simply, living thought raises the problem of whether maximal consistency can be unreasonable. Imagine, for example, being married to a maximally consistent person. A point would arise in that hell in which one declares to one's spouse: 'You are so consistent that there is no reasoning with you. You've become unreasonable'. The short answer, then, is that being constrained to rationality in this way would be a point of rationality ignoring reality. There are many instances in the history of philosophy of wonderfully consistent arguments being out of touch with reality. Adding the concerns of coloniality, the reformulation is that colonising philosophy is also an effort to colonise reason.

The effort to colonise reason leads to a fifth consideration, which is that colonising philosophy is linked to the colonisation of humanity – especially of concepts of what it means to be human. The colonisation of philosophy entails a form of anti-human logic, a commitment to thought as fundamentally misanthropic. The notion of the non-relational human is a case in point. This would make a human being into a thing, a substance, an object. For this to work, the human being most be disaggregated from relations to reality as a thing onto itself. This model of the human is familiar to all who study colonialism. The human becomes a kind of self-contained universal beyond which are universal negatives. It is why colonial logic depends on contraries instead of the interactive, communicative, relational reality of contradictions or dialectical dynamism. The human, in this other sense, is an incomplete reality reaching constantly to reality in the production of meaning. Colonising philosophy militates against this.

4. Market Commodification

The argument thus far is that Euromodern philosophy is rooted in colonisation and develops a concomitant normative life of coloniality. It produces a philosophical anthropology that is at home with capitalism. Here there is a problem whose structure is similar to theodicy. As theodicean arguments eliminate any connection between the divine and its contradictions, many rationalisations of capitalism do the same. Although often confused with a celebration of markets, capitalism is actually against pluralities of markets in favour of an idol that we could call 'the Market' (see Gordon, 2021, and Stingl, 2021). Markets for many millennia were places or relations in which people met to socialise, wherein 'trade' and 'exchange' were not necessarily for profit or extraction. Thus, from a Euromodern colonial perspective, the problem with markets is that they were too human. Eliminating the human through prioritising efficiency and profit leads to a different phenomenon: business. Business deifies the Market, in which legitimation is what facilitates business. Thus, where theodicy rationalises all under the ambit of good within the purview of the deity and bad, evil, or injustice as all that are external, the Market as a god achieves such through legitimation as commodification.

The connection between commodification and colonisation is similar to Eurocentrism. In the realm of producing knowledge, colonisation here takes the form of market commodification of knowledge. It's what sells. But selling an idea could be connected to an infrastructure in which other ideas are impeded or a normative system in which their appearance, despite their link to reality, is illicit. This is a problem in professional philosophy (and many other professional arenas of producing knowledge), where what receives legitimacy is what sells. This is not to say that there is never a convergence of what sells and what is true. Where a process of legitimacy is simply appearing in contexts that function, in effect, as a fetish. In the academy, this is where reviewers look for the tier of the journal or the publishing house or the prestige of the institution in which the academic teaches or researches, instead of actually reading the work or examining the ideas and placing them under the light of evidence, verification, and other practices of assessment.

Beyond the market commodification of professional philosophers and those who seek their recognition, there is also the failure to examine what poses a question *to* or *of* the market but, instead, the *market of* that logic and mode of questioning. Market commodification in this sense colonises philosophy through rendering its capacity to question the Market impotent. It also means that certain areas of philosophy hold sway not on the basis of philosophical reasons and reasoning but, instead, their *marketability*. This is no doubt among the reasons why certain approaches to philosophy become agonal. As a business, they need to 'eliminate' competition.

5. Disciplinary Decadence

The business of professional philosophy is a disciplinary one. Many non-professionals aren't at times even aware that they are producing philosophy, as their goal may simply to be to address an intellectual problem of their concern. Professionals, however, offer their *bona fides*, and this often involves disciplinary membership along with usual forms of certifications – degrees, professional associations, employment, *etc*. This is where the problem of a special form of colonisation emerges from the door opened by what I call 'disciplinary decadence' (Gordon, 2006, 2021).

Disciplinary decadence is when practitioners of a discipline turn away from practices attuned to reality and, instead, treat the discipline and its methodological practices either as complete or, worse, reality itself. In that process, the practitioners treat the discipline as ontological (that is, the way things are), and they lose sight of it as a product of human action and creativity. The result, at the

127

Lewis R. Gordon

metadisciplinary level, is epistemic closure – a judgment in which knowing a part is all one needs to know to determine the whole. This is when the discipline is treated, in and of itself, as all one needs to know. Treating their discipline as complete, the disciplinarily decadent practitioners use it as the basis of absorbing and evaluating all other disciplines, pretty much in the way commodification functions under capitalism. The result is a form of disciplinary nationalism in which natural scientists, from biology to chemistry to physics, criticize those in the humanities and social sciences for not being natural scientists; think of biologists who criticize sociologists for not focusing on biology; anthropologists who criticize economists and historians for not doing anthropology; historians who criticize all others for not being historical; psychologists who criticize the rest for not being psychological; sociologists who criticize the others for not being sociological; and, yes, philosophers who criticize others for not being philosophical – although there are many subfields of philosophy that reproduce this problem in the form of either disciplinary envy, as seen among positivists appealing to natural science, or, within philosophy, epistemologists who criticize ethicists and metaphysicians for not focusing on epistemology; ethicists who criticize social and political philosophers, philosophical logicians, or transcendental phenomenologists for not focusing on ethics; or, across the camps, analytical philosophers who criticize all other forms of philosophy for not being analytical; Eurocontinentalists who reject others as not textualist or historical; and the list goes on. As disciplines focus on producing knowledge, we should bear in mind, however, that epistemology has a special place here because philosophy is a knowledge-producing enterprise. It would be an error, however, to conflate philosophy with epistemology.

Disciplinary decadence is a form of decadence because it exemplifies a decay in the practices that animate forming a discipline in the first place. A discipline is formed when it is developing resources, whether conceptual or methodological, with which to address a problem. This moment of creativity and generation is attuned to reality, with a specific regard for what facilitates understanding versus what does not. There is thus a form of reflective criticality in disciplinary formation. It is a process of learning premised upon developing fertile conditions of continuous learning. When, however, there is a turning away from reality – 'Nothing to see out there' – there is an inward turn in which methods are treated as complete and thus function synecdochally as reality. In effect, reality is thrown to the wayside as the discipline becomes an idol and its methods or method a fetish. Disciplinary decadence therefore

What Does It Mean to Colonise and Decolonise Philosophy?

structures a discipline and its methodological resources as if they were created by gods.

Methodological fetishism at the price of reality is a consequence of disciplinary decadence. This is one of the reasons that a lot of professional disciplinary work can be produced that has no bearing on reality. Less concerned with truth and reality, practitioners are obsessed with whether the method was followed. This fetishism extends to accoutrements that promise methodological adherence. This is why some journals or subfields become metonymic of methodological fidelity and its accompanying forms of epistemic nationalism.

Presuming one sees this as a problem – practitioners rarely ever do – the question that follows is whether it can be transcended. Some critics may offer interdisciplinarity as a solution. A problem with that response, however, is that this could involve a set of decadent disciplines meeting one another as ontologically whole. The problem is similar to the one presented earlier of looking at human beings as substances instead of communicable relationships. Having a group of children playing separately in a sandbox offers the illusion of a group activity. As Husserl famously put it in 'Philosophy as Rigorous Science', too often the philosophers meet but not the philosophies (Husserl, 1965). Similarly, the practitioners of disciplines could meet without their disciplines doing so. For disciplines to meet, there must be a form of openness at the disciplinary level, including its methodological assumptions, that facilitates communication. In effect, the practitioners must have the humility to admit that their disciplines, as human created phenomena, are incomplete, and what may occur through communicating with other orientations on reality offered by other disciplines is the possibility of epistemic growth in the form of new disciplines. Transcending disciplinary decadence therefore requires being willing to go beyond one's discipline in a communicative practice for the sake of reality. The technical term I use for it is a *teleological suspension of disciplinarity*. It means suspending or putting to the side our disciplines so we can focus on relevant problems that may be bigger than they can handle.

Now, there will always be those who reject the idea of reality in the first place. Remember those who place the boulder at the mouth of the cave and report: 'Nothing to see there'. At this point in the discussion, the critique of substance-metaphysics and by extension, reductive ontologies, is that reality is not a thing. Reality relates to us through our efforts and practices and understandings in which our limitations are realized while developing our awareness of our experience only being part of a larger story.

Lewis R. Gordon

In philosophy, a teleological suspension of disciplinarity takes the form of a teleological suspension of philosophy. It is teleological in a small 't' sense, since it refers to purpose animating from specific problems instead of an overarching *telos* ('purpose', 'goal', or 'end'). This effort leads to something seemingly paradoxical. Philosophy must be willing to go beyond philosophy, ironically, not only for the sake of reality but also, in doing so, philosophy.

This paradoxical effort – of philosophy being a project of being willing to go beyond itself for the sake of reality – is in fact what many of those who produced major and at times revolutionary contributions to philosophy did, not only within philosophy but also in how they came to philosophy from other disciplines. They came from architecture, astronomy, chemistry, engineering, geography, law, medicine, physics, poetry, and more. For example, in medicine there are Imhotep (c. 2667–2600 BCE), Lady Peseshet (between 2500 and 2400 BCE), Aristotle (384–322 BCE), Ge Hong (283–343 or 363), Tao Hongjing (456–536), Abu al-Walid Muhammad ibn Ahmad ibn Rushd (1126–1198), John Locke (1632–1704), Anton Wilhelm Africanus Amo (c. 1703–c. 1759), Mary Seacole (1805–1881), Zhang Xichun (1860–1933), William James (1842–1910), Leo Tolstoy (1854–1936), Karl Jaspers (1883–1969), Ludwig Wittgenstein (1889–1951), and Frantz Fanon (1925–1961) among many others. Some of these, like Wittgenstein, also practiced architecture and engineering; Hypatia was a mathematician and astronomer; St. Augustine (354–430) was a theologian and bishop; Abu Nasr Muhammad Al-Farabi (870–950) was a lawyer; Christine de Pizan (1364–c. 1430) was a poet, historian, and more; René Descartes (1596–1650) was a lawyer who also became a mathematician and natural scientist; Gottfried Leibniz (1646–1716) contributed to so many disciplines, including diplomacy, that a list here would be too long; David Hume (1711–1776) studied law and contributed to history and economics; G.W.F. Hegel (1770–1831) was a theologian; Friedrich Nietzsche (1844–1900) was a philologist, poet, and composer; Edmund Husserl (1858–1938) was a mathematician; Alfred North Whitehead (1861–1947) was a mathematician; his student, Bertrand Russell (1872–1970), studied mathematics and economics; Rosa Luxemburg (1871–1919) was an economist; Sri Aurobindo (1872–1950) was a poet, journalist, and yogi; C.L. James (1901–1989) was an historian; and this non-exhaustive list is marked by how many canonical names I've not mentioned.

Philosophy, in other words, is imperilled where commitments to truth and reality fall sway to disciplinary and methodological allegiances the result of which is a set of siloed practices. It is most healthy when its practitioners have the humility to admit that their discipline, as they've received it, doesn't contain the answers to everything but can instead serve as a point of departure to learn beyond what it initially offers.

6. Solipsism and Problematic Redemptive Narratives

That disciplinary decadence is a manifestation of solipsism is evident from all its premises. Epistemic closure leads to the false conclusion of an ontological reality into which all possibilities are squeezed. We imperil philosophy when we attempt to force reality into it instead of regarding it as a search or journey for what always exceeds it. To make philosophy the world – in a word, a complete encapsulation of reality – requires nothing short of the colonisation of reality.

Additionally, such an effort offers a form of normative effort of self-justification. Put differently, to colonise the world serves as redemptive narrative of the necessity of one's being and, correlatively, the practices that rationalise it. This is a familiar response to an awful truth. Reality doesn't give a damn about us. Worse, no one's existence was necessary, although our coming into the world is not always accidental. Deliberate and necessary are not, however, identical. The outcomes, however, raise the question: are they worthy of being?

There is something ridiculous in this question. Given the lies and suffering wrought from colonisation, that need lingers, and there is no shortage of rationalisations in response to that question: was it worth it?

As there are so many alternatives to what unfolded, I won't belabour this consideration. At the heart of it is a problematic narcissism. I add 'problematic' because narcissism is not in-and-of-itself an evil. Humanity is, after all, a narcissistic idea from a narcissistic species. We spend most of our time looking at, thinking about, and negotiating human phenomena because, harkening back to philosophical anthropology, emergence in symbolic life makes us creatures of meaning. We live, in other words, in and through an ongoing disclosure of human reality always haunted by realities that transcend it. Colonialism and coloniality are, however, not about disclosure and relating to reality but, instead, about covering over reality's displeasing truths. Leaping into the arms of those pleasing falsehoods include redemptive narratives of an affirmative response to, again, the question whether it (coloniality) is worth it.

7. Decolonising Philosophy

Decolonising philosophy is clearly more than an attunement or attitude. The clearly relational arguments offered throughout this reflection entail that philosophy should consider being true to its roots of connectedness and relations to reality instead of normative appeals to 'purity' and reductive reasonings of translating reality into a singular domain. This means that philosophy, as articulated in the discussion of teleological suspensions of disciplinarity, must be willing to go beyond itself. This, of course, means drawing upon the openness of multidimensional, multirelational, and creolising (see Gordon, 2014, and Monahan, 2022) approaches to the study of reality. As we have seen, the question of what is meant by 'reality' is raised here, but we should bear in mind how it plays out with the term '*human* reality'. The 'human' in that formulation, as we have seen, is not closed – that is, it is not a well-formed-formula – but, instead, an ongoing openness of becoming that also constitutes meaning. This insight is present in many languages and the symbols they use to articulate humanness, humaneness, and humanity. For example, the Chinese word *Rén* (人) is the word for human being or person. Notice that the symbol is open. In Mdw Ntr, it is *anx* (symbolized by a sandal with flowing water and a human figure poised to stand up). Another word for mankind or human in that language is *rmT* (symbolized by a human figure or at times a male and female figure or three figures poised to stand up). As meaning is at work in these portraits of human reality, we could easily see that the vessel model of reality (the ontological model of a thing) should be questioned into the unfolding model in which there is always more. As Keiji Nishitani (1982, p. 16) beautifully observed, even Being has a nasty habit of covering reality.

At this point, some readers may wonder about the political dimensions of these reflections. The idea of non-political colonialism and coloniality would rightfully seem odd. The critical concern, in light of these reflections, is not to approach political questions in a decadent way, wherein philosophy would be criticised for not seeking its legitimacy in political terms. There is, however, a non-disciplinarily decadent way of raising the question of political concerns in decolonising philosophy. This requires addressing a dimension of what it means to be political to which Euromodern liberal philosophical thought is for the most part allergic – namely, power.

As with the discussion of the notion of the modern, power has received its share of colonised interpretations in the history of Euromodern philosophy. For the most part, it has been treated in the Hobbesian tradition through to the neoliberal present as a coercive dynamic. Yet, power, whose etymological roots lie in the Latin *potis* (think of 'potent'), whose roots point back to the Mdw Ntr *pHty*, which refers to the divine abilities and strength of pharaohs, is the ability to make things happen through access to the conditions of doing so. Notice the relational understanding here. An ability without conditions achieves nothing. *PHty*, for example, cannot be activated without *HqAw* or *heka*, which activates the *ka* (which has no singular equivalence in English, but 'activator', 'life force', 'soul', 'spirit', and 'womb' are among its meanings). This is curiously transcendental. The conditions of activating our abilities include social reality, physical reality, and more for human beings, and the organization of such conditions with concomitant abilities in the form of institutions takes many forms, including what we call governing. But what animates governing and other organizations of life, including how to live together despite conflicts, is also called, from Greek, *politeia*, which in English we call politics. The link with power reveals technologies of human reality. In our reduced physicality, our ability to make things happen – power – is a function of our physical reach of our physical bodies. Technologies of speech, expanded into a social world of culture and its many meanings and production of meaning, enable us to make things happen – affect reality – beyond our physical location. This extraordinary development can go in multiple directions. Generated outward, it could serve as the conditions for other possibilities. Generated inward, it can affect not only our embodiment but also our imagination.

When power is directed not as a condition of possibility for new meanings and growth but instead to impede possibilities, power hordes conditions through the disempowering of others. Where this limits the options, abilities are restricted; choices and meaning are trapped within; and oppression looms. Colonialism limits the options by which meaning in the form of livable lives can be produced. This is the coercive model of power. That, however, is not the only manifestation of power.

Access to the conditions of making things happen is empowerment. Increasing those conditions is a feature of political life. It is power for the empowering of human living. This aspect of power affords one of the unfortunate realities of political life. As power can be used to disempower; politics can be used to depoliticise – in effect, close off empowering potential – the human world and, consequently, dehumanise it. This observation brings light to the question of the political dimensions of decolonising philosophy. Such a task requires the ability to make decolonisation happen, which requires access to conditions of doing so. Those conditions are not only conceptual, but they are also institutional. They are institutional conditions in which free critical thinking, a crucial feature of the philosophical enterprise from antiquity to the present, can live and flourish.

Decolonising philosophy, then, is not simply an aspiration *for* philosophy. It is a crucial aspect of philosophical practice. It requires practitioners, then, to take on a form of responsibility akin to political responsibility, and this takes us back to the Allegory of the Cave. Political responsibility involves the undertaking of producing what is always greater than the practitioner and is thus, in the end, an inheritance across time to those who are, ultimately, anonymous to those who produce it. Such an effort requires abandoning the lie of 'Nothing to see here' and embracing the possibility and courage not only to see, hear, and understand, but also to learn and keep learning.

References

Inscription of Antef, quoted in Théophile Obeng, 'Egypt: Ancient History of African Philosophy', in Wiredu (ed.), *A Companion to African Philosophy* (Malden, MA: Blackwell Publishers, 2004), 35.

Jane Anna Gordon, *Creolizing Political Theory. Reading Rousseau through Fanon* (New York: Fordham University Press, 2014).

Lewis R. Gordon, *Disciplinary Decadence. Living Thought in Trying Times* (London: Routledge, 2006).

Lewis R. Gordon, *Freedom, Justice, and Decolonization* (London: Routledge, 2021).

Edmund Husserl, *Cartesian Mediations. An Introduction to Phenomenology*, Dorion Cairns (trans.), (The Hague: M. Nijhoff, 1960).

Edmund Husserl, 'Philosophy as Rigorous Science', in Quentin Lauer (trans. and intro.), *Phenomenology and the Crisis of Philosophy. Philosophy as Rigorous Science, and Philosophy and the Crisis of European Man* (New York: Harper and Row, 1965), 71–147.

Gorav Kalyan and Rohan Kalyan, *Badiou* (Documentary Film, 2018): https://www.badioufilm.net/.

Nelson Maldonado-Torres, *Against War. Views from the Underside of Modernity* (Durham, NC: Duke University Press, 2008).

Walter Mignolo and Catherine Walsh, *On Decoloniality. Concepts, Analytics, Praxis* (Durham, NC: Duke University Press, 2018).

What Does It Mean to Colonise and Decolonise Philosophy?

George Misch, *The Dawn of Philosophy. A Philosophy Primer* (Cambridge, MA: Harvard University Press, 1951).

Michael J. Monahan, *Creolizing Practices of Freedom. Recognition and Dissonance* (Lanham, MD: Rowman & Littlefield, 2022).

Eric Nelson, *Chinese and Buddhist Philosophy in Early Twentieth-Century German Thought* (London: Bloomsbury, 2019).

Keiji Nishitani, *Religion and Nothingness*, Jan Van Bragt (trans.), (Berkeley, CA: University of California Press, 1982).

Peter J. K. Park, *Africa, Asia, and the History of Philosophy. Racism in the Formation of the Philosophical Canon, 1780–1830* (Albany: SUNY Press, 2013).

Alexander Stingl, *Care, Power, Information. For the Love of BluesCollarship in the Age of Digital Culture, Bioeconomy, and (Post-) Trumpism* (London: Routledge, 2021).

How Philosophy Can Support Community-Led Change: Reflections from Bristol Campaigns for Racial Justice

JOANNA BURCH-BROWN

Abstract
How can philosophy expand to be a discipline via which young people from diverse backgrounds feel they can make a direct and positive contribution to their communities? In this chapter I suggest some creative methods by which philosophers can support community-led change. Collaborators and I have been developing the approaches described here through work on issues of racial justice, but they can be applied to campaigns or public debate on any topic. Developing more community-led, socially engaged methods has the potential to make philosophy a more attractive discipline for young people from diverse backgrounds who are keen to use their skills to make a positive difference to their communities.

1. Introduction

In this paper, I would like to share some of the ways in which I have been approaching my role as an academic and philosopher working on issues of racial justice. Over a number of years, I have been involved in community organizing and campaigns for racial justice in Bristol, England. This has given me the opportunity to learn from leaders from a wide range of social locations and backgrounds, and to learn how to apply philosophical training to campaigning and community organizing. I distil here some simple methodological insights and ideas which I hope may inspire other philosophers, and in particular young people or mature learners coming into philosophy from backgrounds currently underrepresented in the discipline, with a desire to make a positive change in their communities.

I would like to see my home discipline grow in new directions. When I was younger, I found it perplexing that great social movements that have transformed society – movements for gender equality, race equality, LGBTQ+ pride, urban development and so on – had barely begun to be discussed in my home discipline. These have been amongst the most significant social movements of the

doi:10.1017/S1358246123000127

past century and have transformed the shape of society in numerous countries, and yet ethics, political philosophy, and social philosophy seemed to have had relatively little to say about them. Those who were tackling these topics, like Lewis Gordon, Sally Haslanger, and Tommie Shelby, were pioneers. Like many others coming into the discipline in my generation, I wondered why relatively few philosophers were engaging with questions emerging from these social movements. Consider, by contrast, the formidable tradition of American sociologists studying race and class dimensions of concentrated urban poverty, such as William Julius Wilson, Alford A. Young, Robert Sampson, and Annette Lareau (e.g., Wilson, 1987; Young, 2011; Sampson, 2012; and Lareau, 2018).[1] These sociological literatures raise important questions for ethicists and political and social philosophers, and yet philosophers are only beginning to address these topics in a meaningful way (see for instance, Shelby 2005, 2016 and Haslanger 2012, 2014).

I have wanted my own work to make a meaningful contribution to social and cultural change for racial equality. I am hopeful about the possibilities for practice-based, socially engaged philosophy. There is no need for philosophy to be detached from our rich social movements. We should be growing into a discipline which says to young people and mature learners – particularly learners coming from non-traditional backgrounds – that this is a place where they will be able to hone their skills to make significant contributions to their communities.

This paper outlines opportunities for philosophers to do socially meaningful work, supported by shifts in outlook and methodology. Social change takes place through whole ecologies of activity. Working on community campaigns and community organising can open the opportunity for philosophers to collaborate with community leaders, youth workers, poets, film-makers, graphic designers, web developers, events organizers, artists, dancers, historians, educators, politicians, institutional leaders, everyday people, and academics from other disciplines in the arts and humanities, sciences, law, or social sciences. I am curious to see how philosophy grows as a discipline as a critical mass of philosophers begin working in more community-led ways; with more philosophical researchers coming from disadvantaged communities; greater direct guidance from disadvantaged communities about what is needed to make things better; and greater input from social science methodologies.

[1] With tremendous thanks to William Baker for guiding me through this sociological research, and for helping to think through many of the ideas in this paper.

2. Methodologies

Philosophy can support community campaigns through purpose-driven and community-led research questions, with action-based research, and input from a wider range of methods from social sciences such as discourse analysis, semi-structured interviews and ethnography.

Philosophers often take their conversations with each other as the starting point for their research questions. One approach I have found fruitful is to instead take conversations in the public sphere as the starting point for my work, with the contours of public debate as it exists scaffolding the directions tackled and the topics to be addressed. When I first got involved with the Countering Colston campaign, I had what I now recognize as a simplistic view of the contours of the debate. It seemed common sense to me that the Colston Hall should be renamed, and I could not understand why anybody would disagree unless they were overtly racist. Surely only an overt racist would want to enjoy their music in a concert hall named after Edward Colston, an individual who had been involved in bringing tens of thousands of African people into slavery in Caribbean plantations. I did not initially foresee the range of ideas and views people would bring in challenge to the idea of renaming the Colston Hall. If asked at the time what the main counterarguments would be, I would have given a very undeveloped summary.

Over the course of the Countering Colston campaign, fellow campaigner Mark Steeds gathered hundreds of letters that came to the (then right-leaning) regional newspaper, the *Bristol Post*, almost all of which opposed renaming the Colston Hall. I analysed 55 of these letters in detail. As I did so, my understanding of the contours of public debate grew and changed. I created a spreadsheet, and every time a letter-writer made a new kind of argument, I created a column; and I then ticked or added quotes each time a new letter-writer made the same argument. I identified 27 different arguments being made, and I clustered these into groupings. The most common kind of argument concerned political culture and universalizability; these included concerns that it was 'PC gone mad', that it was 'a slippery slope' (if we rename one building we'll have to rename them all), that it was 'elites or non-Bristolians deciding' and so on. The next most common kind of argument was about history and included the idea that we should not erase or sanitize history, that we cannot change the past, that it is our heritage and we should learn from it 'warts and all' and that changing the name was an injustice to a great Bristolian. The third most common kind of argument focused on parity, and included arguments that white people were exploited too, that it is unfair that injustices to black people are being highlighted while class injustices to white people are ignored, that Africans sold fellow Africans and are therefore the real ones to blame, and that changing place names or removing statues is a waste of energy that could be better spent on contemporary issues like modern slavery.

Clearly, many of the arguments were inflected with racist attitudes. Others were not inflected with racism and reflected genuine concern with the best method for a society to educate new generations about the most difficult parts of its past. Crucially, the range of arguments was not what I would have predicted if asked beforehand. By doing this analysis we were able to ensure that our arguments and efforts directly addressed the questions that people on the opposing sides of the issue were finding salient.

I wrote a short article for the local press, in which I gave simple, neutral statements of the ten most common objections, with simple replies (Burch-Brown, 2017a). This informed many conversations with members of the public across the political spectrum. I expanded on this material in academic articles (Burch-Brown, 2017b, 2020), but it was crucial that the public exchange and action-based learning came first and underpinned those articles. The benefit of starting by studying the contours of existing public debate was that it helped make the research useful for institutional decision-makers who were needing to navigate demands from a fractured public, and they were better able to anticipate how different actions might be perceived in different corners. This in turn supported the campaign objectives. For instance, I worked with the editor of the *Bristol Post* to look at their editorial strategy in covering the Colston topic including the Colston statue fall; I was amongst those advising the Dean of the Cathedral around measures to address Colston in the Cathedral, and amongst those advising the Colston Hall as they went through the process of renaming to become the Bristol Beacon. These activities then fed into developing guidelines for public bodies reviewing contested heritage (Burch-Brown, 2021a, 2021b).

The basic model described above would be an easy methodology for philosophers to pick up and develop more fully. It would be straightforward for philosophers to gain training in social scientific or historical methods of discourse analysis, carry out social scientific research relevant to an initiative identified by a community as important, and then work philosophically with findings. The model requires a willingness to attentively listen to views on opposing sides of a debate, then state key views in simple and neutral terms, work through arguments and counterarguments and share these back to collaborating groups, institutional partners, and a wider public.

Another approach I have found meaningful is to start by finding community partners who are doing promising work on the ground, and listening to what they say are the most important priorities locally. I then get involved in initiatives that community-based partners have identified as top priorities. I pay attention to philosophical questions as they emerge and get worked through. This can be thought of as 'action-based' philosophical research.

The method of listening and investing resource into what community partners say is important is built into the main project I am now working on, which is the development of a public educational project and social enterprise called 'Bridging Histories'. We began developing Bridging Histories as part of the work of the Bristol History Commission, in response to the task we were set by the Mayor after the fall of the Colston statue in 2020, to 'help the city understand where we have been, so we can better decide where we want to go'. Bridging Histories approaches this task in a grassroots-led way by inviting people anywhere to join in six activities – writing poetry on the theme 'I am from', sharing recipes, street history, and family history, being a monument detective, and being a person or community changemaker. Anybody can get involved and then share what they make in public events or our online gallery. With funding from the ESRC, UKRI, AHRC, and the London Mayor's Office, we have sponsored a growing community of 30 Bridging Histories Ambassadors, who have each been awarded grants to get people from their different communities involved in creative activities related to any of the six activities.

Bridging Histories gives a framework through which anybody can join in learning from the past and making positive change for the future. The structure was inspired in part by conversations with Esther Stanford-Xosei on her theory of reparative justice, which emphasizes the importance of community empowerment alongside financial compensation in holistically repairing the harmful legacies of injustice. It was also inspired by Bree Picower's *Using Their Words: Six Elements of Social Justice Curriculum Design for the Elementary Classroom* (2012) which suggests that social justice education works best when it starts with priming learners with self-love and respect for others, before looking at a historical injustice and learning how people overcame that injustice, then sharing learning more widely and finally inviting people to engage in their own concrete changemaking activities on a present-day issue that matters to them. Bridging Histories is co-directed by George Francis, a community organizer and youth worker from St Pauls, Bristol, who initially became involved as an ambassador, and together we have been developing methods for asset-based community development, involving both community-based and university-based collaborators (Bridging Histories, 2021). The team are in continual communication around the ideas, ethos, and practicalities of the projects we are doing. This collaboration gives direction to my philosophical research questions and the contours of my academic work.

You might similarly find you slot into a team of collaborators and can then start working together. As you work, you might then keep an eye out for a) philosophical questions that are pivotal to the issues at stake, which you may be able to help reason through, b) philosophical understanding that is being generated by campaigners or organizers through their ground-up efforts, which you may be able to support, for instance by amplifying voices, and c) the opportunity to help systematize a messy public debate, which can often generate a sense of relief and open the door to greater mutual understanding amongst parties on separate sides of an issue.

It is crucial in such work that skilful judgement and sensitivity are exercised to navigate both practicalities and social positions to achieve genuinely egalitarian collaboration. Class, ethnicity, educational background, professional background, university regulations and the highly localized, unique network structures of communities all play a role in the power dynamics around collaboration. For an introduction to key considerations around power and positions, see *Common Cause Research: Building Research Collaborations between Universities and Black and Minority Ethnic Communities* (2018), and *Creating Living Knowledge. The Connected Communities Programme, Community-University Relationships and the Participatory Turn in the Production of Knowledge* (2016). There are also more topic-specific resources, like the *Principles of Participation* developed by the International Network of Scholars and Activists for Afrikan Reparations (2021). It can also be beneficial to look at how colleagues in adjacent disciplines are creatively working with participatory methods. In Bristol, a UKRI grant has brought together four 'citizen science' projects on reparative justice, which has given us a chance to learn from each other's methods (UKRI, 2021). Jessica Moody, Cleo Lake, and Kwesi Johnson are working with community dancers to create a 'decolonizing memory' project involving dance memorialization (Decolonizing Memory, 2021); Marie-Annick Gournet is working with a team of school teachers to develop inclusive pedagogies for teaching history of enslavement; Richard Stone and Cassandra Gooptar are working with community-based historians to trace compensation records from the 1838 Abolition of Slavery Act; and George Francis and I are facilitating grassroots-led reparative initiatives via Bridging Histories (University of Bristol, 2021). Philosophical methods for working with community initiatives are less well developed than methodologies in these other disciplines, but can be informed by their examples.

It is possible for academic input to help campaigns and community initiatives succeed. I have heard from both campaigners and institutional leaders about the benefits of bringing philosophical input to a public debate or a campaign. Institutional leaders have explained that having philosophical analysis of views helped them more easily assess the arguments and address them with other institutional leaders in a way that had previously been difficult because of how polemical the debate had become. Having neutral, simple statements of the most plausible versions of key arguments in a public debate is helpful for institutional decision-makers.

Campaigners, on the other hand, have said that it is valuable to have the contribution of time and reasoning power to work through topics within a campaign. Most campaigners have short windows in which to carry out the research for a campaign. Academics have dedicated time in which to give campaign questions a sustained focus, so they can take advantage of this to contribute to the intellectual footing of a campaign. What is not helpful to campaigners is having researchers who drop in for their own interest, purely to address a research question set independently, study what is happening, and then leave without a contribution in return. By contrast, what is helpful is when a researcher asks what is needed and directs research towards helping organizations achieve those socially important aims. For philosophers, a contribution is a particular kind of clarity of thought, so a significant contribution that philosophers may be able to make is to listen attentively to different considerations, think patiently through counterarguments, and reflect back to their collaborators a simplified, clarified outline of the key positions and issues. In doing so, it is important not to see the academic as the main expert. Instead, often it is the campaigners or community leaders who are the most acute critical thinkers, with the most long-standing expertise on the topic at hand, and they will have worked through many subtle philosophical issues in the course of their organizing. However, the community group may or may not be able to articulate their insights in a way that is easily absorbed or seen as legitimate to decision-makers. A philosophical researcher who takes the time to listen attentively over a sustained time can synthesize key insights and expertise from the group, lobby for that group, and put their insights in terms, styles, and formats that institutional leaders are more likely to learn from and take on board.

For scholars to whom these approaches sound intriguing or attractive, my suggestion is to start by listening closely to what people say are the live issues in a community with which you have some natural connection. Get involved in an effort that seems worthwhile, and then look for where the philosophical questions are within the issue as it is playing out on the ground. Look at the contours of the public debate and see if you can give simple statements of views that capture the positive intentions behind opposing sides. Look at who is having a hard time making themselves understood by institutions, regardless of where they are politically, and articulate those views to help them be better heard.

Above, I highlighted potential for action-based methods in practical ethics and social philosophy. It is also worth thinking about the ways in which we could make better use of the core methodologies of social sciences. Recently, philosophers have taken an interest in 'ex-phi', or philosophy informed by experimental psychology and cognitive science. However, to date it seems to me that philosophers have not yet appreciated the philosophical potential in standard qualitative social science methods, such as use of semi-structured interviews (interviews using open-ended questions) or ethnography (being based in a particular community over a period of time, and writing on this basis).

Semi-structured interviews and ethnographies are both ways to gain a vivid detailed understanding of a particular social world. Experiences that are described in semi-structured interviews could be a fertile basis for philosophical reflection and exploration. Without such source materials, we often tackle social philosophical topics from our own standpoint without sufficient input from others. We end up reflecting philosophically based on our own experiences or abstract suppositions about other people's experiences. This can feed into the tendency for philosophical debates to become detached from common sense and from real-world problems as people actually face them. More use of qualitative methods as a source material for philosophical reflection might lead to social philosophy, ethics, and political philosophy that stays anchored in common sense and is more answerable to people's everyday lives and the problems that need addressing.

Qualitative social sciences differ from quantitative social sciences in that quantitative research collects data to be measured and counted, whereas qualitative research seeks to generate more nuanced and fine-grained understanding. You can generalize from a well-designed quantitative study to a whole population; but for the study to be tractable, you have to stick with predefined answers (yes or no, multiple choice, scale of 1–5 *etc.*) or else be prepared to go through resource-intensive processes of coding qualitative answers to arrive at quantitative results. By contrast, qualitative methods are open-ended and give rich information about a small number of individuals or environments. For instance, they include semi-structured interviews, where people are asked open-ended questions which they then discuss freely; and ethnographic methods, where a researcher is based within a community over a long period of time and writes about it. It is often impossible to generalize from qualitative surveys to claims about whole populations, because the sample size will not be statistically significant. However, they give 'possibility' proofs, vivid examples of how an individual might see or experience things, or of how dynamics and patterns might sometimes play out in lived experience. They allow researchers to develop richer descriptions and insight into subtle details that cannot be captured in quantitative data.

We used both qualitative and quantitative research in shaping recommendations to the Bristol City Council about the future of the Colston statue. In 2021, the Bristol History Commission worked with Bristol City Council to do a survey of what people wanted for the future of the Colston statue. The survey was promoted alongside our temporary exhibition of the statue at the MShed museum. We had displayed the statue lying down with graffiti intact, beside a wall of BLM placards and a timeline explaining the history of the statue itself, from the time it was put up to the time it was brought down. Above the statue, we projected a series of three-part dialogues designed to help people reflect on their own views and those of others. For instance, one voice would be projected on the wall over the statue saying, 'I was euphoric when the statue came down'. The next said, 'Really? I was horrified'. The first voice returns and says, 'For me it was like a great weight was lifted'. Then finally a question is posed to the viewer, 'How did you feel when the statue came down?' The series of dialogues were drawn based on the ideas we knew were common at the time in Bristol (Burch-Brown, 2021b).

In the survey, we asked people what they wanted for the future of the Colston statue, what they wanted for the Colston plinth, and how they felt when the statue came down. 14,000 people replied, the largest survey to date carried out by the Bristol consultation and engagement team. The most striking result was that there was a high level of agreement, much higher than might have been expected from treatment in the media. 1 in 5 (80%) of Bristol-based respondents said that the statue should be in a museum, and 5 in 8 (65%) said they felt positively about the statue coming down. The other most striking result was that age was the key factor determining how people felt. Ethnicity made little difference to whether people felt positively or negatively about the statue coming down; and their feelings also couldn't be predicted by whether they lived on a wealthier street or a less wealth street. Age, on the other hand, was a great predictor of attitude. Young people were almost universally positive about the statue coming down, whereas about 7 out of 10 people in the oldest cohort felt negatively about the statue coming down. Age mattered; ethnicity didn't (Burch-Brown and Cole *et al.*, 2022).

Reflecting on these findings as a philosopher, what is striking is that there are ethical upshots of our findings that age mattered to people's attitudes while ethnicity didn't. If there is a social conflict over statues, it is not between people of different ethnicities, but between people of different ages. This suggests that there is a civic need for space for intergenerational communication and exchange, healing and understanding. Such findings can be very useful for informing ethical, political, and social philosophical conclusions.

We also were able to learn from the comments people wrote in response to open-ended questions, which often revealed more about their thinking than the quantitative survey did. The open-ended comments were also a source of valuable statements of views: 'It should be in a museum. Statues are celebratory, museums are educational'; or 'It is not 'rewriting history' to remove a statue if its preserved in a museum in an appropriate context'; 'The law is the law and must be respected'; 'Direct political action accomplished what bureaucracy couldn't'; 'It was hard for any black person to walk past every day'; 'It shouldn't have been vandalized as it is a work of art'; 'A beautifully powerful act' (Burch-Brown and Cole *et al.*, 2022, pp. 20–25). Qualitative surveys used judiciously can be a way of gathering ideas from the crowd, and the most important ideas can then be explored philosophically. These are just a few examples of how philosophy can engage in supporting community-led initiatives, campaigns, and public debates.

3. Conclusion

To return to my starting point, I would like to see my discipline expand so that young people who want to make a difference in their communities recognize a place for themselves within philosophy, and see that they can use it to make a difference. One of the important features of entrenched inequalities is that people affected by concentrated disadvantage often have difficult experiences with the education system. One in four children in Bristol is growing up in poverty, rising to one in two children in our most disadvantaged neighbourhoods. In the least well-off parts of Bristol, there are schools where not even a single child in the history of the school has been to university. The most acute forms of disadvantage are the most important ones for society to address. The people experiencing that disadvantage have situated expertise about its contours that nobody else has. Yet in the absence of formal further or higher education, it may be impossible for many people to make their views heard, understood, and taken seriously by people in institutional roles. There is a collective responsibility to overturn entrenched inequalities, including supporting people to transform their own circumstances in ways that empower them, and one step is to create more bridges between people who are experiencing the effects of entrenched inequalities and people who have greater access to institutional resource and influence. If philosophy as a discipline began to grow a cohort of young scholars developing methods for community-based scholarship in an egalitarian and collaborative way, we could greatly increase our direct contribution to communities we serve. I imagine the disciplinary conversations would broaden, and the discipline itself would start to be much more attractive to diverse young people interested in making positive change in communities, who would be able to see how their disciplinary skills can support community-led change.

Acknowledgements

The work discussed here has been highly collaborative and I am grateful to many more people than I can name individually, so I must begin with warm thanks to the many people who have supported me or expanded my thinking beyond those named here. I am deeply grateful to my family, including Will Baker, Sean Baker, Katie Lou Baker, Ann Kilkelly, Frank Burch-Brown, Carol Burch-Brown, and Jack Burch. I am especially grateful to Will Baker for his wonderful loving support, for guiding me in relevant social sciences, and helping me think through ideas over the course of many years. It is a tremendous honour to thank Bridging Histories' co-leader George Francis, for the positive change he is constantly working for in the St Pauls community, and for inspiring and challenging people all around him to aim higher. I am grateful to all Ambassadors and collaborating partners from Bridging Histories and the St Pauls Community Forum including but by no means limited to Derek Edwards (Patwa), Rob Saunders (Splendid Web), Jasmine Coe (Coe Gallery), Ash Bond, Bandele Iyapo, Trini Layne, Sister Nwanyi, Tappis the Poet, Fazey, //Kabbo Hue-Ferdinand, Wiz, Caroline Thake, Shaun Clarke (Urban Word Collective), Garry Atterton and Alexander Smith (Barton Hill History Project), John O'Connor, Vanessa Melody, Valentina Pas Huxley, Jagun Akinshegun, Judit Davis, Rowan Lund, Kinsi Abdulleh (Numbi Arts), Trisha McCauley, Juma Harding-Dimmock, Nurull Islam (Mile End Project), Troy Richards and Imaan Samson (Museum of Diversity), Gbemi Isimi (Culture Tree Centre), April Richmond, Leigh McKenna, Shani Whyte, James Boyd (SSGB), Glen Crooks (Glen's Kitchen), Ras Bandele, Malcolm Hamilton, and Ben Stephenson. It is a pleasure and honour to thank Cleo Lake, Marti Burgess, Katie Finnegan-Clarke, Mark Steeds, Ros Martin, and other excellent Countering Colston campaigners whom I will leave unnamed here, as well as Tristan Cork from the *Bristol Post*. I am lucky to thank fellow researchers from 'Citizens Researching Together' (UKRI Citizen Science grant BB/ V013378/1): Olivette Otele, Marie-Annick Gournet, Cleo Lake, Jessica Moody, Richard Stone, Cassandra Gooptar, Nathaniel Adam, Tobias Coleman, and Kwesi Johnson; and Dee Smart, Kate Miller, and Ben Meller from Public Engagement. I thank colleagues at Kuumba, BSWN, MX, Rastafari Cultural Centre, Barton Hill History Group, INOSAAR (International Network of Scholars and Activists for Afrikan Reparations), the Legacy Steering Group, Afrikan Connexions Consortium, Centre for Black Humanities at University of Bristol, Migration Mobilities Bristol, Rising Arts Agency, and organizers of 'Celebrating Santuary' Refugee Week Bristol. I thank the London Mayor's Culture Team and London Commission on Diversity in the Public Realm, especially Hassan Vawda, Melissa Bennett, Kirsten Dunne, Robert Bevan, and David Bryan. I am deeply grateful to Steve Mallinson for invaluable therapeutic support. It is a pleasure to thank Bristol History Commissioners Tim Cole, Shawn Sobers, Estella Tincknell, Edson Burton, Nigel Costley, Steve Poole, Madge Dresser and David Olusoga, and Bristol City Council officers supporting the commission including Ray Barnett, Amber Druce, Simon Fenn, Jon Finch, Fiona Gilmour, Lisa Graves, Laura Martin, Barry Norris, and Jon Severs. It is an honour to thank leaders from whom I have learned including Mamokgethi Phakeng, Marvin Rees, Sarah

How Philosophy Can Support Community-Led Change

Robertson, Sandra Stancliffe, David Hoyle, Mike Norton, Roger Griffiths, Edward Mortimer, Tim Ryback, Marie-Louise Ryback, Lawrence Hoo, Jendayi Serwah, and Sado Jirde. I have benefited from outstanding support from the University of Bristol Research Enterprise and Development team, including Julian Jantke, Lorraine Fairbanks, Emily Crick, Heather Williams, Andrew Wray, Les Finnemore, Alice Malhadour and colleagues; Liam McKervey for guidance around research ethics; and University of Bristol Design and Print Services team Shirine Watts, Ben Dynamou, Lawrence Flavell, and Rob Mitchell. I have been lucky to learn from Will Baker's colleagues linked to the School of Education including Rafael Mitchell, David Rawlings, Julia Paulson, Leon Tickly and Arathi Sriprakash, as well as Foluke Adebisi, Terra Glowach, Remco Merbis, Su-Lin Lewis, and Alvin Birdi, and colleagues in the Anti-Racist Steering Group at University of Bristol. It is a pleasure to thank all teachers, students, and organizers contributing to our 'Arts, Activism, Social Justice Summer School' and the MA in Black Humanities. I am grateful to philosophy colleagues including Ten-Herng Lai, Chong-Ming Lim, Eric Hatala Mathes, and Alfred Archer. Finally it is a great pleasure to thank the wonderful University of Bristol Philosophy Department, School of Arts, and Faculty of Arts for their support, with particular thanks for conversations and practical support from Anthony Everett, James Ladyman, Giles Pearson, Seiriol Morgan, Zara Bain, Ji-Young Lee, Leia Hopf, Rebecca Buxton, Ana-Maria Cretu, Tuomas Tahko, Megan Blomfield, Chris Bertram, Tzuchien Tho, Martin Sticker, Richard Pettigrew, Havi Carel, Fiona Jordan, Debbie Hughes, Alison Johnston, Lisa Turner, Debra Squires, Emma Cook, Polly Gitsham, and Sharon Beehan. I am grateful for the exceptionally generous support given by Julian Baggini and Hannah Laurens as I was preparing this paper.

This research has been supported by ESRC IAA grant number ES/M500410, UKRI Citizen Science grant number BB/V013378/1 'We Are Bristol: Reparative Justice through Collaborative Research', and AHRC Impact Accelerator Award 'Bridging Histories in St Pauls: Heritage, Place and People', grant number AH/X003094/1.

References

Bridging Histories. Nurturing Futures through Histories (2021), accessed 15 February 2023: www.bridginghistories.com.

Joanna Burch-Brown

David Bryan, Katherine Dunleavy, Kery Facer, Charles Forsdick, Omar Khan, Mhemooda Malek, Karen Salt, and Kristy Warren, *Common Cause Research: Building Research Collaborations between Universities and Black and Minority Ethnic Communities*, accessed 14 February 2023: https://www.commoncauseresearch.com/report/.

Joanna Burch-Brown, 'Speaker's Corner. Defenders of Colston are the Ones Airbrushing the Past, says Bristol University Academic', *Bristol Evening Post*, 30 April 2017 (2017a): https://www.bristolpost.co.uk/news/bristol-news/defenders-colston-ones-airbrushing-past-40454.

Joanna Burch-Brown, 'Is It Wrong to Topple Statues and Rename Schools?', *Journal of Political Theory and Philosophy*, 1 (2017b), 69–88.

Joanna Burch-Brown, 'Should Slavery's Statues be Preserved? On Transitional Justice and Contested Heritage', *Journal of Applied Philosophy*, 39:5 (2020), 807–824.

Joanna Burch-Brown, 'Reflection and Synthesis. How Moral Agents Learn and Moral Cultures Evolve', *Journal of Philosophy of Education*, 55:6 (2021a), 935–948.

Joanna Burch-Brown, 'Edward Colston Museum Display. What Happens Next for the Fallen Statue', *The Conversation*, 8 June 2021, (2021b): https://theconversation.com/edward-colston-museum-display-what-happens-next-for-the-fallen-statue-162376.

Joanna Burch-Brown and Tim Cole *et al.*, *The Colston Statue. What Next? We Are Bristol History Commission Short Report*, Bridging Histories: Bristol (2022), https://bridginghistories.com/heritage-resources.

Tristan Cork, 'Colston Statue Should Stay in a Museum Decide People of Bristol: The Overwhelming Majority Say It Should Be a Museum Piece to Help Tell the Story of the Transatlantic Slave Srade', *Bristol Post*, 3 February 2022: https://www.bristolpost.co.uk/news/bristol-news/colston-statue-stay-museum-people-6596017.

Decolonising Memory. Researching and Countering Bristol's Memory of Enslavement through Dance (2021), accessed 14 February 2023: https://decolonisingmemory.co.uk.

Keri Facer and Bryony Enright, *Creating Living Knowledge. The Connected Communities Programme, Community-University Relationships and the Participatory Turn in the Production of Knowledge*, accessed 14 February 2023: https://connected-communities.org/wp-content/uploads/2016/04/Creating-Living-Knowledge.Final_.pdf.

International Network of Scholars and Activists for Afrikan Reparations. Principles of Participation, (2021), accessed 14 February 2023: https://www.inosaar.llc.ed.ac.uk/en/principles-participation.

Sally Haslanger, *Resisting Reality. Social Construction and Social Critique* (Oxford: Oxford University Press, 2012).

Sally Haslanger, 'Studying While Black. Trust, Opportunity, and Disrespect', *Du Bois Review: Social Science Research on Race*, 11:1 (2014), 109–136.

Annette Lareau, *Unequal Childhood. Class, Race and Family Life* (London: Routledge, 2018).

Bree Picower, 'Using Their Words. Six Elements of Social Justice Curriculum Design for the Elementary Classroom', *International Journal of Multicultural Education*, 14:1 (2012), 1–17, accessed 14 February 2023: https://files.eric.ed.gov/fulltext/EJ1105049.pdf.

R.J. Sampson, *Great American City. Chicago and the Enduring Neighborhood Effect* (Chicago: University of Chicago Press, 2012).

Tommie Shelby, *We Who Are Dark. The Philosophical Foundations of Black Solidarity,* (Boston, MA: Harvard University Press, 2005).

Tommie Shelby, *Dark Ghettos. Injustice, Dissent, and Reform* (Boston, MA: Harvard University Press, 2016).

UKRI, Citizen Science Awards to Put Public at Heart of Key Research (2021), accessed 15 February 2023: https://www.ukri.org/news/citizen-science-awards-to-put-public-at-heart-of-key-research/.

University of Bristol, 'Exploring How the Legacy of Transatlantic Slavery Continues to Impact Bristolians', 24 May 2021, accessed 15 February 2023: https://www.bristol.ac.uk/news/2021/may/we-are-bristol.html.

William Julius Wilson, *The Truly Disadvantaged. The Inner City, Underclass and Public Policy* (Chicago: University of Chicago Press, 1987).

Alford A. Young Jr., *The Minds of Marginalized Black Men. Making Sense of Mobility, Opportunity, and Future Life Chances* (Princeton: Princeton University Press, 2011).

Grammars of Listening: Or On the Difficulty of Rendering Trauma Audible[1]

MARÍA DEL ROSARIO ACOSTA LÓPEZ

Abstract

What would it mean to do justice to testimonies of traumatic experience? That is, how can experiences which do not fit the customary scripts of sense-making be heard? Whereas processes of official memorialization or legal redress often demand that victims and survivors convey their experiences through familiar modes of narration, in my project on 'grammars of listening' or 'gramáticas de lo inaudito' I want to ask how it might be possible to hear these experiences on their own terms and what the challenges are that we encounter when trying to do so. What I ultimately want to argue is that doing justice to trauma requires a profound philosophical questioning of the conditions that allow us to listen to testimony, and a true reckoning of the responsibility that we bear as listeners.

[1]   This paper is a brief overview of my current research project entitled 'grammars of listening' or 'gramáticas de lo inaudito'. The project has resulted mostly from the work I have had the opportunity to do outside academia with survivors of state-sponsored violence. I thank the National Historical Memory Center (CNMH) in Colombia and the Chicago Torture Justice Center (CTJC) in Chicago for giving me the chance to learn how to be a memory worker. I most of all thank all the survivors that shared with me their stories and allowed me to listen to them, that participated in the various memory workshops organized in the above-mentioned centres, and that have shown me with their strength, generosity, and creativity the importance of a radical form of listening. The current version of the essay is the updated and edited version of the lecture I gave for the Royal Institute of Philosophy on February 2, 2022, as part of their series *Expanding Horizons*, following the invitation of their former director Julian Baggini. Since what I am presenting here is an ongoing research project, parts of this paper (and mostly, other versions of some of the same arguments) have been published elsewhere (cf. particularly Acosta López 2019b, 2020a, 2021a, and 2022a), and will also be part of my forthcoming book on the subject (cf. Acosta López 2023, 2024). I'll offer the corresponding references throughout.

doi:10.1017/S1358246123000048   © The Royal Institute of Philosophy and the contributors 2023

María del Rosario Acosta López

1. Introduction

What would it mean to do justice to testimonies of traumatic forms of violence? In my research I argue that listening to the kind of trauma that results from specific (and extreme) forms of political violence is not just a question of having the disposition to do so. Even when we are willing to listen, even when institutions are willing to change their requirements to listen to testimony and make them as open as possible (for instance, in the case of Truth Commissions all over the world, as it is also happening right now in Colombia), this often comes with an unspoken, tacit, demand that survivors convey their experiences through familiar modes of narration – or, to begin to introduce some of the key terms of my project, that their testimonies 'fit' and make use of the usual grammars that are already at our disposal to organize and make sense of the world around us.

When I say grammars here, I not only mean the rules that organize our discourse, I also mean the frameworks that arrange our perception, and the hierarchies that govern our senses. In my project I want to ask how it might be possible to hear these testimonies – and even what might seem, at first, as the lack of testimony – in their own terms and what the challenges are that we encounter when trying to do so. The task is one of listening, because it is not a question of finding words on behalf of those who have suffered traumatic forms of violence, nor of speaking for them, but rather of seeking ways to listen to how they communicate such world-shattering experiences – while truly understanding how much those shattering effects affect the way someone perceives and makes sense of the world around them.

My inquiry wants to emphasize that one of the central aspects of traumatic violence is that it is not only an assault on life but on the conditions of production of sense that make life legible as such (cf. Acosta López, 2020a and 2022a). To bear witness to these testimonies, then, to truly listen to them, does not mean to find ways of rewriting them within the frames we already feel familiar with, but rather of doing justice to the way in which they radically challenge our grammars.

Testimonies of traumatic violence often go unheard – not only in the sense that they run the risk of never being told or remembered, and in many cases of being explicitly erased and made inaccessible, but also in the sense that if and when we truly want to listen to them, they appear unbelievable, impossible, or nonsensical – precisely because of their challenge to our existing frames of sense and to what we think is even possible, if not even imaginable, in the world we inhabit. They often disorder our senses and present themselves, as Hannah Arendt would put it when speaking about the testimonies coming out of the Nazi death camps, as 'horribly original', as unheard of, requiring new grammars to be truly understood, believed, rendered audible and legible (cf. 2004, p. 309).[2] All of this in addition to the fact that those grammars governing the usual frameworks of meaning and distribution of sense are also reproducing and enforcing the erasures that do not allow for testimonies of traumatic violence to come to light – at least not in their own terms. The kind of erasures that traumatic forms of violence impose are not only described as an explicit obliteration of the archive or an enforced silence on survivors; they are also operative at the epistemic and aesthetic levels, that is, both at the level of our cognition and the concepts we use to describe the world, and at the level of our senses and the perceptions that first organize and decode our sensible connection to our surroundings. This means that traumatic forms of violence and the kinds of erasure they often enforce ultimately determine what is legible, and thus audible, to us. Consequently, what I ultimately want to argue is that doing justice to trauma requires a profound philosophical questioning of the epistemic and aesthetic conditions that allow us to listen to testimony, and a true reckoning of the responsibility that we bear as listeners.

2. Context: From Colombia to Chicago

Before I get into the conceptual details of the project, let me start first by sharing a bit of the kind of experiences that have prompted me to

---

[2] Some of my claims are therefore very close to the secondary literature on epistemic injustice and epistemic violence, beginning with Miranda Fricker's work (2007), and continuing with authors such as Dotson (2011), Medina (2012 and 2013), and Ruiz (2020). I am however interested in adding to the literature on testimonial and hermeneutical injustice the question of what kind of listening is required in the particular case of traumatic forms of violence and the specific forms of epistemic and aesthetic silencing that need to be brought to light, confronted and dismantled in such cases, as well as the particular forms of responsibility and 'hermeneutical virtues' (Medina, 2012) that are demanded by them. I also agree with Ruiz (2020, p. 701) that there is no epistemic injustice without epistemic violence, and that speaking of the former without diagnosing the latter (and understanding it as grounded on it) is just another layer of the kind of erasures that come with colonizing forms of violence. I have developed some of these connections in Acosta López, 2019a and 2020b. Recently, Medina has also generously connected my project to a larger version of this tradition (see Medina, 2022).

María del Rosario Acosta López

ask the questions that give shape to it, and the specific historical and political situations that deeply inform my approach – particularly, as I hope to show, with an emphasis on the erased and silenced memories and histories of violence and the injustice of their access to representation. My project develops in close connection to my context, namely, Colombia's more than 70-year-long armed conflict and the unspeakable horrors plus normalizing forms of violence that characterize the last century of the country's history, together with the institutional silences that have accompanied this history. The country is currently going through what some may describe as a transitional justice process, which started in 2005 by way of an agreement between the government and the larger paramilitary groups in Colombia (the AUC, Autodefensas Unidas de Colombia), and continuing in 2016 with the peace agreement process with the country's larger guerrilla group, Colombian Armed Revolutionary Forces (better known as the FARC).[3]

In this context, much is being done to address one fundamental side of any transitional justice process, namely, the development of institutional and non-institutional forms of memory as reparation. As part of this process, the Colombian Historical Memory Center (CNMH) was created in 2005 and designated as the entity in charge of recovering the memories of the Colombian conflict with a special emphasis on victims and survivors.[4] I was given the opportunity to work with the CNMH for a few years. As part of this work, I had the privilege of getting trained as a memory practitioner with the tools that had been developed for this purpose by some of the Colombian researchers that had founded the Center (see Riaño and Wills, 2009, and Riaño and Uribe, 2016). I also participated in the production of written reports and documentaries that seek to make audible at a larger scale the kinds of violence that many isolated communities had gone through during the peak of the paramilitary regime. This involved an extensive fieldwork process, including workshops and interviews with survivors of mass atrocities. The memory workshops were designed, and allowed for communities, to give an account of the events in their own terms, with their own

[3] For more on this context, see the contributions to the most recent publication on the subject, Acosta-López y Acosta López (2022).

[4] For a history of the Center and the process of its institutionalization, see Stern (2018). In Acosta López (forthcoming) I emphasize this history in terms of the legacies the Center's work left for current memory initiatives in Colombia, including interviews with some of its founders and researchers.

cultural resources and their own tools for interpretation. These forms of memory building were also often perceived and articulated as political forms of resistance to the ongoing forms of violence operating around them.

After my work in Colombia, I took this set of tools with me and continued this kind of work in Chicago in connection to the Chicago Torture Justice Center (CTJC) and the Chicago Torture Justice Memorials (CTJM). The CTJC was created in 2015 after an ordinance from the city of Chicago that officially recognized a group of 96 African-Americans as having been tortured by police between the years of 1972 and 1991 under police chief John Burge, and ordained (for the first time in the history of the United States) a package of economic and symbolic reparations including the creation of the Center, a memorial for the survivors and their families in the city of Chicago, and the mandate to teach the case in every public school in the city in 8th and 10th grade.[5] I had the opportunity to work with the team that put together the Center and that started the process towards the memorial. The tools I had learned in Colombia helped me imagine, together with the survivors, who are the real force behind the Center, a space for healing and remembering – together with a number of activities that I had the honour to be a part of, such as the production of an oral histories archive, and training survivors as liberatory memory workers.[6]

This experience outside academia was all-decisive for the kind of philosophical work I am currently doing: on the one hand, having the chance to share political spaces and to conduct memory workshops with survivors of traumatic forms of violence, listening to their stories and trying to figure out how to make them audible in a more public context, to gain both legal and historical recognition for the harm inflicted on them; on the other hand, learning the importance of producing *counter-memories* for the official and institutional versions which, at least in these cases, had almost entirely

---

[5]   See the City of Chicago ordinance, together with information about the group of survivors and activists (CTJM) that got the ordinance passed in 2015 after a long political and legal battle, at https://chicagotorture. org/. See also detailed information about CTJC, together with their history and current projects leaded by survivors, at http://chicagotorture-justice.org/. See also the interview I conducted with Elizabeth Deligio, co-founder and current board member of CTJC, as part of Acosta López (forthcoming).

[6]   For a historical account of the connections between CNMH and the creation of CTJC see also Zornosa's contribution in Acosta López, (forthcoming).

erased survivors' perspectives, replacing them with official 'records' that usually criminalize survivors and justify state violence as legitimate and legal.

As much as there is already here, as one can expect, a problem of translation – how to make the testimonies audible to a larger audience without falling into a betrayal of what those stories are recounting – the first difficulty that truly arose in the context of this kind of work was how to truly *listen* to what was happening and being passed on in these encounters. Not merely words – and their failure to name properly the experiences in question – were being communicated, but also profound and eloquent silences, grounded in a kind of harm and pain that accompanies a shattering of language when it comes to speaking about what had happened (cf. Acosta López, 2018). On many occasions – including in later work with police torture survivors on the Southside of Chicago – it became clear that, beyond the demand for listening and the challenge of inscribing the breakdown of language itself in the record, what is especially needed is a further experience of being *believed* in spite of the fragmentary, sometimes contradictory forms of narrative that emerge in and as testimony, and which were rendered 'illegible' by official and instituted grammars. The kind of violence that many of these communities have had to endure is so extra-ordinary – and yet also so structural and pervasive – that the testimonies coming out of these contexts seem sometimes 'unreal', even to those who are telling their stories.[7]

---

[7]   It is important to recognize that there are, indeed, structural forms of violence that operate in and on everyday life, and which complicate the distinction between the 'exceptionality' of trauma and what Lauren Berlant calls the 'overwhelming ordinary' or 'crisis ordinariness' (2011, p. 10). I agree with Berlant that sometimes the 'exceptionality' of trauma is used to hide and erase these overwhelming ordinary forms of violence, and that it is essential for a critical historical outlook to 'put catastrophe back into the ordinary' (p. 54). I would, however, also like to insist on the extra-ordinary character of certain forms of violence, and particularly on their effects on one's life, as well as on the conditions of meaning production and the tools that are available to make sense of these lives. If we let go of this exceptionality, we also lose the critical capacity to signal, name, denounce, and even historize (I would argue here against Berlant) what otherwise remains erased from experience. I would say that, like Berlant, I am looking for the 'genres' that can turn into historical experiences (into 'events' in the language of Berlant, see p. 16) the kinds of violence that, without a genre, remain untold – unheard, inaudible.

It is in this context that my project on grammars of listening started to take shape. Even though at first it seemed that philosophy had not prepared me at all to deal with the difficulties that were raised in these encounters, I then understood that the challenge was precisely to make philosophy speak and participate in these conversations. I did not do it with an optimistic view of what philosophy can do in these contexts, but rather with the conviction that it has a responsibility to react creatively and actively participate in the critical task of transforming the grammars that define our political and ethical worlds, and of bringing to light the forms of violence that are perpetuated and result from not taking this task as seriously as one should.

3. Listening to Trauma: A Philosophical Perspective

Let me start by considering briefly the following story – or to be more precise, the story of a somewhat failed encounter between testimony and listening. The following excerpt is taken from the fieldwork notes made by Alejandro Castillejo, who used to be a field researcher for the CNMH and was until its very end one of the members of the recently concluded Colombian Truth Commission.[8] It describes a meeting held between a witness – known here only as the 'old man' – and a team of field researchers appointed by the district attorney's office to collect information to support one of the investigations regarding the actions of paramilitary groups near the town of Puerto Gaitán:[9]

[8] For more on Castillejo's work and his involvement on memory initiatives in the Colombian transitional justice process, see the interview I conducted with him as part of Acosta López (forthcoming).

[9] I thank Julian Baggini for suggesting adding here, for the sake of clarity, an 'example' of the kind of breakdowns and fractures I describe as populating testimonies of traumatic forms of violence. No example is ever enough, and it is in response to the singularity of testimony, each time anew, that I propose we must develop grammars of listening. Testimonies do not serve therefore as examples in my work, and I rarely include them in my academic texts, since I am aware of the privilege and confidence that has been offered by those who have shared them with me, and I also do not consider them or want to treat them as 'objects of study'. That's why in this case I offer someone else's fieldwork notes. I thank Tania Ganitsky for her translations of these fieldnotes, which I reproduce with permission of their author. See also a version of this testimony and its context in Castillejo, 2014, pp. 228–229.

María del Rosario Acosta López

Yet again, this story revolved around displacement and his son's murder [...]. The man weeps, he breaks down in tears, yet he is very reserved. He continues talking. Now and then he would leave us for a few seconds. His story got denser and slower as time passed; it was hard to listen to. The scene was touching, but the team did not know how to deal with the situation, with the sheer awkwardness produced by the encounter. His story consisted of nothing but violence. There seemed to be no light at the end of the tunnel. Not only was what he was saying stark, but also the way he was saying it.

The team members listened to him respectfully, but the experience his words originated from made what he said virtually incomprehensible. [...] The team is not used to narratives like this. They do not know how to deal with them. These stories say a lot, yet not enough, not what they *need* to say. How do these stories record, interpret, contextualize and relate to the paramilitaries' crimes? The old man jumps indiscriminately from one moment to another. Although he is trying his best to help the investigation, the word[s] spoken that afternoon, within temporalities that go beyond the frames established by the law, was almost incomprehensible for a legal outlook [mirada judicial]. Thus, the old man's story had to be literally *left out* of the *historical record*. (emphasis added)

These words powerfully illustrate the different aspects of the kind of challenges, both aesthetic and epistemic, that are raised in the context of listening to testimonies resulting from traumatic forms of violence. On the one hand, the description of the encounter, as recounted by Castillejo, allows us almost to 'hear' and witness the complicated relationship between experience and communicability in cases of traumatic memories. The story of the old man maintains its own pace and conflicting temporalities. It is not only *what* he says that matters, since perhaps there are truly no words that can *communicate* the experience he is recounting. This (apparent) failure is not only a failure of language, but also and moreover, of the grammars that frame what is being communicated – ones so different in kind, it seems, that the old man's testimony cannot be recorded by the members of the research team. Patiently, they listen to his story without being able to 'do' anything with it.

On the other hand, what we encounter here is the problem of the different and sometimes conflicting ways of doing history and taking a step from trauma and testimony into memory. The legal outlook, in this case, frames and orients a form of listening that cannot be attuned to the nuances, singularities, and specific forms of temporality taking place in the old man's testimony. What the legal record can document does not coincide with what an ear attuned to other registers may be able to hear. The answer is perceived as evasive, partly because of the necessary ambivalence it needs to perform, partly because the question it is answering is a different one, and lives in different registers, temporalities, and conceptions of history, from the question asked.

My initial reaction to the encounter with these difficulties, as mentioned above, was paralyzing. I had neither the tools nor the proper training to offer anything beyond my willingness to listen – a listening, however, that was more and more aware of its failures and limitations to do justice to what was being shared. The philosopher in me, however, felt the need and the responsibility to investigate further, fully aware of the radical challenge these experiences posed to more traditional philosophical accounts of experience and its communicability. The problem, I insisted, needed to go further than pointing out language's limited ability to name the horror. The issue here is not only a lack of words and cannot be addressed only in terms of how un-representable and in-communicable trauma is. These two features are commonly acknowledged in trauma studies; but renouncing the possibility of understanding trauma on its own terms and giving up the chance to listen to the voice that comes out of these experiences and is claiming to be heard (even if the claim is silent or can only express itself in silence) is, in my opinion, avoiding our ethical responsibility to render trauma audible.

What one hears in testimonies coming out of traumatic forms of violence is the shattering of all available grammars to make sense of what is being communicated. This is due, on the one hand, to the unprecedented forms of violence to which they bear witness (forms of violence that many times are also directed towards destroying and controlling the means for their representation, see Acosta López, 2022a), and thus to the lack of available categories that can properly render intelligible (even audible) what is being conveyed. It is also due, on the other hand, to the fact that the form of experience struggling to communicate itself is one we are not accustomed to recognizing *as* experience, since it radically challenges the frameworks that allow us to make sense of a story in its telling (see also Acosta López, 2019b).

Considering all these levels of difficulty, I would say that a philosophical perspective on the question of listening to traumatic forms of violence leads therefore at least to three main key or guiding points:

María del Rosario Acosta López

(i)   First, the question must focus on the conditions that first make possible the task of listening to testimony in contexts where violence deeply affects the very possibility of production of sense. By production of sense I mean precisely what I was indicating before in terms of 'grammars'. Namely, what is involved here is the recognition of how deep traumatic forms of violence affect those who survive it, not only at a corporeal and existential level, and in their profound psychological and psychoanalytic effects, but also at the level of an aesthetic and epistemic disruption of the frameworks that usually organize our experience and shape our broader sense of the world and of ourselves within it. How much then – we ought to ask – may the available tools at our disposal prove insufficient to render audible the experiences coming out of trauma? How much will the frameworks that structure our perception as well as our conceptual judgements about the world (epistemic and ethic alike) need to be revised – and perhaps even disrupted and produced anew – to allow for survivors to tell their stories, but also to allow us to truly listen to their testimonies? My project wants to emphasize this latter side since it is mostly concerned with our ethical responsibility towards the kinds of harm left by trauma in the fabric of our world – a world we are all responsible for.

(ii)   Thus, in my project, this is translated into the possibility of imagining and offering what I call a 'radical form of listening', capable of tuning our ears to the silences, erasures, and fragmentary meanings produced by traumatic forms of violence and very often reproduced and intensified by the 'historical violence' of their forgetting (see Acosta López, 2018, 2019a, and 2019b).

(iii) This comes too with a philosophical and not a medical/pathologizing approach to trauma. Traumatic violence needs to be understood in its deeply devastating effects, not only on survivors' lives but also on their worlds of perception and meaning. Trauma, on the other hand, needs to be addressed as a singular type of experience, resulting from but not reduced to these effects. The voice coming out of trauma is one capable of producing, while also demanding, its own grammars in order to be rendered audible and communicable (see Caruth, 1996, Martínez Ruiz, 2020, and Acosta López, 2021b).

Now, if we take seriously the effects that trauma has on whomever survives it (i), and if we take up as a responsibility the task of understanding not only the damage trauma causes, but the form meaning might take as a result of its effects (iii), then a philosophical perspective on the question of listening in traumatic contexts (iii) leads to the need for a *critical analysis of the criteria and conditions of possibility for becoming audible*. That is, the criteria that determine (many times in advance, and without us even realizing it) what fulfils or does not fulfil the conditions for what we regard as intelligible (audible, even believable). Only when we listen to something as making sense can we truly render it audible, that is, only then we can offer, too, a site for believability as a precondition for its remembrance. In the specific case of traumatic forms of violence, as I was suggesting, these criteria require a revision of the very structures that determine experience and render it legible, recognizable, including its spatial-temporal frames.

Thus, when I speak about rendering trauma audible, I mean by this, too, understanding it as meaningful, listening to it as 'making sense' instead of discarding it as nonsensical or renouncing the possibility of its communicability. I mean, ultimately, not only listening to the ways in which trauma speaks, but also listening to it as believable without questioning its legitimacy, and as rememberable, as worthy of being registered and recognized as historical truth (see Acosta López, 2020a and 2022a). For that to be possible, we also need to revise what we mean by historical truths, what we consider worthy of remembrance, and how memory and history are intertwined with our criteria for believability and audibility (see Acosta López, 2022b). Hence, once again, my emphasis on attending to the grammars that govern the way in which we perceive, shape, and understand our experiences and those of others, which are, too, the grammars that govern our listening.

4. Grammars of Listening or Gramáticas de lo Inaudito

Let me recap a bit first: traumatic violence brings about what Nelly Richard, a theorist and sociologist in post-dictatorship Chile, aptly calls a 'catastrophe of meaning' (2007, p. 13). There are certain types of violence, Richard argues, that cause 'the collapse of traditional categorial orders' (p. 13) all while introducing unprecedented forms of violence whose excess has not yet been – and perhaps is not entirely meant to be – made intelligible. Not only are these realities horribly original (to remind us once again of Arendt's dictum, see

María del Rosario Acosta López

2004, p. 309), but their originality is also meant to remain unthought, since their attempt is not only to destroy life but also the tools by way of which we make sense of the world and interpret it, denounce it, remember it.

Now, it is important to keep in mind here that while this is the intended effect of traumatic forms of violence, they do not necessarily succeed in doing so, that is, in stripping away our capacity for understanding and for the production of meaning. The force displayed by resistance in these contexts is never to be taken for granted, since it is born in conditions designed to impede it – but it is also precisely where the most creative, unexpected, and admirable forms of resistance, subversion, and resilience take place. Giving testimony in the contexts I have mentioned above is one of these instances of resistance where everything – including the mechanisms designed to 'give voice' to victims and survivors – ends up, once again, silencing them, erasing them, or presenting their testimony as illegible. In spite of all, survivors do speak – the question is how we can truly listen.

How then to properly listen *at the site* of trauma, that is, from out of that open wound that addresses us and claims our listening (see Caruth, 2016)? How to hold on to the experience to which these testimonies bear witness without translating, betraying – leaving aside the breakdown of language – the erasures and the absences that are also part of the story to be told (see Hartman, 2008)? And most importantly, how to carry the voice and produce the conditions of possibility for its audibility without speaking for another?

My project thus proposes to inquire into the kinds of grammars that need to be inaugurated – and that testimonies do actually inaugurate – each time anew in order to render audible what otherwise remains unheard as a consequence of traumatic forms of violence and their capacity to silence, erase, hide, and deny their own shattering effects. In Spanish I call them 'gramáticas de lo *inaudito*', since the word 'inaudito' points both to the unheard and the unheard of, namely, what hasn't (yet) been rendered audible and what confronts us as ethically unacceptable (see Acosta López, 2022a). There is a close connection between the two in my work: my claim is that it is precisely because traumatic violence inaugurates unprecedented forms of harm – forms of harm absolutely unheard of and which thus challenge our ethical imagination in radical ways – that we do not *yet* have the grammars to approach them properly and make them audible, much less intelligible or even believable. And with this, we risk doubling the effect of forgetfulness and inaudibility that trauma usually imposes on its survivors.

A grammar of 'lo inaudito' opens thus a site for listening to what does not 'make sense' as meaningful within available and hegemonic frameworks of meaning. While signifying and opening a site for audibility, it is also capable of denouncing erasure, concealment, and silencing. And in this capacity to denounce and remind us of the responsibility to listen to the unheard of, it also finds ways of interrupting and subverting the structures that have made the erasure inaudible by having presented it as illegible, unbelievable, unrecognizable and thus forgettable, not worthy of remembrance, not legitimate enough to be heard and documented as true.

These are all central aspects of my project. It is important for me, then, to insist that my search is not only for the inauguration of sites for audibility, and for the conditions that may allow for testimony to be shared and be heard. My inquiry is also about a form of critique that the search for those grammars enacts, about the kind of structural violence it wants to denounce, and, equally important, about the creative possibilities embedded in the forms of resistance that are both produced and demanded in these contexts in order to subvert, interrupt, and irrupt into the regime of the audible. By no means I want to be understood in terms of reinforcing the wrong (and very wrongfully applied) idea of passive survivors who need to be 'translated', be 'made audible', 'helped out' of their trauma. This is not what I mean here by the responsibility to listen to the unheard of.

It is true that trauma leaves its survivors exposed to a very particular kind of vulnerability, one that requires us all to understand the responsibility it bears on all of us as listeners, and as responsible for a world where that kind of harm needs to be taken up by all.[10] However, as I have mentioned above, the background of this project is very much connected to the work being done with, and mostly by, resilient, creative communities, capable of rendering their own voices loud and clear, but whose stories are permanently being shut down by systems of meaning that are supported, enacted, and permanently imposed by political and historical structures that need to be dismantled. The approach needs to move therefore from what can be understood initially as a psychoanalytic and perhaps more figurative understanding of trauma towards a greater emphasis on its historical, material, and political dimensions.

A few clarifications are thus in place, just to finish with what I think is essential in any philosophical endeavour, but particularly in the

---

[10] For recent developments of this radical notion of responsibility, see Ferber (2016), and connected to the harm of 'not being heard', see above all Jill Stauffer's concept of ethical loneliness (2015).

María del Rosario Acosta López

kind I have been presenting above; that is, a recognition of the project's scope and its limitations. First, what I am proposing is to change the perspective from what would be, broadly speaking, a focus on the conditions of possibility (or impossibility) for the production of testimony in the context of memory production (and particularly in the context of the production of counter-memories) to the conditions of possibility for the task of listening to testimony. In other words, I propose to reflect on the kind of 'hermeneutical sensibility' (see Medina, 2012, p. 207) that is required to listen to what can't be communicated in already given and available grammars; namely, to the kind of openness and creativity – both at the conceptual and aesthetic level – that is required to perceive, understand, and interpret realities that can challenge in radical ways our own. This emphasis puts the weight of the responsibility on the listener. However, this does not mean that the listener is also responsible for producing 'meaning' in these contexts: it is not our job as listeners to provide a narrative for what can otherwise not be told. It is our responsibility, rather, to guarantee conditions for audibility so that testimony can be told in its own terms and without having to reach a demand for translation into already available meanings. In this way, the task of listening is more connected to providing resonance than to the production of sense. And it requires a development of an acute ear for other forms of meaning that are usually not made audible within our already predetermined sensory registers.

Second, I am also interested in proposing a shift from the focus on veracity and verifiability of testimony to a focus on credibility. To foster grammars of listening in these contexts means to imagine modalities of memory building and possibilities of historical register that break with the criteria dependent on a verification of the past and its location in the archive. To produce spaces for credibility means to open in the present a space for the production of a past that has not yet been produced and/or recognized, and whose history of violence continues operating in the present, saturating the latter with the meanings that such structural violence imposes over and against other grammars of sense (see Zambrana, 2021).

Third and last, the experience of a radical form of listening must not be understood as a linear process of progressively revealing, discovering, and unveiling that which has been silenced and erased, as if the task were to broaden the spectrum of what should be made audible within our usual frameworks. If we understand traumatic violence in its radicality and complexity, what becomes clear is that listening to its testimony is not the task of unveiling a truth that otherwise remains hidden, nor it is about unblocking its passage towards memory – it is rather the task of subverting the criteria for audibility, including therefore the criteria for producing historical knowledge and for what it means to remember.

This latter point must lead in turn, I contend, to an understanding of history as invention and of memory as resistance. I do not have the time to go into detail about these other sides of my project (which I usually refer to as the need for decolonizing history and memory, see Acosta López 2020a, 2022a, and 2022b). Let me just mention before finishing that, from this point of view, the act of listening and of making oneself heard are, at the same time, the act of producing a world that was not but should have been. This is a subversive act of invention whereby invention is not opposed to history but rather actualizes it, making possible resistance to structural forms of oblivion.[11]

The first step towards this, is the demand for reclaiming the memory of what should not have happened. Grammars of lo inaudito, therefore, should also be conceived of as the articulation of frameworks of sense capable of granting us access to this ethical face of both history and memory. This is the resistance to acceptance that memory must exercise in the face of violence and its radical forms of destruction. The resistance to admit the world as it is, and the political task of imagining and producing an otherwise – for the present, for thought, and for the sake of a past that is not yet over.

References

María del Rosario Acosta López, 'La narración y la memoria de lo inolvidable. Un comentario al ensayo 'El narrador' de Walter Benjamin', in Maria Mercedes Andrade (ed.), *Walter Benjamin, aquí y ahora* (Bogotá: Universidad de los Andes, 2018), 175–196.

María del Rosario Acosta López, 'One Hundred Years of Forgotteness: Aesth-Ethics of Memory in Latin America', *Philosophical Readings* XI:3 (2019a), 163–171.

María del Rosario Acosta López, 'Gramáticas de la escucha: aproximaciones filosóficas a la construcción de memoria histórica', *Ideas y Valores* 68: 5 (2019b), 59–79.

[11] I owe this interpretation of the notion of 'invention' to Karera's work on Fanon (forthcoming), and its connection to a decolonial approach to history to Gualdrón's work on Édouard Glissant (2019).

María del Rosario Acosta López

María del Rosario Acosta López, 'Gramáticas de la escucha como gramáticas descoloniales: apuntes para una descolonización de la memoria', *Eidos* 34 (2020a), 14–40.

María del Rosario Acosta López, 'Perder la voz propia: de una fenomenología feminista de la voz a una aproximación a la violencia política desde la escucha', in Luciana Cadahia and Ana Carrasco Conde (eds.), *Fuera de sí mismas. Motivos para dislocarse* (Barcelona: Herder, 2020b), 121–156.

María del Rosario Acosta López, 'From Aesthetics as Critique to Grammars of Listening: On Reconfiguring Sensibility as a Political Project', *Journal of World Philosophies* 6 (2021a), 139–156.

María del Rosario Acosta López, 'Grammars of Addressing: On Memory and History in Cathy Caruth's Work', *Diacritics* 49: 2 (2021b), 147–157.

María del Rosario Acosta López, '*Gramáticas de lo inaudito* as Decolonial Grammars: Notes for a Decolonization of Memory', *Research in Phenomenology*, 52:2 (2022a), 203–222.

María del Rosario Acosta López, '*Hamaca Paraguaya* de Paz Encina: notas sobre la resistencia *de* la memoria', *Huellas* 110 (2022b), 100–109.

María del Rosario Acosta López, *Gramáticas de lo inaudito: pensar la memoria después del trauma* (Barcelona: Herder, 2023).

María del Rosario Acosta López, *Memory Work in Colombia: Past and Present Experiences, Legacies for the Future* (World Humanities Report: South America (CHCI), (forthcoming).

María del Rosario Acosta López, *Grammars of Listening: On Memory after Trauma* (NY: Fordham, forthcoming, expected 2024).

Juana Acosta-López and María del Rosario Acosta López, '¿Por qué una mirada retrospectiva a la justicia transicional en Colombia?', in J. Acosta-López and M.R. Acosta López (eds.), *Justicia transicional en Colombia: una mirada retrospectiva* (Bogotá: Planeta and Universidad de la Sabana, 2022).

Hannah Arendt, 'Understanding and Politics', in *Essays in Understanding* (New York: Schocken, 2004), 307–327.

Lauren Berlant, *Cruel Optimism* (Duke University Press, 2011).

Alejandro Castillejo, 'La localización del daño: etnografía, espacio y confesión en el escenario transicional colombiano', *Horizontes antropológicos* 20:42 (2014), 213–236.

Alejandro Castillejo, 'Giving a Place to the Dead and Reassembling the Present', in Acosta López (ed.), *Memory Work in Colombia: Past and Present Experiences, Legacies for the Future* (World Humanities Report: South America (CHCI), forthcoming).

Cathy Caruth, *Unclaimed Experience: Trauma, Narrative and History* (Baltimore: Johns Hopkins University Press, 1996, ed. 2016).

Elizabeth Deligio, 'Memory Work Needs to be Infused with the Power of Imagination', in Acosta López (ed.), *Memory Work in Colombia: Past and Present Experiences, Legacies for the Future* (World Humanities Report: South America (CHCI), forthcoming).

Kristie Dotson, 'Tracking Epistemic Violence, Tracking Practices of Silencing', *Hypatia* 26:2 (2011), 236–257.

Ilit Ferber, 'Pain as Yardstick: Jean Améry', *Journal of French and Francophile Philosophy* XXIV:3 (2016), 3–16.

Miranda Fricker, *Epistemic Injustice: Power and the Ethics of Knowing* (Oxford, 2007).

Miguel Gualdrón, 'To 'Stay Where You Are' as a Decolonial Gesture: Glissant's Philosophy of Antillean Space in the Context of Césaire and Fanon', in J. D. Webb, R. Westmaas, M. del Pilar Kaladeen, and W. Tantam (eds.), *Memory, Migration and (de)colonisation in the Caribbean and Beyond* (University of London Press, 2019), 133–152.

Saidiya Hartman, 'Venus in Two Acts', *Small Axe* 12:2 (2008), 1–14.

Axelle Karera, 'Frantz Fanon and the Future of Critical Phenomenology in an Anti-Black World', *Political Theology* (forthcoming).

Rosaura Martínez Ruiz, 'Collective Working-Through of Trauma or Psychoanalysis as a Political Strategy', *Psychoanalysis, Culture and Society* 25:4 (2020), 595–611.

José Medina, 'Hermeneutical Injustice and Polyphonic Contextualism: Social Silences and Shared Hermeneutical Responsibilities', *Social Epistemology* 26:2 (2012), 201–220.

José Medina, *The Epistemology of Resistance* (Oxford: Oxford University Press, 2013).

José Medina, 'Estéticas de la resistencia: reimaginando la filosofía crítica desde las gramáticas de lo inaudito de María del Rosario Acosta López', *Estudios de Filosofía* 66 (2022), 155–165.

Pilar Riaño and María Victoria Uribe in 'Constructing Memory amidst War: The Historical Memory Group of Colombia', *International Journal of Transitional Justice* (2016), 1–19.

Nelly Richard, *Fracturas de la memoria. Arte y pensamiento crítico* (Buenos Aires: Siglo XXI, 2007).

Pilar Riaño and Maria Emma Wills (eds.), *Recordar y narrar el conflicto: Herramientas para reconstruir memoria histórica* (Bogotá: Comisión Nacional de Reparación y Reconciliación, 2009).

María del Rosario Acosta López

Elena Ruiz, 'Cultural Gaslighting', *Hypatia* 35:4 (2020), 687–713.

Jill Stauffer, *Ethical Loneliness: The Injustice of Not Being Heard* (NY: Columbia, 2015).

Steve Stern, *La memoria nos abre camino. Balance metodológico del CNHM para el esclarecimiento histórico* (Bogotá: Centro Nacional de Memoria Histórica, 2018).

Rocío Zambrana, *Colonial Debts* (Durham, NC: Duke University Press, 2021).

Laura Zornosa, 'How We Remember: Memory Work in Chicago and Colombia', in Acosta López (ed.), *Memory Work in Colombia: Past and Present Experiences, Legacies for the Future* (World Humanities Report: South America (CHCI), forthcoming).

In the Mood: Why Vibes Matter in Reading and Writing Philosophy

HELEN DE CRUZ

Abstract

Philosophers often write in a particular mood; their work is playful, strident, strenuous, or nostalgic. On the face of it, these moods contribute little to a philosophical argument and are merely incidental. However, I will argue that the cognitive science of moods and emotions offers us reasons to suspect that mood is relevant for philosophical texts. I use examples from Friedrich Nietzsche and Rudolph Carnap to illustrate the role moods play in their arguments. As readers and writers of philosophical texts, we do well to attend to mood.

1. Introduction

In the Preface to the *Genealogy of Morality*, Friedrich Nietzsche muses about philosophical mood:

> If anyone finds this script incomprehensible and hard on the ears, I do not think the fault necessarily lies with me. It is clear enough, assuming, as I do, that people have first read my earlier works without sparing themselves some effort: because they really are not easy to approach. With regard to my *Zarathustra*, for example, I do not acknowledge anyone as an expert on it if he has not, at some time, been both profoundly wounded and profoundly delighted by it, for only then may he enjoy the privilege of sharing, with due reverence, the halcyon element from which the book was born and its sunny brightness, spaciousness, breadth and certainty. (Nietzsche, 1887 [2006], p. 8)

Nietzsche's point is that his writings are not always easily accessible: a full appreciation of them requires effort on the part of the reader. If she truly wishes to be an expert on his work, she must be prepared to be 'profoundly wounded and profoundly delighted by it'. The form of Nietzsche's prose is essential to understand it. You cannot be an expert on his work if you aren't affected by the moods invoked in it.

doi:10.1017/S1358246123000073   © The Royal Institute of Philosophy and the contributors 2023

Royal Institute of Philosophy Supplement **93** 2023

Helen De Cruz

Nietzsche is far from the only philosopher who plays with his readers' feelings. Many classic and beloved philosophical works have a distinctive mood. We can think of (among many others) playful Zhuangzi, earnest Augustine, or speculative Pascal. The moods these works evoke have helped to cement their enduring appeal in the history of philosophy. You flutter along with Zhuangzi to experience what it's like to be a butterfly. You groan inwardly as Augustine obsesses over a few stolen pears. You sense, along with Pascal, horror at the vastness of the universe. What wisdom or insight is gained when these texts carry us away?

In this paper, I examine the role of mood in philosophy – moods such as sorrow, nostalgia, unease, excitement, playfulness, strenuousness, adventurousness, and pathos. On the face of it, they contribute little to a philosophical argument. When we give feedback on student essays, we do not caution them to pay attention to the mood of their writing. If anything, better prioritize clarity and precision over rhetoric and feeling! A typical book review of a philosophical monograph will rarely assess the mood it evokes. However, as I'll show, the cognitive science of moods and emotions offers us reasons to suspect that mood is relevant for philosophical texts. As readers and writers of such texts, we do well to attend to it.

2. What is Philosophical Mood?

2.1 Philosophical and Psychological Views on Mood and Emotion

To get a better grasp of what philosophical mood might be, let's first look at the general concept of mood, as it is discussed in philosophy and cognitive science. In this literature, a distinction is drawn between mood and emotion. Robert Roberts (2003, p. 112) argues that moods, unlike emotions, do not have clear propositional content; they are not 'about' something. You can be depressed or elated, without having a definite object to be depressed or elated about. Roberts argues that we have reasons for our emotions (e.g., a gift makes us grateful or joyful). On the other hand, moods tend to have causes rather than reasons, e.g., a happy tune puts us in a happy mood, but the tune doesn't give us a *reason* to feel a happy mood, unlike the gift. Adam Morton (2013, pp. 29–36) also distinguishes moods and emotions based on their content. Emotions are about things that happen or that we imagine might happen. In Morton's view, an emotion might be the fear that your house will burn down or that you might catch a deadly disease. Moods, by contrast, are not tied to concrete situations or imaginings, but are diffusely in the background. Take the mood of fearfulness, a mood that is in the vicinity of the emotion of fear. Consider a mother in the US who brings her child to school in the days after a school shooting once again made the national news. The first days, she might feel fear the same thing might happen at her child's school. Gradually, the fear ebbs away as it usually does. But the mood, which persists for much longer, does not. Lodged in her stomach remains an inchoate sense of dread, an uneasy feeling she cannot seem to shake, even as she cheerfully bids the other parents good morning.

What is the inspiration for these distinctions? Both Roberts and Morton draw on the folk concept of mood. Morton (2013, p. 32) distinguishes between emotion and mood 'on intuitive grounds, without experimental evidence'. He notes that emotion researchers have not carefully distinguished mood from emotion. Until the late 1990s, psychologists indeed used 'mood', 'emotion', and 'affect' interchangeably. However, contemporary psychologists distinguish between mood and emotion. According to a standard distinction (see Ekkekakis, 2012, for an overview), emotions are a complex set of interrelated sub-events. They involve a core affect (e.g., feeling sad), associated behaviors such as smiling or crying, heightened attention toward that object, and neural and endocrine changes. Moods, by contrast, are longer lasting, and are 'about nothing specific or about everything—about the world in general' (Frijda, 2009, p. 258). They influence our global appraisal of situations and specific events, without being specifically directed at events or objects.

The distinctions between moods and emotions in philosophy and psychology remind us of how those words are used in everyday contexts. Beedie, Terry, and Lane (2005) compared the usage of the word 'mood' of authors of psychology textbooks with non-specialist English sources, such as cooking books and novels. Both groups distinguished moods from emotions as follows: moods are longer-term, more nebulous, less intense, less focused, and less tied to specific situations than emotions. Given how well folk psychology and psychology textbooks agree on this, I take moods to be a kind of feeling that is not situationally specified, can persist over long periods, and that do not have a clear target. The distinction between moods and emotions is not absolute and admits of degrees. Many philosophers use 'mood' and 'emotion' interchangeably. To ensure some uniformity, I will treat as philosophical mood affective states that are not emotions (i.e., not clearly directed) and that are elicited in readers or listeners when they engage with philosophical works.

Helen De Cruz

2.2 Nietzsche and Carnap: Two Examples of Mood in Philosophy

Here are two examples of philosophical mood in two very different philosophers: on the one hand, Friedrich Nietzsche, filled with pathos, verve, concerned with the brilliant individual in a faceless mass. On the other, lucid, clear Rudolph Carnap, worried about the ascent of the far right, concerned with working-class people and their rights. In spite of their differences, both philosophers were faced with a similar problem: what if your philosophical outlook is *radically different* from the mainstream, particularly the political mainstream? How do you convince your audience? Friedrich Nietzsche makes mood (*Stimmung*) central to his critique of the prevailing morality of his time, particularly in *Daybreak* (also sometimes translated as 'Dawn', originally *Morgenröte – Gedanken über die moralischen Vorurteile,* 1881 [1997]). Rebecca Bamford (2019) argues that mood plays a central role in Nietzsche's overarching philosophical project. Mood is not incidental to his work, but serves to 'identify, and counter, the highly problematic and deeply entrenched authority of the morality of mores' (Bamford, 2014, p. 56). In *Daybreak* 9, Nietzsche argues that people obey the morality of customs (or mores) out of a society-wide prevailing sense of fear. This mood of fearfulness has two bad consequences: it further entrenches the customs, and it discourages people from innovating in the moral domain.

> Every individual action, every individual mode of thought arouses dread; it is impossible to compute what precisely the rarer, choicer, more original spirits in the whole course of history have had to suffer through being felt as evil and dangerous, indeed through feeling themselves to be so. Under the dominion of the morality of custom, originality of every kind has acquired a bad conscience; the sky above the best men is for this reason to this very moment gloomier than it need be. (Nietzsche, D 9)

Anticipating research on the psychology of mood (as we will see in the next section), Nietzsche argues that the mood of fearfulness stultifies our appetite for action. We need to feel in a positive mood, we need to rid ourselves of this background sense of dread, in order to do something that goes against the grain, to pull ourselves together and become truly innovative, original thinkers. For Nietzsche, joyous moods were crucial: 'The good mood was placed on the scales as an argument and outweighed rationality' (D 28).

Nietzsche harnesses mood as a counter-attack against the dominant dread that entrenches our customs. He notes that we have words for extreme emotions such as love, dread, compassion, and pain, but not for milder, more diffuse moods (D 115). This makes it hard to coin new words that would help us to break free of customary morality and the implicit moods it drives on. The moods Nietzsche evokes in his philosophical works serve to counter the entrenched mores of his time. We should counter the fearful mood of customary morality with a mood of 'cheerful resolution' (D 28), a mood that engenders within us a joyful resolve to act (Ansell-Pearson and Bamford, 2021, pp. 57–58).

Indeed, Nietzsche goes as far as to recommend deliberate mood-management: '"Create a mood!" – one will then require no reasons and conquer all objections!' (D 28), i.e., we must counter mood with mood when we engage in ethical theorizing. Nietzsche's appeal to mood is primarily strategic: if philosophical works are to challenge entrenched ideas, and moods are an important part of the entrenchment, then incorporating a countervailing mood can be beneficial. However, this tactic leaves open the question of whether moods are also beneficial *to help us think*. I'll return to this in section 4.

Rudolph Carnap's *Preface* to the first edition of *The Logical Structure of the World* (Carnap, 1928 [2003]) shows a different mastery of philosophical mood. Carnap was a proponent of logical positivism and a member of the Vienna Circle. Its members regularly met at the University of Vienna in the 1920s to discuss fundamental questions on the nature of science, how logic could improve our thinking, the limits of reason, and what makes a statement meaningful. They were strongly committed to clarity of thought. Many of them were left-leaning and concerned with improving the lives of working-class people. During this period, Austria increasingly came in the grip of emotionally charged Nazi propaganda, populism, and antisemitism. This rhetoric had no basis in fact but was very effective in stirring people's emotions. Carnap, like other members of the Vienna Circle, wanted to counteract this propaganda, but interestingly, he did not want to do away with mood. Rather, like Nietzsche, he wanted to fight mood with mood. In his *Preface*, Carnap states that a 'requirement for justification and conclusive foundation of each thesis will eliminate all speculative and poetic work from philosophy' (p. xvii) – eliminating metaphysics from philosophy is an important element of his overarching project, which aims to engineer concepts with utmost precision and clarity (Dutilh Novaes, 2020). At the same time, Carnap acknowledges that philosophers are emotional beings, and that emotions – like purely intellectual rationality – will always play a part in how we engage with philosophy:

> The practical handling of philosophical problems and the discovery of their solutions does not have to be purely intellectual, but will always contain emotional elements and intuitive methods. The justification, however, has to take place before the forum of the understanding; here we must not refer to our intuition or emotional needs. We too, have 'emotional needs' in philosophy, but they are filled by clarity of concepts, precision of methods, responsible theses, achievement through cooperation in which each individual plays his part. (Carnap, 1928 [2003], p. xvii)

So, in Carnap's view, the thirst for clarity is part of a distinctively philosophical mood. This mood 'demands clarity everywhere, but [...] realizes that the fabric of life can never quite be comprehended' (Carnap, 1928 [2003], p. xviii). We can see this mood expressed in other areas of human creativity, such as music and architecture. Carnap had a strong connection with Bauhaus, a modernist architectural movement that prized functionality, rationality, order, and the use of technology to help organize life (Potochnik and Yap, 2006). In a guest lecture he gave at Bauhaus Dessau (the Bauhaus school of art, design, and architecture) on 15 October 1929, he argued that philosophy of science and architecture are two manifestations of a single way of life. Logical positivists and Bauhaus architects shared the same opponents: members of the religious right, nationalists, nativists, and Nazis (Galison, 1990). Carnap characterizes this philosophical Bauhaus mood as follows:

> [T]here is an inner kinship between the attitude on which our philosophical work is founded and the intellectual attitude which presently manifests itself in entirely different walks of life. [...] It is an orientation which demands clarity everywhere, but which realizes that the fabric of life can never quite be comprehended. It makes us pay careful attention to detail and at the same time recognizes the great lines which run through the whole. It is an orientation which acknowledges the bonds that tie men together, but at the same time strives for free development of the individual. Our work is carried by the faith that this attitude will win the future. (Carnap, 1928 [2003], p. xviii)

What is this Bauhaus mood in the *Logical Structure of the World*? It is not just a mood of clarity and dispassion, nor merely achieving a balance between analytic and synthetic styles of thinking. It is also, and perhaps more importantly, a mood of fellow-feeling, co-operation, and optimism about modernism and the positivist research agenda. This mood is not just dispassionate. Rather, it involves an *active rejection of passion*. It encourages composed coolness, lucidity, and level-headedness that helps to ground readers and prevents them from being swept away by grand and vague rhetoric, such as that of the Nazis.

Nietzsche and Carnap both hold that philosophical mood matters. They recognize that their philosophical work has a distinctive mood, and that these moods contribute to it. Both compare the mood of their philosophies with that of their intellectual opponents: the joyful resolve versus the dread and fear of custom in Nietzsche, and the clear and dispassionate internationalist mood against the opacity and wild appeal to emotions by members of the political right in Carnap. Carnap also held that his philosophical mood fits within a broader intellectual climate, which, if implemented, would ameliorate the political situation as well (Dutilh Novaes, 2020). He further hints at a function of mood in our thinking: it makes us 'pay careful attention to detail and at the same time recognizes the great lines which run through the whole' (p. xviii). As we will see in the next section, Carnap's remarks prefigure cognitive psychological findings that indicate that mood indeed influences cognitive processing styles. Feel a different mood, and you will process information differently.

3. The Influence of Mood on the Appraisal of Philosophical Ideas and Arguments

3.1 Two Hypotheses on Mood and Cognitive Processing

As we saw previously, moods are not clearly directed at objects or events. A nostalgic mood does not mean we are nostalgic for something, we just feel a vague sense of longing for we-know-not-what. Nevertheless, mood has a strong influence on our motivations and on our evaluation of situations and ideas. For example, it influences our appraisal of the difficulty of a task and our ability to succeed in it. A chore that might seem insurmountable when we are in a negative mood can look eminently feasible when we are in a positive mood (Gendolla and Brinkmann, 2005).

Mood has a significant influence on our evaluation of persuasive communications, a finding that is of interest to marketing specialists as well as philosophers. A happy mood tends to make participants more vulnerable to accepting weak arguments. Participants in a sad mood give lower ratings to weaker arguments than happy participants; sad people can differentiate better between stronger and weaker arguments than happy people (Bless, Bohner, Schwarz, and Strack, 1990). Negative moods tend to enhance both attention to detail and critical thinking. But positive mood also has positive aspects. For example, positive moods enhance creativity and focus, and increase cognitive flexibility (Baas, De Dreu, and Nijstad, 2008).

How does mood influence cognitive processing styles? This is a matter of continued debate among cognitive scientists. An influential proposal (Blanchette and Richards, 2010) holds that positive moods promote big-picture appraisals of a situation, and hence lead to schematic, goal-oriented, global thinking, whereas negative moods help us to focus on details, and to resolve specific problems.

Cognitive psychologists have offered two main hypotheses on how mood and evaluative attitudes relate, and why positive mood promotes schematic and global thinking, and negative mood encourages paying attention to details. The *affect-as-information hypothesis* states that 'affect assigns value to whatever seems to be causing it' (Clore and Huntsinger, 2007, p. 393). Differently put, cues from the environment influence our mood, and that mood gives us affective and valuable information about our surroundings. For example, if we are in an environment that induces a mood of fearfulness (even if we can't quite identify the specific triggers for why we should be afraid), that mood provides valuable information that we are in a dangerous situation. Applied to evaluative attitudes in philosophy and other contexts: if an argument puts us in a positive mood, we are more likely to evaluate it positively than if it puts us in a negative mood. Our current feelings guide cognitive processing, with positive feelings promoting greater reliance on accessible information. For example, an atheist scholar reads a paper that tells her that atheists are better at analytic thinking than theists. Because the paper makes her feel good about herself, she does not critically look at potential weaknesses in the experimental design of the study.

The *alternative mood-as-priming hypothesis* (Bower, 1981) states that moods prime us to recall information stored in long-term memory that is relevant for the given situation. A sorrowful mood focuses us on negative memories that elicited those moods in the past, whereas a joyful mood makes us think of earlier positive occasions when we felt happy that are similar to the situation we are confronted with. Here the link with the environment and our moods is less direct than in the previous hypothesis. If, for some reason, a feature in our environment triggers a memory that evokes a mood, that mood will colour our evaluation of our current situation. For example, you sit in a restaurant eating escargots and you suddenly feel sad, without knowing why. The escargots bring to memory the last time you ate them (years ago), which was when your boyfriend texted you to break up with you.

These two hypotheses point at potential pathways through which mood can influence our evaluation of philosophical ideas. The affect-as-information hypothesis indicates that mood tends to influence our judgments directly, by serving as experiential and bodily information regarding how one feels about the object of judgment. The mood-as-priming hypothesis also points to the value of mood, but in this case the mood depends less upon the object and more upon analogous situations in the past. One could simply evoke a positive or negative evaluation of an object by inducing the relevant mood. At present, the affect-as-information hypothesis enjoys better empirical support (Clore and Huntsinger, 2007). For this reason, I use this hypothesis as the psychological theoretical background to think about the importance of mood in philosophy, though many of the claims I will make would stand with the mood-as-priming hypothesis as well.

3.2 Heidegger's Stimmungen

The affect-as-information hypothesis has a striking parallel in Martin Heidegger's work on mood (*Stimmung*) and its ability to shape our sense of being in the world. Lauren Freeman (2014, p. 446) characterizes Heideggerian *Stimmungen,* or moods, as follows:

> Moods are not mere mental states that result from, arise out of, or are directly caused by our situation or context. Rather, moods are fundamental modes of existence that are disclosive of the way one is or finds oneself [*sich befinden*] in the world. Mood is one of the basic modes through which we experience the world and through which the world is made present to us.

Heidegger holds that human beings are not impartial spectators who can gaze upon the situations they find themselves in from an idealized perspective. We never hold a view from nowhere, but are always situated, fully immersed in the world. Some things present themselves to us because of their practical significance, whereas others remain irrelevant and invisible. This practical significance is a holistic web of significance relations – things are not significant or insignificant to us in isolation. This web of significance depends on mood. For Heidegger, moods are like lenses through which we see the world.

Helen De Cruz

They are not some colourful add-on or extra, but are a part of how we are basically constituted (Freeman, 2014). We are always in some mood. With his account of *Stimmung*, Heidegger rejects the commonplace view that mood merely colours our experiences.

> The fact that moods can deteriorate [*verdorben werden*] and change over means simply that in every case *Dasein* always has some mood [*gestimmt ist*]. The pallid, evenly balanced lack of mood [*Ungestimmtheit*], which is often persistent and which is not to be mistaken for a bad mood, is far from nothing at all. (Heidegger, 1927 [1962], 29, p. 175).

For Heidegger, finding ourselves in a world is a precondition for having objects of experience, and we would not find ourselves in a world without mood (Ratcliffe, 2013, p. 159). Mood is an essential element of being-in-the-world, 'It comes neither from 'outside' nor from 'inside', but arises out of Being-in-the-world, as a way of such Being' (Heidegger, 1927 [1962], 29, p. 176). Differently put, there is a dynamic interaction between an agent and her environment, and mood arises because of that interplay.

Through mood, we get attuned to our environment. This shapes our experiences, thoughts, and beliefs. In this respect, mood is more fundamental than even beliefs or desires, as moods shape what beliefs and desires we might form in a given situation. Freeman (2014) observes that this embodied framework of mood is largely missing in contemporary cognitive psychology. Nevertheless, there are important ways in which Heidegger's account resonates with findings in cognitive psychology. Take the observation that our appraisals of the difficulty of a task and probability of success are influenced by mood. It's so much easier to get anything done when you're in a happy mood than when you feel a bit down. When you are depressed, tasks that are trivial for others, such as filling in a form, answering an email, or putting a letter in the mail, can become formidable. Mood is contagious: Kramer, Guillory, and Hancock (2014) showed how affects can be transmitted through social networks such as Facebook, even in the absence of direct verbal cues and direct interaction.

The Heideggerian picture of mood also agrees with the extensive literature on mood management and on mood disorders, such as bipolar depression. In neurotypical people, mood varies throughout the day and shapes their engagement with the world. They scaffold moods using music (Krueger, 2014), listening to epic orchestral music, light classical music, or hip-hop as they go through their everyday tasks. Somewhat surprisingly, people sometimes deliberately

180

seek out fictions and music with a negative mood, such as tragedies and sorrowful music even when they don't feel happy (Mar, Oatley, Djikic, and Mullin, 2011). Perhaps it is because we feel the mood of tenderness when we listen to sad music, and we find comfort and solace in that feeling (Oliver, 2008). However, mood disorders disrupt this mood management. In bipolar depression, for example, patients experience swings between elevated moods and depressed moods, with depression being the hallmark of the disorder. As one patient describes his periods of low mood (cited in Mitchell and Malhi, 2004, p. 531):

> Profound melancholia is a day-in, day-out, night-in, night-out, almost arterial level of agony. It is a pitiless unrelenting pain that affords no window of hope, no alternative to a grim and brackish existence, and no respite from the cold undercurrents of thought and feeling that dominate the horribly restless nights of despair.

This mood disorder has a wide range of effects. It leads to low self-perception, inability to get simple tasks done, negative evaluation of neutral social interactions, among many others. Sometimes people who suffer from mood disorders are told by unsympathetic acquaintances to 'just pull yourself together'. But, using Heidegger's framework, we can say that this doesn't work. Mood constitutes a way of being, it fundamentally preconditions how we experience the world.

4. Why Mood Matters for Philosophizing

Taking together the psychological and philosophical ideas on mood in the previous sections, we now begin to see how mood is fundamental for how we evaluate situations. Mood influences our thinking, and it influences how we appraise certain arguments. In this section, I'll show that philosophers who pay attention to the mood of their work help their readers to evaluate it. Readers who are attuned to the mood of a philosophical work, likewise, are better able to evaluate it.

For the longest time, I had difficulties reading French phenomenologists such as Maurice Merleau-Ponty and Jean-Paul Sartre, trying to puzzle out their thoughts and lines of argument. But my difficulties vanished once I realized that you need to read French phenomenology 'on vibes', feeling along with the various moods the authors evoke. I'll now look more closely at *how* moods can help us to read and write better philosophy: control of background mood, making us care, and transforming us in the long term.

Helen De Cruz

4.1 Better Control of Background Mood

As we saw, moods can influence thinking styles (global and schematic versus attention to detail and critical), and this influences the appraisal of philosophical texts. We come to a philosophical text, like we come to anything, while we are in a particular mood. For example, you might be in an anxious mood because of many teaching and administrative tasks ahead, or in a nostalgic mood because you were just reminded of a happy school day. This baseline mood that we bring to the text will influence how we appraise it. It will make some aspects of the text more salient, and help us make certain connections. Since, as an author, you have no control over the background mood readers bring to the text, the influence of the initial moods of the readers on their initial appraisal of your text is unpredictable and variable. However, if you write a text in such a way as to instill a mood that is congruent with the aims of your paper, this can help to draw the reader's attention to relevant aspects of your argument.

The affect-as-information hypothesis helps us see why: an appropriate mood allows us to better attend to the author's intent. Moods point us to relevant aspects of the text and draw our attention to it. Philosophy texts tend to be obtuse. For example, a recent quantitative study found a higher number of hedge words (probably, possibly, *etc.*) in philosophy compared to other disciplines, and these words hinder comprehension (Hartley, Sotto, and Fox, 2004). An appropriate mood can help the reader grasp the main lines of an argument better. Since we also pay attention to other aspects that help the reader grasp the argument, such as clarity of structure and sentence-level prose, we should pay attention to mood as well, for example, by ditching hedge words and using more evocative examples.

4.2 Giving a Sense of Why a Philosophical Position Would Matter to Us

Intellectually grasping an idea is not the same as fully grasping *why* it matters or why we should care. As Heidegger suggested, moods are prior to desires and beliefs. They shape which desires, beliefs, and appraisals we form in a given situation. An appropriate philosophical mood puts us in a better position to fully appreciate a philosophical position and its wider ramifications by shaping our beliefs and appraisals. This allows countercultural gadflies such as Nietzsche to counteract prevailing moods that a reader is subject to, such as the background sense of dread that stifles creativity, or an internationalist positivist such as Carnap to counteract the emotionally-charged propaganda of the Nazis.

We can see the persuasive function of mood in the method of cases in recent analytic philosophy. The method of cases involves writing vivid thought experiments that help a reader see how an abstract point can play out in different situations, thus eliciting intuitions. Why do philosophers rely on fanciful scenarios to make philosophical points, rather than laying it out straight (e.g., Norton, 1996)? While Herman Cappelen (2012) has argued that thought experiments and their appeal to intuitions are merely a form of hedging, other authors (e.g., Nersessian, 1992) argue that thought experiments can stir our imagination and help us construct mental models. If these latter authors are right, the moods thought experiments evoke is not incidental, but central to the overall argument. Take the mood evoked in Judith Jarvis Thomson's people-seeds thought experiment:

> Suppose it were like this: people-seeds drift about in the air like pollen, and if you open your windows, one may drift in and take root in your carpets or upholstery. You don't want children, so you fix up your windows with fine mesh screens, the very best you can buy. As can happen, however, and on very, very rare occasions does happen, one of the screens is defective; and a seed drifts in and takes root. (Thomson, 1971, p. 59)

This is one of three vivid thought experiments to get us to think about the ethics of abortion. They evoke a mood of horror and disquiet which is in tune with the sense of horror one might feel at the prospect of an unplanned, perhaps unwanted, pregnancy. These weird fictions help to set the mood, and the mood helps the reader to grasp the argument. Crucially, none of the arguments require the reader to have the biological characteristics to become pregnant. Any reader can appreciate the dark, uncanny mood of these pieces. This helps to scaffold the reader's mood, and in this way, shapes his attunement to the paper he's reading, and through this, his appreciation of Thomson's argument in favor of abortion. Paying attention to mood and making mood consonant with the point one makes thus increases the effectiveness of the way we communicate philosophical ideas.

4.3 Mood and Philosophical Self-Transformation

Think about works of fiction you have read that have transformed how you think, that have deeply influenced you and resonate with

Helen De Cruz

you long after you put them down. Such works are transformative, to use L.A. Paul's (2014) terminology. Reading them is a transformative experience: they change both who we are and what we know. How does this transformation happen? A large literature indicates that narratives can radically change their readers' outlook on life. For example, nineteenth-century novels by authors such as Charles Dickens and Harriet Beecher Stowe were able to help overcome stubborn empathic bias against people from different social classes and racial groups. They have helped to overcome prejudice and effect societal change (Harrison, 2011). Can we discern whether mood played a role in this? Experimental studies have attempted to tease out the importance of mood (as evoked by the quality of writing, the effectiveness of setting, the atmosphere of the text) versus the pure effect of the plot itself in such personal transformative situations. In one study, participants read either Chekhov's short story *The Lady with the Toy Dog* or a control text with similar plot, length, and complexity, but without the artistic qualities of the original story (Djikic, Oatley, Zoeterman, and Peterson, 2009). Participants who read Chekhov's original short story experienced greater changes in personality (as assessed by a 'Big Five' questionnaire before and after the study). Moreover, they reported feeling more moved than control participants.

In a similar vein, mood in philosophy can help us to achieve self-transformation. But for that, we need to have a philosophical practice that allows us to shape the moods of our readers. The remarks about professional philosophy that Arthur Danto made in his presidential address to the Eastern APA in 1984 still ring true today. Philosophy, he pointed out, has become homogenized and standardized in academic papers and monographs, at the expense of a plenitude of genres that all come with their own, distinctive moods. We used to have dialogues, genealogies, *pensées*, ramblings, rants, letters, essays, autobiographies, aphorisms, plays. Now, most we have is 8,000-word papers and 80,000-word monographs. (Indeed, I am aware of the irony of writing this within the limits of an 8,000-word paper.) The peer review process, meant to make the evaluation of philosophy less prone to bias, also dampens our writing, turning it into cookie-cutter philosophy, devoid of mood and personality. As Danto complained,

> The journals in which these papers finally are printed [...] are not otherwise terribly distinct from one another, any more than the papers themselves characteristically are: if, under the constraints of blind review, we black out name and institutional affiliation,

there will be no internal evidence of authorial presence, but only a unit of pure philosophy, to the presentation of which the author will have sacrificed all identity. This implies a noble vision of ourselves as vehicles for the transmission of an utterly impersonal philosophical truth, and it implies a vision of philosophical reality as constituted of isolable, difficult but not finally intractable problems. (Danto, 1984, p. 7)

Yet, as Danto goes on to point out, this author-effacing vision of philosophy is an illusion, because it discounts the fact that philosophy texts are being *read*. Reading is not a passive process of absorption; we're not sponges soaking in philosophical knowledge. Rather, we actively think along with the author. As we think and read along with a work such as Descartes' *Meditations*, we identify not with the protagonist of a fiction that we are in the thralls of an evil demon, but with the author who carefully devised this thought experiment. Through this identification, we can become transformed in our philosophical outlook.

As Richard Pettigrew (2020) points out, when we choose to transform ourselves, we will seek out a social environment that is conducive to this change. Although we do not meet the authors of philosophical texts that transform us in the flesh (at least, not in the moment of reading), we can be transformed by identifying with them through their writing. Mood can facilitate this process of identification, and thus deepen our understanding of a philosophical work. Pettigrew provides some examples of how self-transformation works in typical cases where we consort with people we wish to emulate. Take, for example, the case study of Giang, a man who values seriousness but who would like some levity and light-heartedness in his life. To become more frivolous, he hangs out more with his friend Gail, whom he feels strikes the right balance (Pettigrew, 2020, p. 5). This is achieved in part through social contagion of moods: the playful mood of Gail can help Giang become more attentive to fun and frivolous situations in his life. In a similar vein, imagine a philosopher who, for many years, has deepened her expertise in analytic philosophy, but who would now want to work more in continental philosophy. She might do well to seek out continental works that aid her self-transformation, and that, through their specific moods, get her more into the mindset of continental philosophy in the specialization she is interested in (e.g., phenomenology) and less in the analytic tradition she usually works in (e.g., philosophy of mind). This shows how mood-management in philosophical texts is a bi-directional process. The author can frame the work's mood such that the reader becomes more receptive to her arguments. The reader can deliberately seek out works with a particular mood to facilitate her self-transformation.

My remarks are tentative and speculative. Future experimental philosophical studies may allow us to see if mood indeed aids personal transformation. I predict that a text by Nietzsche or Zhuangzi has a greater transformative effect upon the reader than a control text with similar philosophical content, length, and complexity that is devoid of mood. Philosophical mood helps to countervail existing moods and tendencies that a reader might be subject to. The joyous and irreverent mood of Nietzsche's *Daybreak* and other works counters the mood of fearfulness and dread invoked by custom, and makes us braver, hence better able to take his radical ideas serious, rather than dismiss them out of hand. Zhuangzi seeks to free his readers from the earnestness of Confucianism. His playful and cheeky scenarios, such as the expert butcher who cuts up an ox in front of an impressed king, help readers to free themselves from the rigid demands of living up to one's social role. The mood that Nietzsche and Zhuangzi evoke in their work frees the imagination from the grip of customary morality and makes freer thought possible. This helps their readers become different people who walk through life with a lighter step (Moeller and D'Ambrosio, 2017).

5. Should we Worry about the Use of Mood in Philosophy?

Suppose you are on board with my claim that mood does matter to philosophy, you might still feel a little worried about what this means for our evaluations of philosophical arguments. We can think of this in a broader context: rhetoric aims to persuade, to move the reader or listener to accept your arguments, but is a piece with better rhetoric also more *truthful*? Indeed, we might worry that mood is what Katia Vavova (2018, p. 136) calls an 'irrelevant influence', which she defines as follows:

> An irrelevant influence (factor) for me with respect to my belief that p is one that (a) has influenced my belief that p and (b) does not bear on the truth of p.

We can see irrelevant influences play out in experimental philosophical studies that probe how the framing of philosophical problems influence our appraisals. Take the well-known trolley problem where a participant evaluates if you should (or are allowed to) pull a lever to divert a trolley so that it drives on to kill one person, rather than five if you had not interfered. Schwitzgebel and Cushman (2012) found that the order in which various scenarios are presented (e.g., pushing a lever versus pushing someone from a footbridge onto the track) changes people's evaluation of these scenarios. Not only that, philosophers were also influenced in their evaluation of abstract philosophical principles, such as the doctrine of double effect, depending on which scenario they see first (e.g., switch-first or push-first in trolley scenarios). These order effects persist even if participants can think about the task, even if they're experts, such as PhD holders in ethics. Given that philosophers likely thought about such principles as the doctrine of double effect before they enrolled in the experiment, these effects are surprising. How to explain them? Mood may play a key role. In one study (Valdesolo and DeSteno, 2006), participants received a positive or neutral affect (mood) induction, by watching either a happy or a neutral video. Immediately after watching these videos, participants were presented with footbridge and switch trolley dilemmas. While there was no difference in evaluation of the switch trolley dilemma, participants in the happy condition were three times more likely to say it was appropriate to push a large man off a footbridge to save five people from a hurtling trolley than those in the neutral condition. Strohminger, Lewis, and Meyer (2011) used a similar set-up and found that mirth (evoked by humorous audio clips) increased the perceived permissiveness of pushing a fat stranger off the footbridge, whereas elevation (evoked by inspirational narrations) did not. Given this influence of background mood on our evaluation of philosophical positions, readers and writers of philosophical texts should pay *more*, not less, attention to mood.

Okay, you might say, I can see why mood is important for philosophical texts, but isn't it cheating to mood-manage your readers, rather than try to convince them through the sheer quality of your arguments? My brief answer: it is never just the quality of the arguments. We can read Nietzsche's exhortation 'Create a mood! One will then require no reasons and conquer all objections!' (D 28) as a call to counter mood with mood. Nietzsche thinks that the prevailing mood of fear is so strong we have no choice but to try to counter it with a joyful mood, if readers are to take away anything substantial from his works. This claim needs to be contextualized within his aims in *Daybreak*, namely his campaign against customary morality, where mood can be a practical tool to overcome customs. But we might also read the exhortation as recommending mood in lieu of argument, as a lazy fallback for a philosopher who is unable to convince readers with proper arguments or doesn't bother to convince them but merely massages their moods.

In response to this worry, I want to caution against the construction of philosophy in narrow terms as just arguments. Philosophical arguments have never been pure units of isolable truth. This vision of philosophy does not accord with the sociological reality in which philosophy is practiced, where a variety of factors play a role in how we evaluate philosophical positions. As Danto (1984) pointed out, we aspire to this vision in anonymous peer review, but even then, we are receptive to background cues, such as idiomatic English and citation networks. Moreover, once a paper is published, it's no longer anonymized. Now, we know the author's gender (or can make a good guess at it), their institutional affiliation, and their relative standing in the field. In the social context of practicing philosophy, during events such as the seminar discussion, the colloquium talk, the peer-reviewed journal, the book symposium, we never merely respond to the bare-bones arguments. Our appraisal is influenced by a variety of factors, including the mood of a paper, how evocative a thought experiment is, how engaging the talk is, and the identity of the speaker or author. Philosophical expertise is a complex skill set that involves the ability to make evocative thought experiments, to write in a fluent and persuasive way (Ayala, 2015), to be socially pleasant at professional venues, and so on. The practice of philosophy has a thick, diffuse skill set. Being able to control background mood or to better gauge what the mood of a paper is, is one of the elements in this skill set. It's good to hone skills that are part of a professional practice.

6. Conclusion

I've offered some reasons to think mood is not incidental to philosophy. Mood is essential to provide clarity, focus, and attention for the reader. It scaffolds the reader's attunement and takes away the background noise of varying moods the reader brings to the text. More tentatively, thanks to an appropriate mood, a philosophical text can profoundly transform us. Mood is not just window dressing but an important element of philosophical writing and understanding, which cannot be reduced to the cogency of arguments.

Acknowledgements

Thank you to Julian Baggini, Rebecca Bamford, Johan De Smedt, Ian Olasov, and Will Buckingham for their comments on earlier drafts of this paper, and to the online audience at the Royal Institute of Philosophy lecture series for their helpful suggestions and comments.

References

K. Ansell-Pearson and R. Bamford, *Nietzsche's Dawn. Philosophy, Ethics, and the Passion of Knowledge* (Hoboken, NJ: Wiley-Blackwell, 2021).

S. Ayala, 'Philosophy and the Non-Native Speaker Condition', *American Philosophical Association Newsletter*, 14:2 (2015), 2–9.

M. Baas, C.K. De Dreu, and B.A. Nijstad, 'A Meta-Analysis of 25 Years of Mood-Creativity Research: Hedonic Tone, Activation, or Regulatory Focus?', *Psychological Bulletin*, 134:6 (2008), 779–806.

R. Bamford, 'Mood and Aphorism in Nietzsche's Campaign against Morality', *Pli: The Warwick Journal of Philosophy*, 25 (2014), 55–76.

R. Bamford, 'The Relationship between Science and Philosophy as a Key Feature of Nietzsche's Metaphilosophy', in M. Meyer and P.S. Loeb (eds.), *Nietzsche's Metaphilosophy: The Nature, Method, and Aims of Philosophy* (Cambridge: Cambridge University Press, 2019), 65–82.

C. Beedie, P. Terry, and A. Lane, 'Distinctions between Emotion and Mood', *Cognition & Emotion*, 19:6 (2005), 847–878.

I. Blanchette and A. Richards, 'The Influence of Affect on Higher Level Cognition: A Review of Research on Interpretation, Judgement, Decision Making and Reasoning', *Cognition & Emotion*, 24:4 (2010), 561–595.

H. Bless, G. Bohner, N. Schwarz, and F. Strack, 'Mood and Persuasion: A Cognitive Response Analysis', *Personality and Social Psychology Bulletin*, 16:2 (1990), 331–345.

G.H. Bower, 'Mood and Memory', *American Psychologist*, 36:2 (1981), 129–148.

H. Cappelen, *Philosophy without Intuitions* (Oxford: Oxford University Press, 2012).

R. Carnap, *The Logical Structure of the World and Pseudoproblems in Philosophy* (R.A. George, trans.), (Chicago and LaSalle, IL: Open Court, 1928 [2003]).

G.L. Clore and J.R. Huntsinger, 'How Emotions Inform Judgment and Regulate Thought', *Trends in Cognitive Sciences*, 11:9 (2007), 393–399.

A.C. Danto, 'Philosophy as/and/of Literature', *Proceedings and Addresses of the American Philosophical Association*, 58:1 (1984), 5–19.

Helen De Cruz

M. Djikic, K. Oatley, S. Zoeterman, and J.B. Peterson, 'On Being Moved by Art: How Reading Fiction Transforms the Self', *Creativity Research Journal*, 21:1 (2009), 24–29.

C. Dutilh Novaes, 'Carnapian Explication and Ameliorative Analysis: A Systematic Comparison', *Synthese*, 197:3 (2020), 1011–1034.

P. Ekkekakis, 'Affect, Mood, and Emotion', in G. Tenenbaum, R.C. Ecklundt, and A. Kamata (eds.), *Measurement in Sport and Exercise Psychology* (Campaign, IL: Human Kinetics, 2012), 321–332.

L. Freeman, 'Toward a Phenomenology of Mood', *Southern Journal of Philosophy*, 52:4 (2014), 445–476.

N.H. Frijda, 'Mood', in D. Sander and K. Scherer (eds.), *The Oxford Companion to Emotion and the Affective Sciences* (Oxford: Oxford University Press, 2009), 258–259.

P. Galison, 'Aufbau/Bauhaus: Logical Positivism and Architectural Modernism', *Critical Inquiry*, 16:4 (1990), 709–752.

G.H. Gendolla and K. Brinkmann, 'The Role of Mood States in Self-Regulation: Effects on Action Preferences and Resource Mobilization', *European Psychologist*, 10:3 (2005), 187–198.

M.C. Harrison, 'How Narrative Relationships Overcome Empathic Bias: Elizabeth Gaskell's Empathy across Social Difference', *Poetics Today*, 32:2 (2011), 255–288.

J. Hartley, E. Sotto, and C. Fox, 'Clarity across the Disciplines', *Science Communication*, 26:2 (2004), 188–210.

M. Heidegger, *Being and Time* (J. Macquarrie and E. Robinson, trans.), (Oxford, UK, and Cambridge, MA): Blackwell, 1927 [1962]).

A.D. Kramer, J.E. Guillory, and J.T. Hancock, 'Experimental Evidence of Massive-Scale Emotional Contagion through Social Networks', *Proceedings of the National Academy of Sciences USA*, 111:24 (2014), 8788–8790.

J. Krueger, 'Affordances and the Musically Extended Mind', *Frontiers in Psychology*, 4:1003 (2014), 1–12.

R.A. Mar, K. Oatley, M. Djikic, and J. Mullin, 'Emotion and Narrative Fiction: Interactive Influences Before, During, and After Reading, *Cognition & Emotion*, 25:5 (2011), 818–833.

P.B. Mitchell and G.S. Malhi, 'Bipolar Depression: Phenomenological Overview and Clinical Characteristics', *Bipolar Disorders*, 6:6 (2004), 530–539.

H.G. Moeller and P. D'Ambrosio, *Genuine Pretending. On the Philosophy of the Zhuangzi* (New York: Columbia University Press, 2017).

A. Morton, *Emotion and Imagination* (Cambridge: Polity Press, 2013).

N.J. Nersessian, 'In the Theoretician's Laboratory: Thought Experimenting as Mental Modeling', in *PSA: Proceedings of the Biennial Meeting of the Philosophy of Science Association* (Chicago: University of Chicago Press, 1992), 291–301.

F. Nietzsche, *Daybreak. Thoughts on the Prejudices of Morality*, (M. Clark and B. Leiter, eds. and R.J. Hollingsdale, trans.), (Cambridge: Cambridge University Press, 1881 [1997]).

F. Nietzsche, *On the Genealogy of Morality*, (K. Ansell-Pearson, ed. and C. Diethe, trans.), (Cambridge: Cambridge University Press, 1887 [2006]).

J.D. Norton, 'Are Thought Experiments Just What You Thought?', *Canadian Journal of Philosophy*, 26:3 (1996), 333–366.

M.B. Oliver, 'Tender Affective States as Predictors of Entertainment Preference', *Journal of Communication*, 58:1 (2008), 40–61.

L.A. Paul, *Transformative Experience* (Oxford: Oxford University Press, 2014).

R. Pettigrew, *Choosing for Changing Selves* (Oxford: Oxford University Press, 2020).

A. Potochnik and A. Yap, 'Revisiting Galison's 'Aufbau/Bauhaus' in Light of Neurath's Philosophical Projects', *Studies in History and Philosophy of Science Part A*, 37:3 (2006), 469–488.

M. Ratcliffe, 'Why Mood Matters', in M.A. Wrathall (ed.), *The Cambridge Companion to Heidegger's Being and Time* (Cambridge: Cambridge University Press, 2013), 157–176.

R.C. Roberts, *Emotions: An Essay in Aid of Moral Psychology* (Cambridge: Cambridge University Press, 2003).

E. Schwitzgebel and F. Cushman, 'Expertise in Moral Reasoning? Order Effects on Moral Judgment in Professional Philosophers and Non-Philosophers', *Mind & Language*, 27 (2012), 135–153.

N. Strohminger, R.L. Lewis, and D.E. Meyer, 'Divergent Effects of Different Positive Emotions on Moral Judgment', *Cognition*, 119:2 (2011), 295–300.

J.J. Thomson, 'A Defense of Abortion', *Philosophy & Public Affairs*, 7:1 (1971), 47–66.

P. Valdesolo and D. DeSteno, 'Manipulations of Emotional Context Shape Moral Judgment', *Psychological Science*, 17:6 (2006), 476–477.

K. Vavova, 'Irrelevant Influences', *Philosophy and Phenomenological Research*, 96:1 (2018), 134–152.

Fernando Pessoa: The Poet as Philosopher

JONARDON GANERI

Abstract

Fernando Pessoa (1888–1935) lived what was in many ways an astonishingly modern, transcultural, and translingual life. He was born in Lisbon, the point of departure for Vasco da Gama's voyage to India as commemorated by Pessoa's forebear, the poet Luís de Camões. Pessoa grew up in Anglophone Durban, acquiring a lifelong love for English poetry and language. Returning to Lisbon, from where he would never again leave, he set himself the goal of travelling throughout an infinitude of inner landscapes, to be an explorer of inner worlds. He published very little, but left behind a famous trunk containing a treasure trove of scraps, on which were written some of the greatest literary works of the twentieth century, mainly in Portuguese but also a substantial amount in English and French. Pessoa is now acknowledged as one of the greatest poets of the twentieth century, and he has emerged over the last decade as a forgotten voice in twentieth-century modernism, taking his rightful place alongside C.P. Cavafy, Franz Kafka, T.S. Eliot, James Joyce, and Jorge Luis Borges. Pessoa was also a serious student of philosophy and himself a very creative philosopher, yet his genius as a philosopher has as yet hardly been recognized at all.

1. Introduction

Fernando Pessoa (1888–1935) has become many things to many people in the years that have passed since his untimely death. For some, he is simply the greatest poet of the 20th century, certainly in Portuguese and arguably more widely. His poetry, much loved and widely read, has over the years been meticulously edited, published, and translated. For others, he has gradually emerged as a forgotten voice in 20th-century modernism, now finally taking his rightful place alongside giants such as C.P. Cavafy, Franz Kafka, T.S. Eliot, James Joyce, and Jorge Luis Borges. And yet Pessoa was also a philosopher, and it is only very recently that the philosophical importance of his work has begun to attract the attention it deserves. Decisively breaking with the conventional strictures of systematic philosophical writing, the philosophy in his heteronymic poems and his prose anti-novel is a profound and exquisite exploration in the philosophy of self.

Fernando Pessoa lived what was in many ways an astonishingly modern, transcultural, and translingual life. He was born in Lisbon, the point of departure for Vasco da Gama's voyage to

doi:10.1017/S135824612300005X   © The Royal Institute of Philosophy and the contributors 2023
Royal Institute of Philosophy Supplement **93** 2023

Jonardon Ganeri

India as commemorated by Pessoa's forebear, the poet Luís de Camões. Pessoa grew up in Anglophone Durban, acquiring a lifelong love for English poetry and language. Returning to Lisbon, from where he would never again leave, he set himself the goal of travelling throughout an infinitude of *inner* landscapes, to be an explorer of *inner* worlds. He published very little, but left behind a famous trunk containing a treasure trove of scraps, on which were written some of the greatest literary works of the 20th century, mainly in Portuguese but also a substantial amount in English and French. Pessoa's slow reception since his death is largely accounted for by the enormous task of sorting through, reading, and translating the trunkful of notes.

2. Pessoa's Novel Invention

Fernando Pessoa's invention of the concept of a heteronym represents a singular moment in the history of subjectivity.[1] A heteronym is another I, a self that is not one's own. Scattered among his drafts of prefaces to never-to-be-completed editions of his writings and in letters to friends and editors are the few explicit clues we possess as to his intentions. 'The mental origin of my heteronyms lies in my restless, organic tendency to depersonalization and simulation', he writes, already isolating the twin poles around which his philosophy of self revolves, before continuing, 'Fortunately for me and others, these phenomena have been mentally internalized, such that they don't show up in my outer, everyday life among people; they erupt inside me, where only I experience them'.[2] Each heteronym is fully and in its own right a person: 'Ever since I was a child, I've felt the need to enlarge the world with fictitious personalities – dreams of mine that were carefully crafted, envisaged with photographic clarity, and fathomed to the depths of their souls [...]. I intensely conceived those characters with no need of dolls. Distinctly visible in my ongoing dreams, they were utterly human realities for me, which any doll – because unreal – would have spoiled. They were people'.[3]

Pessoa's three most famous heteronyms are the world-class poets he names Alberto Caeiro, Álvaro de Campos, and Ricardo Reis: 'I placed all my power of dramatic depersonalization in Caeiro;

---

[1]   Excellent recent overviews of Pessoa in English include Jackson (2010), Maunsell (2012), Frow (2014), and Visser (2019).
[2]   Letter to Adolfo Casais Monteiro, 13 January 1935, in *Selected Prose* (Zenith, 2007, p. 254).
[3]   [Another version of the genesis of the heteronyms], in *Selected Prose* (Zenith, 2007, pp. 261–262).

I placed all my mental discipline, clothed in its own special music, in Ricardo Reis; and in Álvaro de Campos I placed all the emotion that I deny myself and don't put into life'.[4] As he puts it in a draft preface for an unfinished edition of the *Fictions of the Interlude* (his designation for the complete corpus of his poetic work), 'In the case of the authors of *Fictions of the Interlude*, it is not only the ideas and feelings which differ from mine: the technique of composition itself, the very style, differs from mine. In those instances each protagonist is created as essentially different, not just differently thought out. For this reason, poetry is predominant in *Fictions of the Interlude*. In prose, it is more difficult to other oneself'.[5]

Heteronymy is, as the name implies, an othering of oneself, an awareness of oneself but as other. The contrast with the pseudonym is deliberate: 'Pseudonymous works are by the author in his own person, except in the name he signs; heteronymic works are by the author outside his own person. They proceed from a full-fledged individual created by him'.[6] A pseudonym is a mask, a disguise intended, even if only ironically, to hide the true identity of the author. A heteronym is something else entirely: it is the author writing 'outside his own person' and in doing so transforming himself into an other I. A heteronym occupies the first-person position within the experience of the author and has a defined literary voice and a distinctive power of expression. So to 'write in the name of'[7] a heteronym is not to hide oneself behind a mask but to live in experience as that very person; each heteronym, Pessoa says, is 'lived by the author within himself' and has 'passed through his soul'.[8] A heteronym is 'someone in me who has taken my place'.[9]

---

[4]   Letter to Adolfo Casais Monteiro, 13 January 1935, in *Selected Prose* (Zenith, 2007, pp. 253–254).

[5]   [Preface to *Fictions of the Interlude*], in *Selected Prose* (Zenith, 2007, p. 313).

[6]   [Bibliographical summary], in *A Little Larger than the Entire Universe: Selected Poems* (Zenith, 2006, p. 3).

[7]   [Bibliographical summary], in *A Little Larger than the Entire Universe: Selected Poems* (Zenith, 2006, p. 5).

[8]   [Aspects], in *Selected Prose* (Zenith, 2007, p. 2).

[9]   *The Book of Disquiet* (Zenith, 2002), sketch #351. All references to *The Book of Disquiet* will follow the numbering in Zenith's Portuguese and English editions. The online *LdoD Archive* provides, among other things, for cross-referencing against different editions of the *Livro do Desassossego*. In what follows, any citation attributed to Pessoa from *The Book of Disquiet* should be understood as an attribution to his semi-heteronym Bernardo Soares.

Jonardon Ganeri

In assuming a heteronym one transforms oneself into another I: 'First we must create another I, charged with suffering – in and for us – everything we suffer'.[10] The experiences of my heteronym are both *in* me, in the sense that I am their host, and also *for* me, standing, with respect to me, in a first-personal subjective relationship. When Pessoa writes of heteronymy that it is a subjective state in which 'every felt pain is automatically analysed to the core, ruthlessly foisted on an extraneous I [...]',[11] he exactly formulates the essence of the concept in the idea of experience that is at once irreducibly first personal and yet also alien. A heteronym is a fully formed subject subsisting within one's conscious experience. Heteronyms are, to introduce a notion I will have more to say about later, *virtual subjects*, subjects which are 'well-defined personalities who have incorporeally passed through [one's] soul'.[12] Unlike the target of empathy, which would occupy a second-person position, addressed as 'you', the formal feature that is definitive of heteronymy is that a heteronym occupies the first-person position, spoken of with a use of the first-person pronoun 'I'. A heteronym possesses agency, if only in the capacity to compose verse, and has its own expressive and experiential style. A heteronym is another I, an I who is not me, an othered I: 'But since I am me, I merely take a little pleasure in the little that it is to imagine myself as that someone else. Yes, soon he-I, under a tree or bower, will eat twice what I can eat, drink twice what I dare drink, and laugh twice what I can conceive of laughing. Soon he, now I. Yes, for a moment I was someone else: in someone else I saw and lived this human and humble joy of existing as an animal in shirtsleeves'.[13] Heteronymic simulation is, we might say, the mechanism of self-alienation.

If transforming oneself in simulation into another I is the core of the idea of heteronymic subjectivity, an equally important theme in Pessoa is that of depersonalization. Living through a heteronym, which from one point of view must certainly constitute an enrichment of experiential life, is paradoxically described in terms of a

---

[10] 'Sentimental education', in *The Book of Disquiet* (Zenith, 2002, p. 455).

[11] 'Sentimental education', in *The Book of Disquiet* (Zenith, 2002, p. 456).

[12] [Aspects], in *Selected Prose* (Zenith, 2007, p. 2). I am not alone in appealing to the language of the virtual to elucidate heteronymy: David Jackson calls the heteronyms 'virtual authors' (2010, p. 15) and John Frow describes them as 'virtual selves' (2014, p. 222).

[13] *The Book of Disquiet*, #374.

loss of self: 'Today I have no personality: I've divided all my humaneness among the various authors whom I've served as literary executor. Today I'm the meeting-place of a small humanity that belongs only to me [...]. I subsist as a kind of medium of myself, but I'm less real than the others, less substantial, less personal, and easily influenced by them all'.[14] Again, 'I created a nonexistent coterie, placing it all in a framework of reality. I ascertained the influences at work and the friendships between them, I listened in myself to their discussions and divergent points of view, and in all of this it seems that I, who created them all, was the one who was least there'.[15]

Several distinct claims are intertwined here. The first is that even as he assumes multiple heteronyms, Pessoa is separately conscious of himself in the capacity of medium or meeting-place for them. Unlike a heteronym, which corresponds to a well-defined style of experiencing, this separate self-consciousness is one that is empty of any specific personality or content: it is a depersonalized self-awareness. The use of the first person in relation to this type of self-consciousness is thus quite distinct from that which figures in the self-expression of a heteronym (the use made of it in the formula 'an extraneous I'). Second, one's awareness of oneself as medium or meeting-place is less robust than one's awareness of oneself as another I, in the sense that it does not sustain as strong a sense of presence. Finally, one's self-awareness as meeting-place is associated with a clearly identifiable trait: it at least partially consists in a capacity to observe the heteronyms, both from the outside ('I *see* before me, in the transparent but real space of dreams, the faces and gestures of Caeiro, Ricardo Reis and Álvaro de Campos'),[16] and also, more importantly, from the inside, a partly introspective and partly empathetic capacity to analyse and scrutinize the subjective character of the heteronymic mental life being lived through.

It seems, then, that two distinct kinds of self-awareness are co-present in any act of heteronymic simulation: a *heteronymic* self-awareness which consists in an awareness of oneself as another I, living through a distinctive set of experiences, emotions, and moods; and what I will call a *forumnal* self-awareness, an awareness of oneself as hosting the heteronym, which is at the same time a

---

[14] [Another version of the genesis of the heteronyms], in *Selected Prose* (Zenith, 2007, p. 262).
[15] Letter to Adolfo Casais Monteiro, 13 January 1935, in *Selected Prose* (Zenith, 2007, p. 257).
[16] Letter to Adolfo Casais Monteiro, 13 January 1935, in *Selected Prose* (Zenith, 2007, p. 257).

Jonardon Ganeri

place from which one's experiential life as heteronym can be observed and analysed. It is from the first-person position of the forum that Bernardo Soares, the semi-heteronymic/semi-orthonymic narrator of *The Book of Disquiet*, speaks: 'For me it's never I who thinks, speaks or acts. It's always one of my dreams, which I momentarily embody, that thinks, speaks and acts for me. I open my mouth, but it's I-another who speaks. The only thing I feel to be really mine is a huge incapacity, a vast emptiness, an incompetence for everything that is life'.[17] Pessoa describes Bernardo Soares as a semi-heteronym because 'his personality, although not my own, doesn't differ from my own but is a mere mutilation of it. He's me without my rationalism and emotions. His prose is the same as mine, except for certain formal restraint that reason imposes on my own writing'.[18] And 'Bernardo Soares' is also a semi-orthonym because the name is a 'mere mutilation' of 'Fernando Pessoa', 'Bernardo' differing from 'Fernando' in only two letters, and 'Soares' is almost exactly a syllabic inversion of 'Pessoa'.[19] When Pessoa-as-Soares writes that 'due to my habit of dividing myself, following two distinct mental operations at the same time, it's generally the case that as I lucidly and intensely adapt myself to what others are feeling, I simultaneously undertake a rigorously objective analysis of their unknown self, what they think and are',[20] he shows a keen understanding of the co-presence of these two kinds of self-awareness, a simulated heteronymic self-awareness consisting in 'adaption' to the feelings of another I, and a forumnal self-awareness consisting in 'objective analysis' of what is thereby felt.

The formal structure of Pessoa's philosophy of self is nowhere more clearly set out than in his celebrated late poem *Countless Lives Inhabit Us*:

> Countless lives inhabit us.
> I don't know, when I think or feel,
> Who it is that thinks and feels.
> I am merely the place
> Where things are thought and felt.

---

[17] *The Book of Disquiet*, #215.
[18] Letter to Adolfo Casais Monteiro, 13 January 1935, in *Selected Prose* (Zenith, 2007, p. 257).
[19] A different semi-orthonym exists as an entry in *The Transformation Book*: 'Ferdinand Sumwan (= Fernando Pessoa, since Sumwan = Some one = Person = Pessoa). A normal, useless, lazy, careless, weak individual'. *The Transformation Book* (Ribeiro, 2014, p. 326).
[20] *The Book of Disquiet*, #305.

I have more than just one soul.
There are more I-s than I myself.
I exist, nevertheless,
Indifferent to them all.
I silence them: I speak.
The crossing urges of what
I feel or do not feel
Struggle in who I am, but I
Ignore them. They dictate nothing
To the I I know: I write.[21]

When I think or feel, the first stanza says, it is one of many possible I-s that is thinking or feeling. This heteronymic use of 'I' is immediately juxtaposed with another use of 'I' to refer to the place where things are thought or felt. The second stanza continues with this use, for it is only from the position of the forum that I can affirm that I have more than one soul – each heteronym, taken individually, thinks of itself as a single unified self. The two uses of 'I', heteronymic and forumnal, are again juxtaposed in the final stanza, the urges felt or unfelt are the felt volitions of a heteronym – that is, of myself as another I – but I (as forumnal observer) disregard them.

The poem's disconcerting air of paradox is a deliberate construct, produced by the alternation without explicit indication of two quite distinct uses of 'I'. There is a third use too, almost too pedestrian for Pessoa to mention, the standard and everyday use of 'I' to refer indexically to whomsoever it is that has spoken or written it: as when Pessoa writes in a letter to a friend, 'I submitted the copies required by the Office of Propaganda'.[22] In the poem there is perhaps a trace of this third, indexical, use in the echoing phrases, 'I speak', and 'I write'.

The disconnect between the heteronymic and the forumnal can be heard playing out in another poem, in which 'who I am', my heteronymic self, is contrasted with 'what I am', myself as forum:

I don't know who my soul is.
Nor does it know who I am.
Understand it? It would take time.
Explain it? Don't know if I can.
And in this misunderstanding

---

[21]   In *Fernando Pessoa & Co.: Selected Poems* (Zenith, 1999, p. 137). The poem is dated 30 November 30 1935, just two weeks before Pessoa's death.
[22]   Letter to Adolfo Casais Monteiro, 13 January 1935, in *Selected Prose* (Zenith, 2007, p. 252).

Jonardon Ganeri

Between who I am and what am I
There's a whole other meaning
Lying between earth and sky.[23]

3. Heteronyms as Virtual Subjects

The act of heteronymic self-transformation is quite different from
that of inventing a character in a story. Pessoa alludes to the difference
when, while noting that novelists and playwrights 'often endow the
characters of their plays and novels with feelings and ideas that they
insist are not their own', he adds somewhat gnomically that in the
authorship of heteronyms 'the substance is the same, though the
form is different'.[24] What is fundamental to the notion of a heteronym is that it is an othered I, 'lived by the author within himself',
that is to say, lived first-personally. So a heteronym is not a character
because the relationship an author stands in to an invented character
is a third-personal one. The point in question is analogous to the one
William James makes when he says that 'it is impossible to reconcile
the peculiarities of our experience with our being only the absolute's
mental objects [...]. Objects of thought are not things *per se*. They are
there only for their thinker, and only as he thinks them. How, then,
can they become severally alive on their own accounts and think
themselves quite otherwise than as he thinks them? It is as if the characters in a novel were to get up from the pages, and walk away and
transact business of their own outside of the author's story'.[25] The autonomy here denied to fictional characters is a freedom from the
author who has created them. James's point is that if an individual
human subject were merely the 'mental object' of another mind,
standing in the same relationship to this mind as the fictional character does to its author, it would similarly be without a capacity for autonomous self-expression. The comparison helps to clarify what is so
distinctive and original in the idea of heteronymy. For a heteronym is
not a mental object but a mental subject, a virtual subject transforming its author into another I: 'Why should I look at twilights if I have

---

[23]   In *A Little Larger than the Entire Universe: Selected Poems* (Zenith,
2006, p. 329).
[24]   [Aspects], in *Selected Prose* (Zenith, 2007, p. 1).
[25]   James (1909, p. 69). There is an exquisite treatment of this very issue
in chapter 31 of Unamuno's 1914 novel *Mist*. Here, the character begs the
author to be permitted to live, but to no avail: the author has already
decided that he must die.

200

within me thousands of diverse twilights [...] and if, besides seeing them inside me, I myself *am them*, on the inside and the outside?'[26]

Stephen Crites, by contrast, says of Søren Kierkegaard's pseudo-nyms that nobody 'would mistake them for the voices of real human beings. They are altogether theatrical creations. They are sheer personae, masks without actors underneath, voices' (Crites, 1972, p. 216). Kierkegaard does, sometimes, describe his pseudo-nyms – which he also calls 'polynyms' – in a manner that makes them sound more similar to heteronyms than conventional pseudo-nyms. He is keen to stress that he is simply their producer, or the oc-casion for their production, or a prompter (*souffleur*) for them, but not their author: 'What is written is indeed therefore mine, but only so far as I have put the life-view of the creating, poetically actua-lized individuality into his mouth in audible lines, for my relation is even more remote than that of a poet, who creates characters and yet in the preface is himself the author. For I am impersonally, or person-ally, in the second person, a souffleur who has poetically produced the authors' (Kierkegaard, 2009, pp. 527–528). Yet he goes on to deny that he is himself any of his pseudonyms, and says that he has 'no opinion about them except as third party'; remarks which imply that a Kierkegaardian pseudonym is also still a third party and not an essentially first-personal 'another I'. Pessoa's heteronyms, as John Frow, puts it, 'are not personae, masks through which the poet speaks; they are autonomous figures which allow him to take on quite distinct personalities in his writing' (Frow, 2014, p. 215). Polynyms, again, are multiple names for the same object, and they give rise to puzzles of their own, most famously the puzzle of explain-ing how identity statements containing them can be informative. Solutions to that puzzle, such as distinguishing between the reference of a name and its sense, the mode under which the reference is pre-sented,[27] are of little help, however, in understanding the phenom-enon of heteronymy; for a heteronym is another I, not the same I under another mode of presentation.

One of Pessoa's most basic philosophical concerns is with what I shall refer to as 'the grounding problem for subjects'. This is the problem of accounting for the metaphysical grounds for individual subjects of experience: what it is they exist in virtue of; what they are due to; what they are dependent on for their being.[28] The

---

[26]   *The Book of Disquiet*, #215.
[27]   See Frege (1980).
[28]   As a term of art in contemporary philosophy, grounding refers to a particular sort of non-causal and asymmetric priority between facts,

Jonardon Ganeri

invention of heteronymy serves to underline the fact that there is no solution to this problem in attempts to reduce subjects to merely purely mental objects, such as are the characters in a novel. Neither is it the sort of metaphysical problem that can be solved at the level of linguistic analysis alone.

A closer, if still inadequate, analogy would be with one of those stories in which each chapter has a different narrator writing from a first-person position, such as Orhan Pamuk's novel *My Name is Red* (2001), or William Faulkner's *As I Lay Dying* (1990), or Ryūnosuke Akutagawa's short story *In a Grove* (2011), on which Akira Kurosawa's film *Rashōmon* is based. Each character in one of these stories presents in the first person and is not merely reported on from a third-personal perspective. Each one takes it in turn to occupy the narrator position. And yet a sequence of distinct narrators writing in the first person is *still* not a display of heteronymy. They are distinct characters taking it in turn to speak about themselves in the first person; there is no suggestion that any of them is identical to the author, and neither can any be described as the author as transformed into another I.

Nor does Jorge Luis Borges explicitly describe heteronymy in his brilliant story *The Circular Ruins* (1999). In this story someone, whom Borges describes only as 'the foreigner', sets out to dream into existence another human being, having understood 'that the task of moulding the incoherent and dizzying stuff that dreams are made of is the most difficult work a man can undertake'. Within his directed dreamworld he fashions a youth, whom Borges describes as a 'phantasm' and a 'simulacrum', an individual who is 'not a man but the projection of another man's dream'. Pessoa, too, describes the creation of heteronyms as acts of directed imagining, but the distinction between a simulation and a simulacrum is crucial. For there is no suggestion at any point in Borges's story that the dreamt-up simulacrum is the foreigner himself – an other I of the dreamer – which is what would be required if the simulacrum, a virtual object, were to be a heteronym, a virtual subject, a simulated occupant of the subject position.

Borges ends the story with a twist: the foreigner is given to understand that he is himself a simulacrum, as 'with relief, with humiliation, with terror, he realized that he, too, was but appearance, that another man was dreaming him'. It is within the dream of 'another man' that the foreigner exists, exists as a simulacrum, and in the phrase 'he, too, was but appearance' there is again a clear implication

---

indicated by the use of expressions like 'in virtue of', 'due to', 'based on', 'what makes', and 'because of'. See Correia and Schnieder (2012).

that what is being created is a merely purely mental object. The simulacra in the directed dreams, as the characters in a novel, are virtual objects; a virtual *subject* on the other hand is a simulation, a heteronym, a transformation of the author into another I.

Pessoa anticipates Borges when he writes, 'I begin to wonder if I exist, if I might not be someone else's dream. I can imagine, with an almost carnal vividness, that I might be the character of a novel, moving within the reality constructed by a complex narrative, in the long waves of its style'.[29] What is important to appreciate, though, is that Pessoa is not offering this as a description of heteronymic subjectivity; it is the simpler idea that one might discover that one is, after all, a simulacrum oneself. The grounding problem for subjects begins with the assumption that subjects are not merely apparent, and yet, reluctant to grant them the status of fundamental pieces of the world's furniture, asks what their existence is dependent on. We are more like shadows than hallucinations.

In fact, in *The Circular Ruins* there is a trace of the idea of heteronyms, but it is not to be found in the relationship between 'the foreigner' and his dreamt-up simulacrum. When Borges writes, 'the foreigner dreamed that *he* was in the centre of a circular amphitheatre', the embedded use of the personal pronoun situates the foreigner within his own dream. When one dreams it is not uncommon for oneself to figure in the dream as the one to whom the events in the dream are being presented. The 'subject-within-the-dream' is both a virtual subject and a simulation of the dreaming subject; and for this reason, it would be entirely appropriate to describe the subject-within-the-dream as the dreaming subject's heteronym in the dream. Evan Thompson, in his magnificent book *Waking, Dreaming, Being* (2014), uses the language of virtual reality gaming to make the interesting suggestion that the distinction between subject-within-the-dream and dreaming subject is analogous to the distinction between an avatar in a virtual world and its user: 'We need to distinguish between the dreaming self and the dream ego – between the self-as-dreamer and the self-within-the-dream', he rightly says, continuing,

> In a nonlucid dream, we identify with our dream ego and think, "I'm flying". In a lucid dream, we think, "I'm dreaming", and we recognize that the dreaming self isn't the same as the dream ego, or how we appear within the dream. The dream ego is like

[29] *The Book of Disquiet*, #285. Borges, it would seem, wrote *The Circular Ruins* in the same series in the late 1930s. He spent six weeks in the summer of 1924 living in Lisbon, and this has led to some speculation that Pessoa and he may have met (see Ferrari, 2015).

an avatar in a virtual world; the dreaming self is its user [...]. In a nonlucid dream, we lose the awareness that we're imagining things and identify with the dream ego as the I. We're like gamers who identify so completely with their avatars they forget they're gaming. In a lucid dream, we regain awareness of our imagining consciousness. Nonlucid dreams frame experience from the imagined perspective of the dream ego; lucid dreams reframe experience from the perspective of the imagining and dreaming self. Lucidity can enable the dreaming self to act consciously and deliberately in the dream state through the persona of the dream ego, who becomes like an avatar in a role-playing game [...]. (Thompson, 2014, pp. 109–110)

It is not, though, quite correct to characterize the relationship between the dreaming subject and the subject-within-the-dream as being that there are two distinct subjects whose distinctness is overlooked in an act of mistaken identification. The foreigner dreams that *he* is in a circular amphitheatre and there is no question of an error due to misidentification.[30] It is not that in his dream a certain simulacrum is in the amphitheatre, a simulacrum which is mistaken by the dreamer to be himself. So the analogy breaks down, and instructively so, for the way it does so helps us to understand better the difference between avatars and heteronyms. The difference is that an avatar is a virtual object, a simulacrum, but the subject-within-the-dream is a virtual subject, a virtual occupant of the subject position. What it means to be at the subject position within the dream is indeed that the dream experience is 'framed from the perspective' of this position, and by positioning himself there the dreamer has in effect created a heteronym, an 'I' within the dream. So he cannot 'use' this heteronym as a gamer might an avatar or a master might a slave, because he does not stand in an appropriately third-personal relationship to it. It is literally correct to say 'In *my* dream *I* was flying', and this statement is not a mistaken rendering, based on a false identification with another, of 'In my dream my avatar was flying'.

The idea of heteronymy is much better captured in Yasumasa Morimura's multiple self-portraiture under the assumed identities of famous historical artists, if indeed Morimura would be willing to affirm 'I myself am them, on the inside and the outside'. As in *My Name is Red*, the text for his video piece *Egó Sympósion* has every participant, each of whom is a famous figure in the history of art, taking

---

[30]   On the philosophical concept of immunity, see Prosser and Recanati (2012).

Figure 1. Yasumasa Morimura, *An Inner Dialogue with Frida Kahlo (Hand-Shaped Earring)*, 2001. © Yasumasa Morimura. Courtesy of the artist and Luhring Augustine, New York.

turns to speak for themselves in the first person. The reason this does not reduce to a case of sequential first-person narration by a series of distinct narrators, and the reason it is not merely a case of successive pseudonymous disguise, is that the viewer is never in any doubt that it is Morimura who is assuming – that is, simulating – each participant in turn. Though made up to resemble Frida Kahlo or Johannes Vermeer, Morimura makes no attempt to hide himself or to pretend not to be there. The representation is of Morimura-as-Kahlo not Morimura-as-if-Kahlo, not Morimura pretending to be Kahlo.

The Portuguese novelist José Saramago provides a superb illustration of the idea of the heteronym in a short notebook entry about Pessoa. He imagines Pessoa looking in a mirror and seeing his reflection, in turn as Reis, as Caeiro, and as Campos. 'My name is Ricardo

Reis', 'My name is Alberto Caeiro', 'My name is Álvaro Campos', he declares in turn. When he looks again later that night at the mirror image, he sees that it is of his own face. 'My name is Bernardo Soares', he says, invoking an almost-orthonym:

> [O]n one of those days when Fernando passed in front of a mirror he spied in it, at a glance, another person. He thought this was just another optical illusion, those ones that happen when you're not paying attention, or that the last glass of *eau de vie* had not agreed with his liver and his head, but he cautiously took a step back just to make sure that – as is usually assumed – when mirrors show something they do not make mistakes. This one, however, had indeed made a mistake: there was a man looking out at him from inside the mirror, and that man was not Fernando Pessoa. He was a little shorter, and his face was somewhat dark-skinned and completely clean-shaven. Unconsciously Fernando brought his hand to his upper lip, then breathed deeply in childlike relief: this moustache was still there. One can expect many things from an image that appears in a mirror, but not that it will speak. And because these two, Fernando and the image that wasn't an image of him, were not going to stay watching one another forever, Fernando Pessoa said, 'My name is Ricardo Reis'. The other man smiled, nodded, and disappeared. For a moment the mirror was empty, bare, then right away another image appeared, of a thin, pale man who looked as if he were not long for this world. It seemed to Fernando that this must have been the first one; however, he made no comment, merely saying, 'My name is Alberto Caeiro'. The other did not smile; he merely nodded slightly, agreeing, and left. Fernando Pessoa waited, having always been told that whenever there are two a third will always follow. The third figure took a few seconds to arrive, and he was one of those men who look as if they have more health than they know what to do with, and he had the unmistakable air of an engineer trained in England. Fernando said, 'My name is Álvaro de Campos', but this time he did not wait for the image to disappear from the mirror, but moved away from it himself, probably tired from having seen so many people in such a short space of time. That night, in the small hours of the morning, Fernando Pessoa awoke wondering whether Álvaro de Campos had stayed in the mirror. He got up, and what he found there was his own face. So he said, 'My name is Bernardo Soares', and went back to bed. (Saramago, 2010, pp. 24–25).

A heteronym, finally, let me be completely clear, is not a Cartesian soul. A Cartesian soul is a putative denizen in the actual world, an immaterial mental substance standing in some mysterious relationship with other real entities such as human bodies. Lacking in spatial location, there is nothing to pair particular souls with particular effects: if two souls simultaneously acquire or lose a certain property, there is no way, even in principle, to decide which of the two is the cause of some subsequent event. This is what Jaegwon Kim calls the 'paring problem' for Cartesian souls (Kim, 2001). Then there is, as Bernard Williams puts it, 'absolutely nothing left to distinguish any Cartesian 'I' from any other, and it is impossible to see any more what would be subtracted from the universe by the removal of *me*' (Williams, 1973, p. 42). A heteronym is an aspect of a virtual world, although, as we have seen, it is not a virtual object like an avatar. What is subtracted from the universe by the removal of a heteronym is an entire style of feeling, and styles of feeling are also what is added to the universe by the invention of new heteronyms, new virtual subjects.[31]

References

Jorge Luis Borges, *Collected Fictions*, Andrew Hurley (trans.), (London: Penguin, 1999).

Fabrice Correia and Benjamin Schnieder (eds.), *Metaphysical Grounding: Understanding the Structure of Reality* (Cambridge: Cambridge University Press, 2012).

Stephen Crites, 'Pseudonymous Authorship as Art and Act', in Josiah Thompson (ed.), *Kierkegaard: A Collection of Critical Essays* (London: Anchor Books, 1972), 183–229.

William Faulkner, *As I Lay Dying* (London: Random House, 1990).

Patricio Ferrari, 'Pessoa and Borges: in the Margins of Milton', *Variaciones Borges*, 40 (2015), 3–21.

Gottlob Frege, 'On Sense and Reference', in Peter Geach and Max Black (eds.), *Translations from the Philosophical Writings of Gottlob Frege*, 3rd edition, (Oxford: Blackwell, 1980), 56–78.

John Frow, *Character and Person* (Oxford: Oxford University Press, 2014).

Jonardon Ganeri, *Virtual Subjects, Fugitive Selves: Fernando Pessoa and his Philosophy* (Oxford: Oxford University Press, 2020).

[31] The text for this essay is drawn from my book *Virtual Subjects, Fugitive Selves: Fernando Pessoa and his Philosophy* (Oxford: Oxford University Press, 2020). I thank the publishers for permission to reuse the material here.

Jonardon Ganeri

David Jackson, *Adverse Genres in Fernando Pessoa* (Oxford: Oxford University Press, 2010).

William James, *A Pluralistic Universe: Hibbert Lectures* (New York: Floating Press, 1909).

Søren Kierkegaard, 'A First and Last Declaration', in *Concluding Unscientific Postscipt*, Alastair Hannay (trans.), (Cambridge: Cambridge University Press, 2009), 527–531.

Jaegwon Kim, 'Lonely Souls: Causality and Substance Dualism', in Kevin Corocan (ed.), *Soul, Body, and Survival: Essays in the Metaphysics of Human Persons* (Ithaca: Cornell University Press, 2001), 30–43.

Jerome Boyd Maunsell, 'The Hauntings of Fernando Pessoa', *Modernism/Modernity*, 19 (2012), 115–137.

Orhan Pamuk, *My Name is Red*, Erdağ M. Göknar (trans.), (London: Faber & Faber, 2001).

Simon Prosser and François Recanati (eds.), *Immunity to Error through Misidentification: New Essays* (Cambridge: Cambridge University Press, 2012).

Akutagawa Ryūnosuke, *Rashōmon and Other Stories*, Kojima Takashi (trans.), (North Clarendon: Tuttle Publishing, 2011).

Nuno Ribeiro (ed. & trans.), *The Transformation Book* (Lisbon: Contra Mundum Press, 2014).

José Saramago, *The Notebook*, Amanda Hopkinson and Daniel Hahn (trans.), (London: Verso, 2010).

Evan Thompson, *Waking, Dreaming, Being: Self and Consciousness in Neuroscience, Meditation and Philosophy* (New York: Columbia University Press, 2014).

Miguel de Unamuno, *Mist*, Warner Fite (trans.), (Champaign: University of Illinois Press, 1914 [1955]).

Rehan Visser, 'Fernando Pessoa's Art of Living: Ironic Multiplicities, Multiple Ironies', *Philosophical Forum*, 50 (2019), 435–454.

Bernard Williams, 'Imagination and the Self', in *Problems of the Self* (Cambridge: Cambridge University Press, 1973), 26–45.

Richard Zenith (ed. & trans.), *Fernando Pessoa & Co.: Selected Poems* (New York: Grove Press, 1999).

Richard Zenith (ed. & trans.), *The Book of Disquiet* (London: Penguin, 2002).

Richard Zenith (ed. & trans.), *A Little Larger than the Entire Universe: Selected Poems* (London: Penguin, 2006).

Richard Zenith (ed. & trans.), *The Selected Prose of Fernando Pessoa* (New York: Grove Press, 2007).

Can Aesthetics Be Global?

EILEEN JOHN

Abstract

Philosophical aesthetics is to some extent beholden to what I will call personal aesthetics. By personal aesthetics, I mean the phenomena of individual aesthetic sensitivity: how each of us discerns and responds to elements of experience. I take that sensitivity to be finely woven into feeling to some degree at home in the world. There is something extremely local, and in a certain sense unreflective, about personal aesthetics – it is hard to notice one's own, historically specific aesthetic formation. Philosophical aesthetics, meanwhile, aspires to understand aesthetic life in a more reflective and general way. Aesthetic theories in the Western tradition, like most philosophical theories, try to articulate universally relevant and illuminating theoretical concepts and values. But can a theory of this kind acknowledge what is important at the level of personal aesthetics? Can aesthetic theories find fruitful application while also respecting the locality and variability of aesthetic sensitivity? What kinds of theoretical ambition and humility are called for in philosophical aesthetics?

1. Introduction

This essay considers the scope and aims of aesthetics, a branch of philosophy. I typically take this branch of philosophy – what it is, what counts as 'doing aesthetics' – for granted, roughly because I am immersed in it and find it hard to step back and question the bigger picture. On this occasion, however, I examine a big-picture issue, concerning what happens to philosophical goals when they meet the core phenomena of aesthetic life. Can the following three things be triangulated?

a) The individuality and cultural located-ness of each of our aesthetic lives;
b) the aim of aesthetics to account for aesthetic life in philosophical terms;
c) the aim of philosophy to formulate concepts, principles, and theories with universal relevance.

The partially negative answer that I reach – to the effect that aesthetic life resists some kinds of philosophical theorising – will be paired with some positive suggestions about what aesthetics can fruitfully do. I certainly do not want to cast doubt on the value of aesthetics;

doi:10.1017/S1358246123000061   © The Royal Institute of Philosophy and the contributors 2023

Eileen John

I hope this discussion can even help to indicate and explain its importance. But my argument does suggest that aesthetics is difficult, and particularly difficult when taking the fully wide human world as its domain. Aesthetics calls for care, self-questioning, expanded knowledge and perspectives, and constructive, bridge-building philosophical labour.

Let me note at the outset that this discussion intersects with extensive debates on the problem of imposing, and assuming the validity of, one aesthetic tradition over others. These debates highlight the harms and injustice of entrenching a hierarchy of cultures, nations, races, or classes by aesthetic means – by elevating one socially-politically-economically powerful set of aesthetic values and practices over others. Activities of conquest, colonisation, enslavement, and exploitation have often (always?) incorporated aesthetic expectations and values into processes of control and denigration.[1] Aesthetic demands have been put in the service of unjust domination. But my triangulation question does not take the wrongs of aesthetic domination as its focus. It is a – perhaps unsatisfyingly abstract! – question about meeting the expectations for a philosophical aesthetics, while reckoning with a globe's worth of aesthetic life. Even if thinkers are not motivated or moulded by aims of aesthetic domination, and are motivated to understand and theorise fairly, what philosophical difficulties do they face? My possibly naïve speculative claim – and my hope – is that aesthetic 'global domination' is indeed not realisable. Aesthetic life goes on and evolves without top-down permission and control, despite the huge efforts and impact of political and empire-seeking movements, commercialisation, industrial modes of production, and social media. Ideally, philosophical aesthetics can play a role in helping us to understand, appreciate, and sustain the control-resistant nature of aesthetic life.

2. Philosophy and the Aim of Universality

Turning to the triangulation question, I will start at the bottom of my list and work up, from (c) a basic aim of philosophy, to (b) a basic aim of aesthetics, to (a) the realities of aesthetic life. By positing a basic aim of philosophy, I risk or even doom myself to misrepresenting a multifarious practice with all sorts of aims. For the purposes of this

---

[1]   For a few routes into these debates, see Gates (1988), Shusterman (1989), Blocker (2001), Bhushan (2009), Radano and Olaniyan (2016), Taylor (2016), Maira (2017), and Nzegwu (2019).

argument, I take that risk in order to articulate the problem I am interested in with respect to philosophical aesthetics. But I grant that one way to respond to my argument would be to dispute and reject the universalising ambition that I attribute to philosophy. In any case, this is an aim in the sense of an aspiration and a self-conception: what one conceives of oneself as striving for, when doing philosophy, and how people identify philosophy, rather than a description of what philosophically aimed endeavours actually achieve.

A modest way to articulate the aim I posit for philosophy is to say that philosophy aims to achieve general and deeper understanding of reality. Achieving generality and depth requires offering ideas, principles, conceptual relationships, and evaluative frameworks that give insight into reality, that account for the nature and value of things, rather than describing, recording, causally explaining, and predicting the cornucopia of historically particular fact. Philosophical generality and depth, as aspirations, rest themselves on a somewhat nebulous assumption that there are deeper, general levels of understanding to be had.

Now, how general does philosophical understanding aim to be? The less modest articulation of the aim is that philosophy seeks universal validity. A claim can be general if it avoids attributing properties to a specific individual, but it might do that by concerning a quite limited, contextually focused section of reality. Claims about all carrot cakes from that bakery or about some UK prime ministers are general in that sense (and even logically universal in the cake case), but they are unpromising as philosophical claims. Universality as an aim in philosophy seems both to have to do with the kinds of things considered – broad categories that putatively have application to all people (mind and body, self and other, happiness, knowledge, ethical character, death and immortality, freedom; not carrot cake or UK prime ministers) and with the kind of audience and acceptability they aspire to. This universality is not equivalent to using the universal quantifier ('All Fs are Gs'); a claim such as 'some lies are virtuous' can hold the universal aspiration I am trying to sketch. Such a claim would be offered with the hope or expectation that, given relevant explanation and support, any person could understand the possibility of combining lying and virtue. A philosophical claim aims to have significance and force for people in general, not for a targeted audience (even if the actually interested, engaged audience for a philosophical claim can be pretty small). Trying to avoid the limitations not only of any given individual's perspective and concerns, but of historically limited societies and cultures, a universal philosophical claim would be intended to apply

Eileen John

wherever and whenever the topic of the claim has a foothold in reality (whenever there are minds and bodies, selves and others, conditions that allow for happiness, knowledge, beings that can lie, *et cetera*). The foothold can be partly speculative or hypothetical, engaging with conditions that have not been and may never be realised ('if robots achieve consciousness'; 'if everyone were behind a veil of ignorance'; 'if there were a beautiful world with no minds in it'; 'if the rulers were lovers of wisdom') but that nonetheless can be held to promise insight into real people's concerns. Note that this account of philosophy's aim does build in a limitation in scope by tying philosophy to human concerns. I am taking philosophy to be a human project, one that tries to understand things that figure in and can matter to the reality and experience of human beings.

Universality as an aim sounds outrageous and arrogant. How could one take oneself to be in a position to make claims that could reasonably be thought to apply to or concern anyone? Let me note that philosophers are often cautious about how ambitiously to frame their aims. Philosophy is frequently characterised in terms of the questions it poses – 'the big questions' – allowing for a reserved or non-committal attitude toward the status of the answers.[2] But I take it that the bigness of the questions is implicitly supposed to be met by the bigness of the answers. Exactly how big may often be left unspoken, but if their scope were explicitly limited in certain ways – 'this philosophical thought is pertinent to you, Eileen, right now, but it doesn't matter beyond that' or 'this is pertinent to understanding reality and value in Dakar in 1776 (or Coventry in the 1990s, or Phnom Penh today, or Lima in 2050)' – that would cast doubt on their 'philosophicality'.[3]

---

[2]   A number of philosophy textbook titles refer to 'the big questions' to demarcate the subject. Roger Scruton and others further distinguish philosophy's questions methodologically: 'philosophical questions arise at the end of all other enquiries, when questions about particular things, events and practical difficulties have been solved according to the methods available, and when either those methods themselves, or some metaphysical doctrine which they seem to presuppose, are put in question' (Scruton, 1995, p. 6). Similarly, the 'purpose of philosophy [...] is truth, truth with respect to fundamental and general questions, typically questions whose answering has not yet been made a matter of settled method' (Honderich, 1984, p. 12). 'We are doing philosophy when we engage in dialogue about problems that are important to our culture but we don't agree about the method for solving them' (Van Norden, 2017, p. 142).

[3]   Of course there are difficulties here, e.g., philosophical issues that hang on specific historical conditions and movements (nation-states,

This conception of philosophy is likely to seem stubbornly Euro-Anglo-centric, one of the many legacies of Plato, who has Socrates in the *Republic* distinguish the philosophers – 'those who are capable of apprehending that which is permanent and unvarying' – from 'those who wander erratically in the midst of plurality and variety' (Plato, 2019, 484b). Julian Baggini sees this legacy from Plato, that the ideal of knowledge is 'timeless, placeless, eternal and unchanging' (Baggini, 2020, p. 25), as running up against an inevitable tension: 'the attempt to transcend the particularities of the individual thinker and her time and place can only be made by specific individuals in specific times and places', and he charges Anglophone philosophy with ignoring this tension (Baggini, 2020, p. 24). Baggini argues that philosophy can give up on 'placeless universality' as a goal and still seek objective truth or greater objectivity, by seeking out the 'many clear views' held within different traditions. We can increase objectivity by multiplying and comparing the philosophical views that have made sense to different peoples in different times and places. This process would be able to make manifest the parochial nature of many Western philosophical concerns. Baggini cites as an example the notion of free will that has been central to Anglo-European debates but is not central to or even available in various other traditions; if we can appreciate its limitations by studying other traditions, that will 'contribute to a more objective understanding of human freedom and its limits' (Baggini, 2020, p. 29). Baggini notes Bryan Van Norden and Jay Garfield's call for many philosophy departments to make plain their cultural narrowness and concomitant neglect of many philosophical traditions through renaming, e.g., as 'Department of European and American Philosophy': 'This simple change would make the domain and mission of these departments clear' (Van Norden and Garfield, 2016). Otherwise, 'departments can hide behind the name "philosophy," which represents a topic with cosmopolitan significance, to disguise the fact that their

---

secularism, feminism, artificial intelligence, genetic modification). My claim is that efforts to address these issues philosophically would include, in attending to contextually specific conditions, the aim of making sense of those conditions to anyone. A different difficulty, the fact that philosophers can hold 'particularist' views – e.g., 'a particularist conception of morality [...] which sees little if any role for moral principles' (Dancy, 2004, p. 1) – was suggested to me as evidence that philosophers can reject universality. But a philosopher defending particularism is likely to defend it as *the* way to understand moral judgement, whenever and wherever there is such a thing as moral judgement.

approach is indefensibly parochial' (Van Norden, 2017, p. 35). Like Baggini, Van Norden and Garfield suggest that globally inclusive study of philosophy would multiply our philosophical resources: 'Non-European philosophical traditions offer distinctive solutions to problems discussed within European and American philosophy, raise or frame problems not addressed in [that] tradition, or emphasize and discuss more deeply philosophical problems that are marginalized' (2016). As with Baggini's point about achieving more objective understanding, the suggestion here is that a more globally inclusive philosophical practice would not just increase the diversity of traditions studied, with each preserving its distinct cultural-linguistic affiliations and intellectual concerns. New philosophical activity would be generated, new ideas, questions, and solutions would be available due to the expansion, comparison, and sharing of resources.

It is not easy to say whether the result of such mutual interaction and influence would generate what could be called a global or more global philosophical practice. We have not given this kind of philosophical evolution much of a chance to occur. Rather than speculate about that, let me make a few comments about how to reckon with the diversity of philosophical traditions vis-à-vis aspirations to universality. The first is that the idea of different traditions fruitfully interacting suggests that there is some prospect of doing philosophy with less clear or less committed 'location'. The impact of one's historical and cultural location on one's philosophical orientation is in any case complex, not settling, for instance, whether one is a physicalist or idealist or committed to the centrality of reason, emotion, divinity, or chance. The unsettled or unsettling potential of philosophy is perhaps hinted at in the claims that philosophical problems lack agreed methods of resolution, if this means they are persistently open to new attempts at articulation and reflection. Second, even if philosophical activity is inevitably located in place, time, and culture and is inevitably shaped by that location, that does not rule out that what makes it philosophical is in part the – indeed arrogant – aspiration to reach universally significant understanding. When Van Norden refers to the term 'philosophy' as representing a 'topic with cosmopolitan significance', that could be an earnest identity, despite the great difficulty of achieving such significance. Here is a sample of ideas from different traditions, taken on faith from scholars who know more about these traditions than I do. On Navajo metaphysics, 'Things and beings, events and conditions, processes and powers, are neither good nor evil, or are potentially both good and evil' (Witherspoon, 1980, p. 9). 'The social ideal of

Mencian relational ethics is a harmonious community of persons cultivating themselves to live ethically within a network of relationships' (Tan, 2014, p. 502). 'In India a philosophical system is one which is pertinent to the ultimate supreme value of mankind, the gaining of liberation [...]. What is sought is truth; what truth is is itself a philosophical question' (Potter, 2015, p. 38). Potter continues to note differing Vaisesika and Nyaya systems with different lists of 'the "reals," the stuff of which everything else is made' (Potter, 2015, p. 43). Now, one cannot simply read off a claim to universality from formulations of such ideas, and people often fail to reflect – and get away with not reflecting – on the scope and conditionality of their claims. Exactly what one is committing oneself to may not be transparent to the one making such a claim. My limited point is that part of why these ideas register as philosophical is that they appear to claim universality. They are trying to get at truths that matter to human life in some contextually unbounded way. They seem to aspire to relevance to anyone at any time, and I offer this aspiration as a marker of the philosophical.

Let me close this section by noting that, if we do not attach this aim to philosophy, charges of parochialism seem to lose critical force. If a philosophical view is subject to counterexample and critique when it makes contact with other traditions, that suggests it is supposed to have relevance beyond the social-cultural home in which it emerges. It can be an important objection to a philosophical claim that it unwittingly assumes the validity of merely local and contingent conditions. In any case, highlighting the contextual located-ness of a philosophical view does not seem to rule out counting it against that view if it fails to apply or make sense beyond that context. Now, universality may be a doomed and crazy thing to aim for! Perhaps every philosophical claim from every tradition could look pointless, unilluminating, or false from some other angle. I doubt that this is true, but in any case my preferred view is that universal understanding, albeit arrogant and ripe for presumptuous imposition, is an important human aspiration. It opens us to test and challenge from all comers. The philosopher should not be able to deflect criticism by saying that a given idea makes sense here, 'to us', and does not have to do more than that.[4]

---

[4]   See Mitova (2020), and the special issue of *Philosophical Papers* she introduces, for sharp analysis of the need to undo the 'self-arrogated hegemonic authority' of the Anglo-European tradition (p. 191). My thought here is that it is the hegemonic authority that is the problem that calls for decolonialising projects, rather than the universal ambitions of any philosophical tradition.

Eileen John

3. The Philosophical Aim of Aesthetics

This section sketches a conception of aesthetics that is not the one I want to end up with; it is nonetheless one that I work with and loosely take for granted. It reflects my education and location within Anglo-European philosophy. The point of this sketch is to help show the difficulty of doing what seems to be expected of aesthetics, if understood in these terms. Aesthetics has a reason for being because human life has an aesthetic dimension. If one studied human life and focused on, say, its moral, physical, political, religious, and cognitively significant dimensions, but failed to recognise any aesthetically significant activity, something large – and I would say important – would be left out. Very broadly, the aesthetic dimension of life encompasses our experiential sensitivity and responsiveness. We do not merely acquire information (in some hard-to-imagine, non-aesthetically-encoded way) and then orient ourselves to the world on the basis of that information; we have qualitative experience of the world and respond to that experience. We attend to salient aspects of experience, find patterns, gestalts, contrasts and similarities, feel affectively moved, and assess experience, in everything from mildly pro and con terms to responses of elation and repulsion. Now, even within the limited philosophical tradition I know best, there is not a particularly compelling consensus about what aesthetics does or should concern, given that broad starting point. The aesthetic dimension can be understood to include almost every waking minute of life, given that we are rarely not attending and responding to experience in some way. But usually the focus is taken to be on what can be particularly valuable in experience. This had led to extensive articulation and consideration of specifically aesthetic values, such as the beautiful and the sublime, as well as to approaching aesthetics as the philosophy of art, construing art as a domain devoted to the deliberate shaping of valuable experience.[5] Especially in its attention to art, aesthetics ends up concerning

---

See also Chimakonam (2017) on the issue of globalisation around accounts of justice.

[5] 'Experiences [...] are the starting points for aesthetics, the starting point for reflecting on the nature and value of the arts, the quality of our experiences of the arts, of natural and constructed environments and of various aspects of ordinary life' (Feagin and Maynard, 1997, p. 3). '[A]esthetics is particularly concerned with our experiences of art and natural beauty, in which our perception seems to be especially worthwhile and satisfying in itself' (Higgins, 1996, p. 1). But sometimes art is the primary focus, or

various issues that are less directly focused on qualities of experience, but that matter to how people identify, interpret, and appreciate art in non-experiential terms (e.g., the role of art history, skill, artists' intentions, creativity, truth). As a branch of philosophy, then, aesthetics is where you can turn for study of qualities of experience, experiential responsiveness and evaluation, and the making, experience, interpretation, and appreciation of art.

To specify a dimension of life that 'belongs to' aesthetics does not say much about what the work of philosophical aesthetics would be. I will give one brief example of how a philosopher has built on this starting point, choosing Immanuel Kant as the most influential European aesthetic theorist.

Kant focused on the activity of judging something to be beautiful, specifying the nature of the relevant experience and the conditions under which such a judgement is made. Meeting these conditions, on Kant's view, means that I have had a first-person experience of something's form that supports a free play of my cognitive powers, different from the conclusive cognitive work of applying concepts to experience (unlike 'that is a sock'). I feel a distinctive pleasure, a disinterested pleasure – distinct from the satisfactions of gratifying sensory appetites, instrumental goals, and moral requirements – in this free play. For Kant, this basis for judgement is most purely available to us in experiencing beauty in nature rather than art; his account of finding beauty in art is more complicated. There are many interesting moving parts in this theory, and all of them have been variously interpreted and debated.[6]

The further interesting aspect of Kant's account that I will highlight has to do with the individual yet universal accessibility of this kind of judgement. Kant ties beauty to the combined body-and-mind capacities of humans: 'beauty is valid only for human beings, i.e., animal but also rational beings' (Kant, 2000, §5, p. 95). These capacities are exercised individually and yet representatively: when judging whether 'a garment, a house, a flower is beautiful', '[o]ne wants to submit the object to his own eyes […] and yet, if one then calls the object beautiful, one believes oneself to have a universal voice, and lays claim to the consent of everyone' (§8, p. 101). 'One solicits assent from everyone else because one has a ground for it that is common to all' (§19, pp. 121–2); our apparently

---

even just the evaluation of art, as in Beardsley's account of aesthetics as the philosophy of criticism (Beardsley, 1981, pp. 3–4).

[6] See Wenzel (2009) for routes into this scholarship.

individual pleasure is made to serve 'not as a private feeling, but as a common one' (§22, p. 123).

Clearly there is a lot to argue about here. Fortunately, my present concern is not to defend or attack Kant's view; I offer it as an example of an effort to address some of the difficulty that aesthetic life holds for philosophy. Kant gives us a vision of aesthetic response as a universally shared human capacity, one that, if exercised in the way Kant specifies, manifests a potential for experience and feeling that people have in common. If we went further into the details of Kant's view, we could find more consideration of the roles of knowledge and aesthetic cultivation (emphasised by David Hume in his conception of ideal critics and their cultivation of taste), but Kant's big picture emphasises a basic human readiness for beauty experience. The judgement of beauty does not divide us into idiosyncratic bearers of personal interests and backgrounds, but rather involves activating common experiential, cognitive, and affective capacities, enabling each of us to speak with an aesthetically 'universal voice'.

In making these claims about human capacities, universal human access, and the abstractly characterised conditions for judgement of beauty, Kant is a great example of arrogant, universalising philosophical ambition. Although I have not documented this here, he fully recognises that he is trying to do something philosophically difficult in arguing that the phenomena of individual experiential activity, i.e. each human taking pleasure in experience, can support a practice of judgement with universal validity. However, he does not recognise, it seems, that the whole project of doing things as he does – unpacking the distinctiveness of beauty, positing disinterestedness and free play, minimising the sensory and emotional, tying beauty to certain examples, singling out beauty as the focus at all, emphasising individual subjectivity and autonomy, mostly ignoring the social context in which people experience beauty – can be viewed as a parochial, culture-bound endeavour.[7] Let me agree that his theorising, in its universalising mode, leaves him exposed to criticism at nearly every turn. Still, his view has gripped generations of philosophers and continues to be at the centre of debates in Anglo-European aesthetics. Part of what explains that grip, I speculate, is that it makes itself available to criticism in its universal mode. But for the purposes of argument here, I just want to cite it as a prime example of what philosophical aesthetics can look like. What sort of thing might one

[7]   See Bourdieu (1987) for a sociological takedown of Kantian aesthetic commitments.

do and claim in thinking philosophically about aesthetic life? One might, taking Kant as the example, identify a form of aesthetic value taken to be relevant to all human beings, articulate conditions under which that value is experienced by all human beings, and defend the distinctive role of that value in human life.

4. The Individuality and Cultural Location of Aesthetic Life

If the aesthetic dimension encompasses human beings' experiential sensitivity and responsiveness, philosophical aesthetics will struggle to achieve the kind of universal understanding that Kant and many philosophers may have assumed is possible. Our aesthetic lives resist universality in two ways: through each person's aesthetic formation over the course of a life and through the differing aesthetic influences and norms offered within different cultural contexts. These kinds of differentiating formations are not separable in the living of a life, but they resist universality in somewhat different ways. While these points may seem obvious, I want to take a little time to illustrate the phenomena I have in mind to convey the complexity of individual and cultural aesthetic formation. An overarching claim that I hope to get across is that the aesthetic dimension of life is central to what it is to have a life – it is where 'what it is like to be me' takes shape, in a person's responsive interface with an environment, in the large and small experiential preferences, patterns, limits, and expectations that go into having one's experiential bearings. We persistently orient ourselves to reality aesthetically. This involves responding to our environments through more than conceptual classification, through feeling what is familiar, coherent, out of sync, interesting, boring, mood-enhancing or deadening, glorious, awful, to be shunned or savoured.[8] These experiential responses quickly feed into and bind with cognitive and practical orientations to reality (categorising, comparing, choosing), but those levels of orientation often need or draw on aesthetic orientation. If we ever feel at home in the world, this will in large part be on aesthetic terms. This is not simply a matter of liking the aesthetic possibilities on offer – though presumably we cannot be aesthetically at home if we dislike all of them – but of recognising them, feeling adequate sensitivity to them, and feeling comfortable with one's responses to them.

[8] See Saito (2007) on the pervasiveness and importance of aesthetic responsiveness.

Eileen John

My thinking on this was triggered some time ago by Toni Morrison's novel *The Bluest Eye*, which concerns in part a struggle to be aesthetically at home in the world.[9] But I will refer here instead to some works of autobiographical non-fiction. Each of us has an aesthetic formation, but I think it is rather unusual to be able to evoke aspects and moments of it in words. These passages are all written retrospectively, as attempts to remember scenes or recurrent experiences from childhood or youth. Of course the reader cannot test their experiential adequacy, but I hope they serve to convey the kind of personal aesthetic formation I have in mind. What is displayed here are acute attentiveness, familiarity, and evaluating response within an environment that is somehow of meaning to the speaker. Here is Stuart Hall remembering something of his childhood in Jamaica:

> But I often relive the forbidding climb along precipice-sided potholed roads up into the mountains; then beginning the descent on the other side down towards the north coast, with the aquamarine ocean glimmering seductively ahead through the trees. The wind has a balmy softness in the morning before the sun sets fire to everything. The body unfolds from inside as the day warms up. (I have never really stopped being cold in Britain.) The sea has a powerful, enticing presence in my memory: swimming before breakfast, the water still as glass; or at midday, sliding through the ever-changing green depths at Discovery Bay; or in the afternoon, riding the surging, spume-tipped – and scary – ocean waves at Boston Beach, followed by jerk-pork and festival barbeques. [...] I am still addicted to Jamaican cooking: the creole blend of spices and seasonings – garlic, thyme, pimento, spring onions, Scotch Bonnet hot peppers. [...] These smells and tastes bring back an entire life which, for me in London, is no longer mine. (Hall, 2017, pp. 8–9)

Ben Hamper summons up the quite different cafeteria food and his kinaesthetic-psychological competence on a General Motors assembly line:

> For about five bucks you would receive a slim gray slab of cow-thing, a side of artificial tater goop, a washed-out rainbow of veggies, a rectangle of lime Jell-o and a carton of warm milk. (Hamper, 1986, p. 78)

> The blisters of the hand and the mind had hardened over, leaving me the absolute master of the puppet show. [...] I became so

[9] See, e.g., pp. 19–20 and 45–46 in Morrison (1999).

220

proficient at twirlin' my rivet gun to and fro that the damn thing
felt as comfortable as a third arm. [...] Graceful and indominable.
Methodical and brain-dead. [...] The Rivethead. (Hamper,
1986, p. 94)

Maxine Hong Kingston describes staying late after school one day, a
kind of out-of-bounds moment that leads into trying to force one of
her peers, also from a Chinese immigrant family, to speak:

I and my little sister and the quiet girl and her big sister stayed
late after school for some reason. The cement was cooling, and
the tetherball poles made shadows across the gravel. The hooks
at the rope ends were clinking against the poles. [...] Inside the
playroom the lightbulbs in cages had already been turned off.
Daylight came in x-patterns through the caging at the
windows. [...] She was so neat. Her neatness bothered me. I
hated the way she folded the wax paper from her lunch; she did
not wad her brown paper bag and her school papers. I hated
her clothes—the blue pastel cardigan, the white blouse with the
collar that lay flat over the cardigan, the homemade flat, cotton
skirt she wore when everybody else was wearing flared skirts. I
hated pastels; I would wear black always. I squeezed again,
harder, even though her cheek had a rubbery feeling I did not
like. (Hong Kingston, 1989, pp. 174–177)

Here is John Carey remembering doing errands with his mother in
their London neighbourhood in the 1930s.

At the top of the road [...] was a branch of the United Dairies. A
bell tinkled as you entered, and inside was a temple of immaculate
whiteness, white marble counters, white-tiled walls, and the
ladies who presided were all in white too including their gloves
and hats. I was captivated by their dexterity. If my mother
ordered a pound of butter one of the ladies would take up a
pair of wooden butter pats, slice a wedge from a gleaming
mound on the counter, beat it into a precise rectangular shape,
drop it neatly onto a square of greaseproof paper on the scales,
wrap it with a couple of deft flutters of the white gloves, and
hand the completed artefact to my mother as if it was nothing remarkable. (Carey, 2014, p. 2)

It is interesting to me that I find these descriptions so interesting.
They are not evoking my life, with the exception of Hong
Kingston's attention to the after-school 'feel', but I think they hold
appeal in the way they register a path of experience with such

intensity and care. The passages convey something of how a person was situated in and responsive to reality within the unfolding of a given life (and in Hall's case noting how that past sensitivity still follows him into a very different environment).

We have each followed such a path, with its own patterns, habits, surprises, pleasures, and cumulative impact. For each of us right now there are lived-in settings and patches of earth that are familiar – perhaps loved, perhaps not – and that activate the aesthetic tendencies we have developed. Each of us could offer a different answer about flavours, textures, bodily sensations, kinds of light and shadow, sounds and settings that have been familiar, comfortable, wonderful, or otherwise. This is some of the stuff of aesthetic life. I hope that it begins to look difficult to see how one might conceptualise and generalise about how people respond aesthetically to the world. In these passages some canonically aesthetic vocabulary was used, 'graceful' and more marginally 'neat', and perhaps some artistry was invoked, in the 'master of the puppet show' and the 'remarkable' artefact of the butter parcel. Big aesthetic concepts, e.g., beauty or ugliness, might be able to be applied, but it seems they would bring a loss of acuity and would seem forced. What might I, as an aesthetic theorist, be able to generalise about here, and what would be the point of aiming for universality? The gloss on philosophical universality offered above is that such claims are intended to apply wherever and whenever a topic has a foothold in reality, to have significance and force for people in general. But if the truths of aesthetic life are so individual, so continually developing and sensitive to one's life situation, it is not clear what universal force they could have. The concepts and tendencies needed to state or account for these truths seem pretty closely tied to the things being experienced in that context (the need to rivet quickly, that walk to the beach, the malleability of the butter, the feel of that girl's cheek). I can find these claims interesting, as I do, as evidence of something parallel to – but distinct from – my own aesthetic formation. But to say that they have relevance to me in my status as a person in general and to human life universally seems implausible.

Let me now complicate this first claim, concerning our personal aesthetic formations along individual life paths, with the role of cultural aesthetic formation. In the examples above, though I was emphasising the personal specificity of these aesthetically charged memories, the cultural location of the writers' lives was manifest as well. It is hard to acknowledge the content and influence of cultural contexts without oversimplification and error. I will not attempt to say much about these examples, but the expectations and pressures of a given social community, involving class, race, fashion, immigration and citizenship, and cuisine, were in some way known or felt by these people and contributed to how they experienced and responded to, say, the demure clothing of a classmate, the gleaming whiteness of a dairy shop, or experiences of typical foods. The excerpts above reflect not only individual life paths, but different social and cultural forms that presumably do support some generalisations (standard flavours of Jamaican cuisine, physical and psychological demands of assembly-line labour, clothing possibilities for girls in a given time and place). Our aesthetic lives end up manifesting all sorts of influences – expectations, interests and desires, conceptual categories, evaluative standards, forms of knowledge, the salience of certain stimuli – that we acquire as members of specific groups and cultures. This is yet another broad claim that could be illustrated in many ways.[10] I will turn to some work in aesthetics that I think acknowledges the cultural depth and complexity that can lie behind a way of experiencing things. This will narrow the focus to experience of objects identified as works of art or of fine craftsmanship; such things exemplify particularly well the deep and complex cultural influences that I want to illustrate.

In these examples, philosophers explicitly aim to make Chinese and Japanese aesthetic traditions accessible to people who are not likely to be 'at home' in them. Harold Osborne, discussing the theory and practice of traditional Chinese painting, notes many features that are striking for someone who takes for granted a European painting tradition. The scroll was a paradigmatic structure, to be 'opened gradually and "read" consecutively in time by the observer, not seen in a piece', and monochrome variation and blending of ink and elaborately differentiated calligraphic brushwork ('like tangled hemp' or 'the veins of the lotus leaf') were central to appreciation (Osborne, 1970, pp. 107–108, 123). In terms of the aims and values at work in the practice of painting,

> The Chinese painter was not concerned, except incidentally to the pursuit of other aims, to "imitate" the appearances of things or to represent things ideally as he would like them to be [...]. The cultivation and practice of painting were thought of

[10] Hamper gives such an account of music played at work: 'The music of the Dead Rock Stars is redundant and completely predictable. [It] infinitely mirrors the drudgery of our assembly jobs. [...] the same wearied hepsters who used to dodge economics class for a smoke in the boys' room would later in life become fossilized to the hibernatin' soundtracks of their own implacable youth' (Hamper, 1986, p. xviii).

as a ritualistic activity creating an embodiment of the cosmic force of order which infuses all reality, human society, and the individual personality. [...] his work would be imbued with and would reflect the Tao. (Osborne, 1970, p. 106)

This is an entry into understanding what is relevant to aesthetic life for those participating in this painting practice, whether as painter or appreciator. It signals that deep participation would involve fine-grained perceptual discernment and classification, appreciation of skills and chosen techniques, the action and temporality of looking, and being attuned to the meaning of the ritual and the cosmic order that are at stake in the practice.[11]

Yuriko Saito discusses what she refers to as 'a quintessentially Japanese taste [...] the celebration of those qualities commonly regarded as falling short of, or deteriorating from, the optimal condition of the object'. This long-developed taste has embraced appreciation of 'objects with defects, an impoverished look, or aging effects', such that, for instance, 'impoverished-looking and irregularly shaped Korean peasants' bowls, often with chips and cracks, were highly esteemed' (Saito, 1997, pp. 377–378). Saito's discussion traces complex sources and kinds of meaning for this aesthetic taste. There is the aesthetic potential of contrasts, endings, and wondering about an object's history. The appreciation of imperfection can entwine with yearning for perfection. Saito documents complicated interpretations of this taste's socio-political meaning: it has been viewed as representing a privileged pleasure taken in safely enjoying emblems of impoverishment, as having political value in restraining ostentatious display, and as encouraging the non-privileged to be satisfied with insufficiency – and therefore criticised for putting a positive aesthetic 'spin' on real poverty (Saito, 1997, pp. 379–381). Furthermore, the aesthetics of imperfection has religious and metaphysical meaning in its relation to Shintoism's egalitarian affirmation of things in this world, making no value discriminations, and to a Zen Buddhist ideal of overcoming ego, surrendering to materials and accepting lack of control (Saito, 1997, pp. 381–383).

---

[11]   See Man on the artist and ritual in traditional Chinese painting. '[T]he goal of art-making as such is completely circular: the creation of an art-making agent'; 'art-making can be compared to ritual, especially the genre of rites of exchange and communion, which tends to help articulate complex systems of relationships among human beings, the world, gods, and so on' (Man, 2020, pp. 9, 10).

Saito's and Osborne's essays were important in my own education in philosophical aesthetics, as they were some of the works that introduced me to the issues I am trying to consider here. Saito and Osborne signal the great scope, depth, and intersection of factors that can lie behind being 'at home' with an aesthetic taste or artistic practice. They describe intricately meaningful traditions that have supported forms of aesthetic life. It is great to get some understanding of what could influence and be manifested in the experience of a cracked cup or brushstroke, but it is also overwhelming. To be situated within the relevant tradition could involve artistic, perceptual, political, religious, and metaphysical orientations. Although this kind of cultural formation does not resist universality by resisting generalisation, as perhaps the personally located aspects of aesthetic life do, it does make aspirations to universality of aesthetically relevant concepts and evaluative standards seem intractable. What is appealing about Saito's and Osborne's approaches is that they go deeper into a non-universal aesthetic-cultural form: they try to articulate what is perceivable, conceivable, connected, and valued in a specific tradition. It is hard to see why it would matter if those possibilities of experience and value differ from those in other traditions, and it does not seem one could hold it against these practices if they fail to move or be relevant to people in general.

This is a sweeping overview of phenomena that call for more subtle development. I will not pursue the question of how the individual and the cultural paths combine in a given person's experience, though we have some hints about that in the personal accounts cited above. The broad picture that I hope is in view is that our individual and cultural formations come together in aesthetic life in ways that challenge the feasibility and fruitfulness of seeking philosophically universal aesthetic claims. There is crucial substance in our aesthetic lives, as this is how each of us reckons directly with where we are, what it is like to be there, and what kinds of meaning and value can show up in our experience. But it is not obvious that this substance can be acknowledged, understood, and assessed in universal terms. Can the philosopher's quest for understanding that is relevant to anyone at any time have a point in relation to aesthetic life? Can aesthetics be genuinely global?

5. Prospects for Philosophical Aesthetics

It would be nice if I had a confident answer to my own question, ideally one that would be easy to implement in my own philosophical practice. That is not what I have, but I can explain where this line of thinking has led me so far, and I will make some schematic suggestions. Let me also acknowledge, as I have not adequately done so far, that many other philosophers are alive to these questions and have responded to them in constructive ways.[12] First, thinking about how the universalising aspiration of philosophy can meet forms of aesthetic non-universality opens up a need for more of what might be called meta-aesthetics. What does 'aesthetic life' mean, and what problems face efforts to universalise about it? What is philosophically tractable and otherwise in this domain? I have used the notion of aesthetic life in a universalising way; is that initial move viable? This essay is my own preliminary effort in the meta-aesthetic direction; all of this needs deeper attention. Second, aesthetic theorising in the general but probably not universalising mode is of great importance, and this is a partial way of honouring the philosophical impulse. That is, what Osborne and Saito are doing is crucially generalising about distinctive aesthetic phenomena. In doing so, they will reveal aspects of practice, meaning, and experience that are shared, resonate, or contrast with other stretches of aesthetic life. This kind of generalising study rests on a very demanding base of experience and knowledge; the work of those who have that kind of base should be engaged with as well as possible by those who do not – there is an important division of labour that we can benefit from. Third, the fruits of extending knowledge and reflection on aesthetic life to more and more practices around the world and in time are not yet foreseeable. We have not done enough of the difficult work of becoming more experientially aware and informed about complex aesthetic practices, and of assembling, comparing, and reflecting on different practices. It may be that there is more scope for universalising than I can see at the moment.[13] Finally, as must seem obvious by now, the aesthetic theorist who is moved by

[12]   E.g., in the more globally inclusive contents of anthologies such as Higgins (1996), Feagin and Maynard (1997) – who broach the need for multiple aesthetics – and Hussain and Wilkinson (2006); in the multiple traditions considered in Sartwell (2004); and in Blocker (2001), who probes the problem of constructing a non-Western aesthetics.

[13]   I take Maira (2017) and Sartwell (2004), for instance, to be arguing for the universal significance of beauty. Maira looks hopefully toward an ' 'Age of Inter-Relationality', where it is recognized that all life and social systems are webbed, networked, interconnected, interrelated and interdependent, and where [...] art too must reflect, support and participate in these developments. [...] Not just in India but around the world' (2017, p. 31).

philosophical impulses to say what is true and of universal relevance about some aesthetically interesting domain (e.g., in my own case, fiction or moral learning from art) simply has to be looking out for local and contingent conditions that affect how these things have a 'foothold in reality'. This is a philosophically important habit under any circumstances, but it seems that humility about this ought to be the default attitude for aesthetic theorising. While trying as best I can to reach claims with universal significance and application, I should assume that I am going to end up with something more limited. A further philosophical prospect may then open up, as the limitations of the ideas and phenomena I have considered may help reveal alternatives in a bigger space of possibilities.

6. Conclusion

Let me close with a few summary suggestions. In formulating these in the imperative mood, I am speaking first to myself, but I hope these points hold some combination of reasonableness and provocation for other philosophers.

1. Do not set out to achieve a Global Aesthetics, in the sense of seeking a harmonised conception of aesthetic engagement and set of evaluative concepts that apply universally. Maybe such a thing will emerge over time, but it does not seem we have had good reason to posit one so far.
2. Study the diverse substance of aesthetic life: encounter more than one feels at home with; do not assume convergence and interpersonal agreement; try to compare, translate, and enable access to aesthetic variation, with care, caution, and humility.
3. Defer, or demote concern for, judgement of aesthetic and artistic value. Assessing what is best or most valuable seems unhelpful if not thoroughly intractable; understanding forms of aesthetic life comes first.
4. Explore a space of possibilities, looking to find out what factors can combine in aesthetic life. Given whatever possibilities appear, think about whether any general patterns, tendencies, and common values can be discerned.
5. Attempt to identify and test one's own universalising commitments. This would include, for me, everything I have said here about 'aesthetic life'. Can I assume that aesthetic orientation is central to being at home in the world? That humankind is *the* aesthetically relevant kind? Can I assume that the personal

Eileen John

aesthetic path has weight and is not simply a product of collective pressures and socialisation?

6. Acknowledge and reflect critically on the global movements of aesthetic traditions: their collision, melding, imposition, suppression, elevation, appropriation, 'primitivisation', commercialisation, loss and renewal.[14] Philosophical tools may be particularly helpful when aesthetic practices and discourses come into contact and the claims of different universalising terms and values are put in question.

When thinking about what philosophical aesthetics can fruitfully aim to do, the personally and culturally shaped form of aesthetic life has to be recognised and properly grappled with. If one accepts the importance of aesthetic life to what it is to have a life at all, then it does not seem that philosophy can ignore the aesthetic dimension. However, the universalising ambition that I think indeed characterises philosophy has to be held loosely, self-consciously, and self-critically. The formulation of aesthetic ideas and values needs to be tentative and needs to be based on more inclusive and unsettling evidence than will come easily to any one of us.[15]

References

Julian Baggini, 'Dreams of Utopia: On the Absence of Place', *Think*, 55:19 (2020), 23–32.

Monroe Beardsley, *Aesthetics*, 2nd edition (Indianapolis: Hackett, 1981).

Nalini Bhushan, 'Toward a Development of a Cosmopolitan Aesthetic', *Contemporary Aesthetics*, 0:2 (2009), np.

H. Gene Blocker, 'Non-Western Aesthetics as a Colonial Invention', *Journal of Aesthetic Education*, 35:4 (2001), 3–13.

Pierre Bourdieu, *Distinction: A Social Critique of the Judgement of Taste*, Richard Nice (trans.), (Cambridge, MA: Harvard University Press, 1987).

John Carey, *The Unexpected Professor* (London: Faber & Faber, 2014).

J.O. Chimakonam, 'African Philosophy and Global Epistemic Injustice', *Journal of Global Ethics*, 13:2 (2017), 120–137.

[14] See Nguyen and Strohl (2019) and Young (2021) for some of the ongoing work on these issues.

[15] Many thanks to Julian Baggini, Kirk Surgener, and the audience at the lecture version of this paper.

228

Jonathan Dancy, *Ethics Without Principles* (Oxford: Clarendon Press, 2004).

Susan Feagin and Patrick Maynard, *Aesthetics* (Oxford: Oxford University Press, 1997).

Henry Louis Gates, Jr., *The Signifying Monkey* (New York: Oxford University Press, 1988).

Stuart Hall, *Familiar Stranger: A Life Between Two Islands* (Durham and London: Duke University Press, 2017).

Ben Hamper, *Rivethead* (New York: Warner, 1986).

Kathleen Higgins, *Aesthetics in Perspective* (Fort Worth, Texas: Harcourt Brace, 1996).

Ted Honderich (ed.), *Philosophy Through Its Past* (Middlesex: Penguin, 1984).

Maxine Hong Kingston, *The Woman Warrior* (New York: Vintage Books, 1989).

Mazhar Hussain and Robert Wilkinson (eds.), *The Pursuit of Comparative Aesthetics: An Interface Between the East and West* (London: Routledge, 2006).

Immanuel Kant, *Critique of the Power of Judgement*, Paul Guyer (ed. and trans.) and Eric Matthews (trans.), (Cambridge: Cambridge University Press, 2000).

Shakti Maira, 'The Hollowing of Art and the Call of Beauty', in Kathleen Higgins, Shakti Maira, Sonia Sikka (eds.), *Artistic Visions and the Promise of Beauty: Cross-Cultural Perspectives* (Cham: Springer, 2017), 15–33.

Eva Kit Wah Man, *Cross-Cultural Reflections on Chinese Aesthetics, Gender, Embodiment and Learning* (Singapore: Springer, 2020).

Veli Mitova, 'Decolonising Knowledge Here and Now', *Philosophical Papers*, 49:2 (2020), 191–212.

Toni Morrison, *The Bluest Eye* (London: Vintage, 1999).

C. Thi Nguyen and Matthew Strohl, 'Cultural Appropriation and the Intimacy of Groups', *Philosophical Studies*, 176 (2019), 981–1002.

Nkiru Nzegwu, 'African Art in Deep Time: De-race-ing Aesthetics and De-racializing Visual Art', *Journal of Aesthetics and Art Criticism*, 77:4 (2019), 367–378.

Harold Osborne, *Aesthetics and Art Theory* (New York: E. P. Dutton, 1970).

Plato, *Republic*, Robin Waterfield (trans.), (Oxford: Oxford University Press, 2019).

Karl Potter (ed.), *The Encyclopedia of Indian Philosophies: Indian Metaphysics and Epistemology: The Tradition of Nyaya-Vaisesika*

Eileen John

up to Gangesa, Vol. 2 (Princeton: Princeton University Press, 2015).

Ronald Radano and Tejumola Olaniyan (eds.), *Audible Empire: Music, Global Politics, Critique* (Durham: Duke University Press, 2016).

Yuriko Saito, *Everyday Aesthetics* (Oxford: Oxford University Press, 2007).

Yuriko Saito, 'The Japanese Aesthetics of Imperfection and Insufficiency', *Journal of Aesthetics and Art Criticism*, 55:4 (1997), 377–385.

Crispin Sartwell, *Six Names of Beauty* (London: Routledge, 2004).

Roger Scruton, *A Short History of Modern Philosophy* (London: Routledge, 1995).

Richard Shusterman, 'Of the Scandal of Taste: Social Privilege as Nature in the Aesthetic Theories of Hume and Kant', *Philosophical Forum*, 20:3 (1989), 211–229.

Sor-hoon Tan, 'The Concept of *Yi* in the Mencius and Problems of Distributive Justice', *Australasian Journal of Philosophy*, 92:3 (2014), 489–505.

Paul Taylor, *Black Is Beautiful* (Chichester: Wiley-Blackwell, 2016).

Bryan Van Norden, *Taking Back Philosophy: A Multicultural Manifesto* (New York: Columbia University Press, 2017).

Bryan Van Norden and Jay Garfield, 'If Philosophy Won't Diversify, Let's Call It What It Really Is', *New York Times*, 11 May 2016, https://www.nytimes.com/2016/05/11/opinion/if-philosophy-wont-diversify-lets-call-it-what-it-really-is.html.

Christian Helmut Wenzel, 'Kant's Aesthetics: Overview and Recent Literature', *Philosophy Compass*, 4:3 (2009), 380–406.

Gary Witherspoon, 'Language in Culture and Culture in Language', *International Journal of American Linguistics*, 46:1 (1980), 1–13.

James O. Young, 'New Objections to Cultural Appropriation in the Arts', *The British Journal of Aesthetics*, 61:3 (2021), 307–316.

From Hosting Words to Hosting Civilizations: Towards a Theory of 'Guardianship' and 'Deep Hospitality'[1]

TAMARA ALBERTINI

Abstract

In this paper, I cover some ideas first developed during a research year that took me, among other countries, to Bulgaria, where I enjoyed a Fulbright scholarship in 2018–2019. At a conference in Plovdiv (ancient Philippopolis), I gave a talk entitled 'Neither Clash Nor Dialogue: We Are Each Other's Guardians'.[2] A journalist in the audience became irritated and asked me, 'What do you mean by "neither/nor"? What else is there?' I answered that the explanation was in the subtitle 'We Are Each Other's Guardians'. It proposes a third course, one resting on the notion of 'guardianship' – as a moral obligation. In what follows, I elaborate further on this concept by relating it to the notion of hospitality, not the Derridian variant, but one that is conceptualized as a transformative event for both the host and the guest, which is why I call it 'deep hospitality'.

1. Going Beyond Intercultural Dialogue

The notion of guardianship is not present in Samuel Huntington's *The Clash of Civilizations and the Remaking of World Order* (1996)[3] – how could it be? – and also not among the well-intentioned promoters of civilizational dialogue who approached UN organizations or gave addresses at the UN. There is the example of Austrian philosopher Hans Köchler (b. 1948) who in a Letter to UNESCO

---

[1] I thank Dr Julian Baggini for his gracious invitation. It was truly an honour to be invited to the Royal Institute of Philosophy where Bertrand Russell and many more brilliant philosophers once lectured. I may not have been at the Institute in person, but contemporary technology made it possible for my voice and image to be 'hosted'. The lecture is available at https://www.youtube.com/watch?v=97ZpPfZDI-E.

[2] Available at https://www.youtube.com/watch?v=NELwHzQJKKs.

[3] *The Clash of Civilizations and the Remaking of World Order* was preceded by an article entitled *The Clash of Civilizations?* (1993), which was replied to by Edward W. Said in his famous lecture at the University of Massachusetts in 1996, entitled *The Myth of the 'Clash of Civilizations'*, available at https://www.youtube.com/watch?v=aPS-pONiEG8.

doi:10.1017/S1358246123000139   © The Royal Institute of Philosophy and the contributors 2023

Tamara Albertini

spoke of the 'dialogue entre différentes civilizations' (1972) and eventually received the UN's support in organizing a conference on intercultural dialogue.[4] A famous UN address on the subject was delivered in 1998 by then Iranian president Muhammad Khatami and entitled 'The Dialogue Among Civilizations'. The idea was not without precedents in Iran. We may mention the organization by the same name inspired by French Muslim philosopher Roger Garaudy, of which a branch was founded in Iran under the auspices of the Shahbanou, Iran's last Empress.[5] And there is the even earlier Safa Khaneh Community established by Ḥājj Āqā Nur-Allāh (d. 1927) in Isfahan in 1902. It served as an interfaith centre at a time when no such institutions existed in the West. These were all morally worthy and scholarly commendable initiatives. What I have in mind, however, is not a mere matter of intercultural or interreligious crossings; it goes beyond engaging in dialogue and creating cultural or political alliances. The guardian assumes the *moral responsibility* not only for the continuing existence of other civilizations but also for their thriving and flourishing. Essentially, guardians provide a 'shared home', whether a physical dwelling or a space in the cultural, spiritual, or intellectual life; they make themselves available as 'hosts'.

2. 'Guardian Civilizations': The Different Demands of *Verticality* and *Horizontality*

Before looking into the notion of guardianship as an ethical concept, I will introduce two historical examples of what I call guardian civilizations. One is the Islamic civilization in its classical period (predating the destruction of Baghdad by the Mongols in 1258), and the other is the civilization that the Italian-born Renaissance had aspired to create. In different ways, they both go back to the Platonic Academy, not to its glorious beginning with the larger-than-life founder but, oddly, to the Academy's end. If asked, most people in academia would reply that the school was founded in Athens in or around 387 BC. However, it is unlikely that they know that Plato's Academy lasted continuously till about the time

---

[4] See https://en.wikipedia.org/wiki/Dialogue_Among_Civilizations.

[5] See *The Philosophy of Seyyed Hossein Nasr*, edited by Lewis Edwin Hahn, Randall E. Auxier, and Lucian W. Stone Jr. (2001, p. 34) and Farah Diba-Pahlavi's *Erinnerungen* (2004, p. 248). For more details, see *Dialogue among Civilizations: A Historical Perspective* (2017) by Mohamad Zaidin Mohamad, Sofyuddin Yusof, Ahmad Zahid Salleh, and Abdillah Hisham.

of Cicero. It reinvented itself later but eventually was closed down in the 6th century AD. This historical detail was also pointed out by Bertrand Russell, who remarked judiciously: 'At last, in AD 529, it was closed by Justinian because of his religious bigotry, and the Dark Ages descended upon Europe' (Russell, 1967, p. 61). In other words, the 'inhospitable' Byzantine emperor Justinian could not tolerate an institution that he viewed as a remnant of Paganism. But what happened to the last teachers and students of the Academy?

2.1 The Exodus of Athens's Last Academicians

Some of the Academy's last members escaped to Ḥarrān (today in Turkey), and others to Ctesiphon, the winter capital of the Sassanian Empire. Barely a century later, both Ḥarrān and Ctesiphon were incorporated into the newly formed Islamic Empire. Ḥarrān became *the* centre of translations of Greek scientific and philosophical works into Syriac and eventually into Arabic, while the magnificent city of Ctesiphon suffered irreversible decline after Muslim-Arab troops captured it. Eventually, its palaces and monuments were demolished and used as building materials for a new capital. The city's name was Baghdad. It recycled its predecessor's bricks and marbles – and continued its tradition of scholarship and sciences. Baghdad's famed 'House of Wisdom' (*Bayt al-Ḥikma*) thus served as a library, archive, academy, scientific complex, and translation centre for Hellenistic, Persian, and Indian sources.

It would be overstating matters to claim that the early Islamic Empire might not have become the repository of ancient Greek knowledge without the migration of the last Platonists to Persia; one may never know with any precision how ideas travel nor whether they will be received favourably. Be that as it may, the Islamic world has been a 'guardian civilization' for centuries. It actively preserved the scientific sources of its predecessors and acknowledged its intellectual debt to other nations, especially Greeks and Persians. More importantly, it added substantially to the body of knowledge it inherited from previous civilizations. For a while, some Muslim philosophers and historians, coincidentally many of whom were Shi'ites, even presented a 'chronology' in which Greek and biblical traditions were intertwined as if to say, 'We are all connected'. This is what it looks like:

Empedocles – *King David* or *King Solomon* – *Luqmān* – Pythagoras – Socrates – Plato – Aristotle

Tamara Albertini

In the actual historical sequence, Socrates, Plato, and Aristotle followed the Presocratics with no non-Greeks included into their timeline. Moreover, in Western sources, Empedocles is neither deemed the earliest nor one of the more prominent Greek philosophers. However, according to the Kurdish physician and historian al-Shahrazūrī (13th century), who collected the story from earlier Islamic texts:

> The great and divine philosopher Empedocles, son of Ibn Nādir, born in Agrigento, was one of the greatest and principal sages in the judgment of all philosophers [...]. After he had studied philosophy in Syria with David and Luqmān, he returned to Greece and dedicated himself to the promotion of philosophy. It was also said that he studied with Solomon [...]. (Cited in Palacios, 1978, p. 45)

On this view, Empedocles' fame is connected to his studies with King David and the latter's son Solomon (who actually preceded him by about six centuries). The third figure is Luqmān, a Qur'ānic personage; a chapter of the Islamic scripture is named after him. Later sources state that he was an African sold into slavery but then released by a master who recognized his wisdom. On occasion, he is referred to as a Prophet.[6]

What is the meaning of this encounter between an ancient Greek, two biblical kings, and a Qur'ānic wise man? Since all these figures were said to be sages, the account was likely considered an allegory expressive of a worldview in which wisdom acted as the link between civilizations. In a different Islamic source, Empedocles is himself referred to as a Prophet by use of the term *ghiyāth*, which is derived from Sufism (Islamic mysticism), making him thus partake in a tradition that historically comes later (see Kingsley, 1995, p. 380). One cannot help noticing that this worldview places Islam between two earlier traditions. Moreover, it islamicizes and appropriates historical figures who predate the event of Islam. Nevertheless, it is important to stress that the Islamic *philosophia perennis* tradition does not point out any one tradition as the mother civilization. Wisdom has no beginning; it pervades all cultures.

---

[6] See Heller and Stillmann, 'Luḳmān' in the *Encyclopaedia of Islam*, accessed online on 07 October 2022. The Qur'ānic sura XXXI is named after him.

2.2 The Platonic Academy in Careggi

Centuries later, another revival of Ancient Greek studies took place in a different part of the world. The city where it began was Florence, and the time was the Renaissance. For the sake of brevity, I will focus on Giovanni Pico della Mirandola (d. 1494) only. A fresco by Rosselli at Sant' Ambrogio, Florence (1484–1486) depicts him with Leon Battista Alberti (d. 1472) to the left and Angelo Poliziano (d. 1494) to the right.[7] All three were members of the Platonic Academy in Careggi headed by Florentine philosopher Marsilio Ficino (d. 1499) and sponsored by the Medici family. What artist and art theoretician Alberti, Pico the philosopher, and Poliziano the Aristotelian and poet had in common was Humanism, a teaching that focused on human beings, their true potential, and how to educate for the highest possible human performance, what the Greeks called the 'aretē' (ἀρετή), which can be translated as both the excellence and virtue of man. Unlike Alberti and Poliziano, however, Pico tapped into all civilizations known to the Renaissance.

Among Pico's synthesizing predecessors, one finds Byzantine philosopher Gemistus Pletho (d. 1452/54) who joined emperor John VIII on his trip to Italy in the hope of achieving unity between the Eastern and Western Churches; Nicholas of Cusa (d. 1464), arguably the first Renaissance philosopher and the chief papal diplomat who helped to prepare the Council; and Ficino who translated the entire Platonic corpus, numerous neo-Platonic sources, and also the rare *Chaldaic Oracles* and the *Hymns of Zoroaster*, all from Greek manuscripts. Thanks to his tutor Elia del Medigo (d. 1493), a Jewish scholar, Pico also became the first known Christian philosopher acquainted with the Kabbalah (Jewish mysticism) and Muslim-Andalusian philosopher Abu Bakr ibn Tufayl (d. 501/1185), whose philosophical novel *Ḥayy Ibn Yaqẓān* celebrates a self-taught protagonist who accomplishes himself as an Aristotelian rationalist before turning to Sufism (Islamic mysticism).

Like Ficino, Pico's motivation behind his relentless efforts to study one philosophical tradition after another was driven by the conviction that philosophy dwelled in all world civilizations and that one only needed to find the corresponding pieces in each to reconstruct it. Pico's answer to the question about human excellence is that one must explore all world traditions to find the path of

---

[7] Available at https://www.unigum.it/wp-content/uploads/2019/07/restaurodicosimo1.jpg (accessed 12 October 2022).

Tamara Albertini

self-achievement.[8] That answer was a novelty in a Europe otherwise shaken by century-long debates pitting Platonists against Aristotelians, Christians against Pagans, Theologians against Philosophers, Averroists against non-Averroists, Franciscans against Dominicans, and the Western against the Eastern Church.

The vision that emerges from both the Islamic and Renaissance notions of a *philosophia perennis*, or, as Pico put it, *pia philosophia*, is grandiose and inspiring. However, let us face it, it is one thing to think ourselves the heirs of previous civilizations, which is a way of basking in the light of their achievements, and another to embrace (not merely accept or tolerate) the co-existence with parallel civilizations. While the 'vertical axis' aligns us with the past and lets us take on the convenient role of recipients and keepers of heritage by studying, assessing, and preserving the material and cultural legacy of earlier civilizations, the 'horizontal axis' connects us to contemporary civilizations and implicitly to their and our future. The horizontal axis presents us with the opportunity to not only act as heritage keepers but also to provide a *shared home* for contemporaneous civilizations – without depriving them of theirs. Heritage keepers are essential to preserving historical memory; they act as guardians on the vertical axis, at times with heroic dedication.[9] It seems to me, however, that the role of the guardian on the horizontal axis is yet to be created. I propose to lay out the foundation for this type of guardianship by extracting it from the notion of hospitality, not the Derridian variant, but one that is conceptualized as a transformative event involving both the host and the guest. I call it 'deep hospitality'.

3. Linguistic Hospitality, Guest-Friendship, and 'Hostipitality'

In many ways, every culture and every civilization that has been in contact with other traditions and populations is or has become a host, in whatever modest ways and at least for some period in its history. However, I am thinking about more than just sanctuary

---

[8]   To get a sense of the vastness of Pico's project, see *Syncretism in the West: Pico's 900 Theses (1486). The Evolution of Traditional Religious and Philosophical Systems*, with text, translation, and commentary by S. A. Farmer (1998).
[9]   One such heroic guardian is the Syrian archaeologist Khaled al-Asaad (1932–2015), who together with his staff hid artifacts from the Palmyra Museum and stayed behind alone to face ISIS troops. He paid the ultimate price.

countries as in the case of Persia when it welcomed the last Athenian Platonists or, to move to a different world region, India accepting the Zoroastrians (the Parsis) fleeing forced conversion to Islam. There is a generosity that goes beyond offering shelter and securing survival. What else is there to share?

3.1 From Linguistic Hospitality to Guest-Friendship

French philosopher Paul Ricoeur speaks of 'linguistic hospitality' in the context of translations and emphasizes the ethical dimension of the task. Translators ought to be 'hospitable', i.e., they are to find a new 'home' for what they endeavour to express in another language. The effort is of 'mediation' between the terms in the original text and the ones in the receiving language. Even the most accomplished translator, i.e., the one 'leading across', cannot make every shade of meaning reach the other shore.[10] The art of translating consists of neither entirely absorbing the hosted language – it would make the author disappear – nor surrendering to it, which would erase the reader. Naturally, Ricoeur had more ambitious plans than to solely reflect on the translations of texts:

> Translation sets out not only intellectual work [...] but also an ethical problem. Bringing the reader to the author, bringing the author to the reader, at the risk of serving and betraying two masters: this is to practice what I like to call *linguistic hospitality*. It is this which serves as a model for other forms of hospitality that I think resemble it: confessions, religions, are they not languages that are foreign to one another, which we must learn in order to make our way into them. (Ricoeur, 2006, p. 23, my emphasis).

Ricoeur is quite clear that the lessons to be learned from the hospitable translator extend into other and larger domains. In what follows, I retain his notion of 'linguistic hospitality' to explore the *hosting of untranslated words*, which comes closer to the hospitality extended to *strangers*.

On rare occasions, a country may refuse to *host words* from other languages or attempt to purge itself of traces betraying the presence or influence of another language. One notices this urge in French culture beginning in the sixteenth century when the exclusion of formerly popular 'Italianisms' started. A major factor was also the

---

[10] For the etymology of 'translation', see Davidson (2012, p. 3).

Tamara Albertini

Ordonnance de Villers-Cotterêts (1539), a royal edict that made 'Francien' the country's only official language and was followed by many more laws issued in defence of French to this day. Eventually, the official language politics cleansed a formerly hospitable French of Italian and Occitan vocabulary although it originated in sister languages.[11] Needless to state that this happened at the expense of the expressivity of French. The language that declined to be a host and became, to use Cartesian terms, 'clear' and 'distinct', ended up impoverishing itself; the refusal to host became a culturally costly matter. As is widely known, the more recent efforts to rid French of English words have, so far, failed. The French case, however, is a historical exception. Typically, languages give and receive hospitality. Turkish thus abounds with Arabic, Persian, and (via Venetian traders) Italian words, while much Turkish vocabulary survived in the Balkan countries long after the fall of the Ottoman Empire. An extraordinary case is the hosting of hundreds of Arabic technical terms in European languages, usually via Latin. They are a reminder of an earlier period when Muslims excelled in sciences. These terms are still applied in modern mathematics, medicine, astronomy, chemistry, optics, and many more fields of study. For instance, *algebra, alchemy, algorithm, alkali, almanac, Altair, azimuth, Betelgeuse, borax, cipher, elixir* (originally Greek), *soap, sugar, syrup,* and *zenith*. They are commonly called 'loanwords', as if they were going to be returned one day. If anything, they are on permanent loans. However, if the receiving language is the host, does that not make the language of origin the 'guest'? Like many other languages, Turkish would be both a linguistic host and a guest.

Someone could say, 'Those Arabic scientific terms are already there in European languages'. In other words, it is too late to think of hosting them; the terms in question have already been acclimatized and incorporated. And anyway, how many speakers of English, French, German, *etc.* even know that *Betelgeuse* is derived via French from *yad al-jawzā'* (meaning 'hand of the Gemini')? That is precisely why hospitality needs to be extended – even *post factum*. It accords words like *algorithm, almanac,* or *cipher* a 'guest-home', which transforms a takeover into a welcome that also expresses gratitude towards the culture of origin for enriching one's native vocabulary. Coincidentally, *'cuma'*, etymologically related to 'come', once meant 'guest', and Old English for 'will', i.e., 'willa' (from Proto-Germanic **wiljon-*) means, among other things 'desire',

---

[11] See Scheel's PhD thesis *French Language Purism: French Linguistic Development and Current National Attitudes* (1998).

'joy', and 'delight', making the guest 'one whose coming suits another's will or wish'.[12] Seen in this light, Arabic scientific terms are not absorbed but given a dwelling. To extend linguistic hospitality also implies an acknowledgement that guest terms continue to exist in their language of origin; they have not been taken hostage.[13] The concept that applies here is one of 'guest-friendship', a term that in English translates the Greek '*xenía*' (ξενία). '*Xenos*' means stranger, foreigner, and is also a word for friend. How can strangers be friends? The answer is simple: they become friends once you host them.

3.2 Guest-Friendship: The Ethics and Aesthetics of Hospitality in Ancient Greek and Arab Cultures

When it comes to *hosting strangers*, ancient Greek literature is filled with examples of good and bad guest-friendship. While Jacques Derrida's reflections on hospitality focus on *Oedipus at Colonus*, Sophocles' last tragedy, for reasons to be clarified below, I deliberately choose my examples from *The Iliad* and *The Odyssey*. Both Homeric epics may be read as manuals of hospitality with 'Dos and Don'ts' encapsulated in individual stories. Zeus himself in his role as Zeus Xenios, patron of the strangers, is the embodiment of hospitality and, at times, appears to humans asking them for shelter. In Homer's epic poems, Telemachus and Nausicaa are exemplars of ancient Greek guest-friendship. While the former treats Athena (like Zeus, the protector of strangers) as an honoured guest, only recognizing her divine status upon her departure, the latter offers protection to stranded and naked Ulysses without suspecting his fame and royal standing. According to the etiquette of ancient Greek culture, one was only permitted to ask the guest's name after attending to their basic needs. True hospitality is gratuitous and does not desire anything in return. In the case of Nausicaa's encounter with the King of Ithaca, hospitality also restored the guest's identity: Ulysses became again regal.[14] One should note, however, that there also existed a ritualized form of guest-friendship whereby hospitality

[12] See https://www.etymonline.com/word/welcome.
[13] Derrida too has use for the term 'hostage' but places it in a different context. The guest makes the host hostage, i.e., he is 'the one who keeps him at home'. Also, Derrida derives French 'otage' from *hoste, oste*. See Derrida (2000b, p. 9).
[14] For how hospitality and recognition are linked, see Murnagham's *Disguise and Recognition in The Odyssey* (1987, pp. 92–93).

was reciprocal and cultivated among social equals. It was hereditary between well-to-do families living in different Greek cities and ensured physical and legal protection when they travelled. However, the stories of Telemachus and Nausicaa exemplify an ethics of hospitality that is entirely selfless and spontaneous. This ethics was not unique to the Greeks; think of Arab guest-friendship. It has risen to the level of an art form and continues to be practiced, not only among Bedouins. *Karam*, the Arabic term for hospitality, also means generosity and clearly delineates the ethical standard hosts abide by, even if it should be to the detriment of their families' well-being. To this day, the best compliment one could pay a host is that they are more generous than Ḥātim (*'akram min Ḥātim'*), in remembrance of the pre-Islamic poet Ḥātim al-Ṭā'iyy (sixth century AD) who slaughtered his horse (all he had left) to feed guests, while his own family was starving (see Avempace [Ibn Bajja], 1963, p. 131). In contrast to *xenía*, *karam* has no connotations of 'strangeness' or 'foreignness'. The word for guest (*ḍayf*) simply means the one 'adjoined to the family and fed with them'.[15] As in ancient Greece, however, the code of hospitality included an obligation to offer not only food and clothing but also legal protection since the guest had no rights in a tribe other than his or her own. Later, the ancient Arabian code was islamicized. *Karam* and cognates of this term thus appear forty-seven times in the Qur'ān. In one verse, God himself is referred to as '*Karīm*' (generous).[16] There is also an aesthetic dimension implied in *karam*'s additional meanings of nobility and grace exemplified even in as simple a gesture as the brewing and serving of coffee, which in Arab culture is the privilege of the male head of the household. The gesture expresses a joyful and chivalrous mindset comparable to the medieval ideal of the knight who served his beloved;[17] a recompense would be considered an insult.

I am indebted to Dr Robert Littman, my colleague in Classics at the University of Hawai'i at Mānoa, for this source.

[15] See Lane's *Arabic-English Lexicon* (1863), also available at http://www.tyndalearchive.com/TABS/Lane/.

[16] See https://corpus.quran.com/qurandictionary.jsp?q=krm.

[17] Whereas it is true that the gracious host is honoured in Arab culture, I would not go so far as calling them the 'dandy of the desert', as Toshihiko Izutsu suggests. See Siddiqi (2015, p. 33). The statements collected by Andrew Shryock that speak of hospitality as the sacred and intoxicating 'Arab madness' are closer to my lived experiences in North Africa. See Shryock (2009, p. 34).

In both ancient Greek and Arab cultures, the cultivation of guest-friendship was a way of life. Significantly, while the code of hospitality was culturally mandated, the ideal pursued in practice was one in which the host felt personally rewarded by accommodating the 'stranger-friend' in need of shelter and protection. The ethics of guest-friendship was complemented by an aesthetic dimension that also introduced (the decidedly non-Kantian) element of pleasure, a pleasure derived from the gratuitous act that celebrates the guest and hospitality itself. Oddly, the aesthetics and pleasure of giving are missing in Derrida's reflections on hospitality.

3.3 Derridian Hospitality or 'Hostipitality'?

In twentieth-century Western culture, one needs to turn to Jacques Derrida to find a similarly uncompromising understanding of hospitality, which may be a remnant of his upbringing in Algeria. Some studies suggest parallels between his views and those found in North Africa and the Sahel. Andrew Shryock thus writes: 'Most people do not hear Derrida's accent when he talks about the power of giving and receiving, largely because they do not know how Bedouin sound when they discuss such things'.[18] Knowing the value of *karam* in Arab culture, one may have high expectations of Derridian hospitality. Indeed, the French philosopher agonized over the difficulty inherent in the notion and the very word 'hospitality'. Let us begin with a much-cited passage from his *Of Hospitality*:

> Let us say yes *to who or what turns up*, before any determination, before any anticipation, before any *identification*, whether or not it is to do with a foreigner, an immigrant, an invited guest, or an unexpected visitor, whether or not the new arrival is the citizen of another country, a human, animal, or divine creature, a living or dead thing, male or female. (Derrida, 2000a, p. 77)[19]

[18] Shryock (2009, p. 32). Towards the end of *Of Hospitality* (2000a), Derrida mentions the violence France inflicted on Algeria, but there is no suggestion of a debt, intellectual or cultural, that he felt he owed his birth country. Derrida made his accusations as a Frenchman, not a North African, despite his self-description as 'a little black and very Arab Jew' (see Wise, 2009, p. 27).

[19] In his lecture 'Hostipitality', Derrida freely paraphrases a passage from Martin Heidegger's *What Is Called Thinking?* (1968): 'We might call [*heissen*] a guest [*hôte*] welcome [*Geheiss*]. This does not mean that we

Tamara Albertini

The 'arrival' (or, as Derrida puts it in French, the *arrivant*, i.e., the one in the process of arriving) has not been invited, which would give the host the opportunity to prepare the beginning – and the end – of hospitality. Other than invitation, 'visitation' brings out one's true hospitable nature, if it is there at all. Nevertheless, even when hosts do open their doors to unexpected visitors, Derrida's concern is that guests are overwhelmed by the host's hold. One cannot be in the position of the host without implicitly saying, 'this is mine, I am at home' (Derrida, 2000b, p. 14), which suggests that the guest is not. For Derrida, the philosophical problem at hand lies in the incompatibility between the 'unconditional' law of hospitality and the 'conditionality' of hospitality on the ground:

> To [...] 'bid' someone welcome 'to one's own home', where, in one's own home, one is master of the household, master of the city, or master of the nation, the language, or the state, places from which one bids the other welcome [...] and grants him a kind of *right of asylum* by authorizing him to cross a threshold that would be a threshold <a door that would be a door>, a threshold that is determinable because it is self-identical and indivisible, a threshold the line of which can be traced. (Derrida, 2000b, p. 6)[20]

This is part of the problem as to why Derrida speaks so often of the conditionality of hospitality. The threshold remains a separation even when the guest crosses; the home space is always the host's domain. Derrida was keenly aware of how rigorous his notion of unconditional hospitality was, and that hospitality always included some form of hostility, whether it is the need to overcome one's inner resistance or the urge to translate the guest's 'strangeness' in terms of one's own culture. He, therefore, coined the term 'hostipitality', thereby emphasizing, like French linguist Émile Benveniste, 'host' as the root common to both hospitality and hostility.[21] In reference to

---

attach to him the name "Welcome [*Geheiss*]", but that we call him to come in and *complete his arrival* [my italics] as a welcome friend' (2000b, p. 12).

[20] The gendering of the host in this passage is intentional. Derrida correlates the power imbalance between host and guest with the male assertiveness of the host: 'When Klossowski describes the law of hospitality in speaking of a master of the house, a master of places like the family and a master of the wife, husband of the wife who becomes the stake and essence of hospitality, he is well within the domestic [...] logic which seems to govern this Indo-European history of hospitality' (2000b, p. 13).

[21] See the section on 'Hospitality' in Émile Benveniste, *Dictionary of Indo-European Concepts and Society*, (2016, pp. 61–73). The original

From Hosting Words to Hosting Civilizations

Immanuel Kant's reflections on 'Hospitalität' (also rendered in German as '*Wirtbarkeit*') in *Perpetual Peace: A Philosophical Sketch* (1795), Derrida adds a dark observation placed within parentheses:

> (a word of Latin origin, of a troubled and troubling origin, a word which carries its own contradiction incorporated into it, a Latin word which allows itself to be parasitized by its opposite, 'hostility', the undesirable guest [*hôte*] which it harbors as the self-contradiction in its own body [...]). (Derrida, 2000b, p. 3)

Anthropologist Julian Pitt-Rivers makes a similar observation but focuses on the transformation of the stranger into the guest: 'The inversion implies a transformation from hostile stranger, *hostis*, into guest, hospes (or *hostis*), from one whose hostile intentions are assumed to one whose hostility is laid in abeyance' (Pitt-Rivers, 1977, pp. 101–102). What neither Derrida nor Pitt-Rivers realized is that in English too host and guest are both derived from *hostis*.

4. Mediation Starts from the Middle

On the one hand, the purity of Derrida's ideal of hospitality is the gold standard to keep in mind for anyone seriously considering to be a genuine host. On the other, its unconditionality impedes the implementation of the ideal, which is why he frequently referred to it as the 'impossible'. This is where in a Derridian world the 'hostipitality' that dwells within hospitality traps hospitality. According to the French philosopher, there is 'a non-dialectizable antinomy' between the law of unlimited hospitality and the 'laws' of hospitality, i.e., rights and duties as defined by various cultures in legal, religious, or ethical terms (Derrida, 2000a, p. 77). Be that as it may, it is possible to remove the hegemony of hosts without making them obsolete; there is no hospitality without a host. One must turn to Hegel, the master of dialectics, to find the solution. The way out of the difficulty is not thinking in terms of two but three. And more importantly, rather than focus on the host and guest, which brings up the power imbalance problem, I propose to focus on the notion of guest-friendship as the mediating factor. This precludes the issue of power altogether.

French version appeared in 1969. Derrida acknowledges his debt to Benveniste's method of clustering words pertaining to a 'well-established social phenomenon' such as hospitality (2000b, pp. 13–14).

Tamara Albertini

While Ricoeur suggested a hospitable translator as the intermediate, which only put the burden on one of the players (the other two being the author and reader), I like to use a dynamic Hegelian structure to ensure a built-in mediation process, in which every element is an actor.

In Hegel's famous Lord and Bondsman dialectic, the emphasis is not on the opposites but on a unity that separated into two. That unity for Hegel is self-consciousness. Suppose we substitute self-consciousness with the notion of guest-friendship and understand that it is a relational term, without which there could be neither a host nor a guest. In that case, hospitality is placed in a very different setting. Here is a quotation from Hegel's *Phenomenology of Spirit* in which I inserted the notion of guest-friendship where the original speaks of self-consciousness:

> The middle term is *guest-friendship* which splits into the extremes; and each extreme [*host, guest*, my insertion] is this exchanging of its own determinateness [i.e., being *host* or being *guest*, my insertion] and an absolute transition into the opposite. Each is for the other the middle term, through which each mediates itself with itself and unites with itself; and each is for itself, and for the other, an immediate being on its own account, which at the same time is such only through this mediation. They recognize themselves as mutually recognizing one another. (Hegel, 1977, p. 112)[22]

The ingenuity of the Hegelian dialectic turns each of the three terms into a mediating force. Both the 'host' and the 'guest' realize they need each other. No one is a host without the existence of a guest, and *vice versa* the notion of a guest presupposes a host; neither can exist without the other. What started with the dominant position of the host is transformed into a model in which the positions of host and guest are interconvertible, and transformation follows what Hegel calls '*Aufheben*', meaning both sublation and preservation.

---

[22]   After I delivered my online lecture, I discovered that other attempts have been made to use Hegel's Lord and Bondsman dialectic to explore or salvage Derrida's imbalanced relationship between host and guest. They apply a different methodology and do not recognize that what I call the 'transformative event' requires a third element. See, for instance, Shaul's 'Recognition and Hospitality: Hegel and Derrida' (2019). There are also attempts to work with Hegel to address the question of hospitality regardless of Derrida's dilemma, see e.g., Pagano, 'Recognition and Hospitality' (2019).

From Hosting Words to Hosting Civilizations

The guest is as much a host as the host, and the host as much a guest as the guest. As the two actors in the relationship of guest-friendship recognize each other and themselves in the dynamic setting, they are transformed by the experience and realize that they are both hosting each other and are, therefore, both guests. To apply Hegel's notion of 'sublation-preservation', when guests 'preserve', they become their host's *guardians*, i.e., they host the host; and hosts find themselves their guests' guests. Coincidentally, to 'guard' comes from old or middle French '*garder*', which is derived from Proto-Germanic '*wardōn*' (meaning 'protection', 'attention', 'keeping'), and Proto-Indo-European root '*wer-*' (meaning 'to heed', 'defend').[23] Remarkably, the transformative journey of this ancient Indo-European root that came to characterize the present notion of guest-friendship has been itself a multiple linguistic guest, while also serving as the host.

By contrast, there are no actors in Derrida's hospitality narrative, only static figures unable to embody the roles they are meant to fulfil. And yet, the notion of a unity that splits into opposites comes up in Derrida's linguistic reflections on hospitality. It lies precisely there where he underlines the common origin of *hôte* (host) and *hôte* (guest); they go back to the same root. However, no transformative event follows the semantic split for the simple reason that *hôte* and *hôte* do not engage each other. The major difference between Derrida's and my reading of ancient Greek hospitality is that I translate it as guest-friendship, which places host and guest in an interactive relationship; there is no friendship without a dynamic framing of the figures involved. The French language does not have an equivalent term, which may have suited Derrida's critique of the poor state of hospitality accorded the stranger, i.e., the North African immigrant in France. But it is not just the language that frames the event of hospitality in his philosophy; Derrida easily ventured into German when it supported his quest. It is significant to understand why he chose the Greek literary figure that he did. Derrida thus focuses on Oedipus as portrayed in Sophocles' *Oedipus at Colonus*; it gives him a protagonist who is never truly at home. Neither in his native Thebes nor his adopted Corinth is the tragic figure in a position to assert, 'This is mine, I am at home'. At the end of his life, the only place that is his is the burial place he chooses himself in the grove of the Erinyes, near Athens. It is about this burial place, where Oedipus believes he will be redeemed

---

[23] See https://www.etymonline.com/search?q=guard. Like Derrida, I, too, learned from Benveniste to apply transcultural etymology.

from his tragic deeds (and where his death will be a gift of peace to the King of Athens who 'hosted' his dead body), that Derrida writes: 'The guest (*hôte*) becomes the host (*hôte*) of the host (*hôte*)' (Derrida, 2000a, p. 125). Sadly, the hosting guest he is referring to is dead Oedipus. In *Adieu to Emmanuel Levinas*, Derrida plays again with a similar formula and imagines a guest becoming the host's host (Derrida, 1999, p. 42). However, what is missing is the transformative event that engulfs both the host and the guest, which is the only means by which the positions can become convertible. Again, mediation must start from the middle.

The plot in the *Odyssey* is very different. Ulysses returns to his palace in Ithaca after twenty years of wandering – as a guest. His son Telemachus receives him graciously without recognizing him. The son honours the stranger in the same way as he had done with the goddess Athena and defends him against the unruly suitor-guests courting his mother. These were uninvited – like Ulysses – but embodied bad guest behaviour. The takeaway message seems to be that Ulysses, who has been the guest of many hosts during his long home-coming, needed first to become a guest in his house before he could again be the host. By first being a guest, he ceases to be a stranger, and, once again, his identity and dignity are restored. However, when he eventually asserts himself as the host, he does not revert to the same position he occupied before he went to war – he becomes the 'host-guest'.

Notably, except for Kant, none of the classical Western ethicists wrote on hospitality. In twentieth-century thought, philosophers typically resort to epic literature and poetry to develop their ideas. Thus Martin Heidegger used Hölderlin's poems as a foil to distil his understanding of dwelling and hospitality (see Winkler, 2017), a device that became a source of inspiration for Derrida. Similarly, Emmanuel Lévinas developed some of his views on the subject as a reflection on biblical stories (see Hatley, 2005; Katz, 2005).

5. Journeying from Being a 'Hostage' to Becoming a 'Guardian Civilization'

I introduced Arab and ancient Greek hospitality as models of guest-friendship. This, however, does not mean that all Arabs or all Greeks have always been hospitable or perfect guests. We may think of Paris, who was Menelaus' guest and stole the latter's beautiful queen, or of the guests who ate Penelope and Telemachus out of house and home;

in both stories, the violation of *xenía*, seen as an insult to Zeus, ends up being punished most harshly. Nevertheless, guest-friendship is understood to be an honoured way of life in both cultures affording individuals a social setting in which to realize themselves as moral subjects, whether in the position of the host or the guest. In current Western civilization, hospitality plays a minor role in the hierarchy of values and, as a result, does not contribute to stronger bonds within the fabric of society or among different societies. We use the expression 'to be a gracious host' but mean by it the kind of generosity extended for a limited time, usually for one evening. Hospitality is not presented as a value to strive for, whether culturally, intellectually, or religiously. We philosophers, at least some of us, praise it in ethical terms, but that does not change anything on the ground. Children are not educated to be hospitable and to delight in taking a step back, and we adults are not exactly acting as exemplary role models. How, then, can we, the nations of the world, become hospitable, which, to put it in no uncertain terms, would expose us to change when we come to reflect our guests and are thus made vulnerable?

Considering the countless past and present conflicts among civilizations and even within one and the same society, resorting to guest-friendship to overcome differences and incompatible claims seems a remote possibility. Nevertheless, in the same way that individuals are able to extend and accept hospitality graciously, the world's civilizations, too, can learn how to be each other's hosts and guests and thus become each other's guardians. Governments may be unteachable; societies, however, are capable of reinventing themselves. Think of post-WWII Germany: apologies, reparations, and collaborations paved the way to friendship with France, its historical enemy, and Israel, where the survivors of the Holocaust and their descendants found a new home.

Let us think of a particularly complicated relationship, such as the sectarian one. How would one get Sunni and Shi'a communities (or Catholics and Protestants in Northern Ireland) to be each other's 'guest-friends'? The opposed parties in both settings are 'hostages' of their respective historical narratives and in need of a 'wrong' version of themselves to support their claim to authenticity. The challenge is to get the 'hostile' camps to think that maybe, just maybe, the other community might be embodying a valid version of the same core teaching. Even if a central authority acceptable to the opposed groups existed, ordering the two communities to give up their narratives would fall on deaf ears. On the one hand, the sectarian narratives are identity-building, on the other, they are also what keeps the communities in question trapped. They fail to recognize that no religion or school of thought is able to completely survey its sources and traditions, which is why there is necessarily a potential for multiple expressions. Thus, societies that reject the possible legitimacy of a competing narrative end up becoming hostages to a self-understanding in which every single feature, every ritual, and every source pertaining to their beliefs are considered 'true' and their sole 'possession'. Any variant is branded *eo ipso* an error, or worse a heresy.

Clearly, the lack of communication between sectarian groups could neither be solved by promulgating a law to enforce hospitality. When Kant insisted on the right to '*Wirtbarkeit*' in *Perpetual Peace*, he had in mind a stranger's right not to be treated with hostility, but he still gave the '*Wirt*' (host) the right to reject the stranger. Although one can appreciate Kant denouncing the 'inhospitable conduct' of European colonial powers and requiring that laws regulate the relationships between states, hospitality as developed in the present narrative, i.e., as 'deep hospitality', needs to mean more than not harming the stranger or salvaging refugees from the sea as it is currently happening daily in most Mediterranean countries. The latter is mandated by international sea law and is, without a question, the right thing to do. Yet, it is different from the rescue provided by fishers who go out individually to save shipwrecked fellow human beings. They would not be breaking any law by staying at home, and yet, they rush out even on a stormy day because they see the refugees who are exposed to the elements as a reflection of themselves. Deep hospitality does not replace societal law regulating international hospitality, and these two do not necessarily complement each other either. They may influence each other mutually, but they operate in a different manner. Deep hospitality generates spontaneous, gratuitous acts of guest-friendship. It is a value, not a matter of being law abiding. However, it would be a mistake to expect that deep hospitality requires the kind of self-effacement and self-sacrifice typically associated with women in traditional societies. One finds this type of value-based model in Lévinas's call to recover the silent and withdrawn 'feminine welcome'; traces of this thought are reflected in Derrida.[24] His valorising of womanhood and maternity places the feminine, whether identified with concrete women or not, in a 'pre-

---

[24]   See Winkler (2017). For a broader discussion of Lévinas's reflections on the feminine, see *Levinas, Judaism, and the Feminine: The Silent Footsteps of Rebecca* by Katz (2003). As for the feminine as the essence of hospitality in Derrida, see footnote 20.

ethical' realm or outside ethics altogether. It is much too close to how Hegel reflected upon the sacrifice of Antigone who followed divine (rather than human) law; it leaves women unable to develop their subjectivity.[25] Lévinas's prose is of an eerie beauty and justly enhances the role women played in the biblical tradition but cannot inspire today's men and women to think of hospitality as a way of life. Men have no desire to renounce their subjectivity (there is no reason they should), and women have been silent much too long.[26]

The question thus remains: how does one evolve from being a 'hostage civilization', which to varying degrees applies to all societies, to being a 'guardian civilization'? Moreover, what is one to think of societies that have deliberately isolated themselves and chosen to ignore other civilizations altogether?

6. An Adaptation of Qustantin Zurayq's Reflections on Change

During its communist period, Albania used to be Europe's hermit kingdom in the way one thinks of North Korea today; it actually drew its inspiration from the latter. Both countries can be considered hostage civilizations. They took hostage of themselves knowing that it would prevent them from advancing; priority was given to shutting out external influence. Qustantin Zurayq (also spelled Constantine Zurayk, d. 2000), a twentieth-century Arab philosopher and diplomat, was confronted with a similar challenge while reflecting on the multiple dilemmas the Arab societies of his day faced. The situation on the ground was less radical than in the hermit kingdoms. There were no closed borders, no economic restrictions, and control was not exerted over all spheres of life. However, on the whole, Zurayq found the Arab world stuck in a solely religiously defined tradition, a glorified historic past never to return, and a culture they were unable or unwilling to invigorate. He identified three binaries: modern vs religious tradition, past vs future, and foreign vs one's own culture. None of the binaries hold a solution; on the contrary, each presents a trap. Zurayq deemed the excessive attachment to the past a nefarious choice for those who wanted to preserve their culture and saw it thus as a matter of 'retrograde reactionism'. Societies end up holding on to the form of tradition at the expense of its content; they attach themselves to the past, which leads to the neglect of the present and with that to the loss of creativity. By the

---

[25] See Hegel in *Phenomenology* (1977, pp. 261, 284) and in *Philosophy of Right* (1967, pp. 114–115).
[26] For a feminist discussion see Anderson (2019).

same token, the negation of one's tradition and one's exclusive orientation toward the future prevents a critical review of the past and triggers the loss of one's cultural identity. Zurayq calls this option 'recalcitrant futurism'.[27] Upon analysing the dilemma 'foreign or one's own culture', he finds that the rejection of a foreign culture in favour of one's own leads to totalitarianism, breeds fanaticism, and generates cultural paralysis. Surprisingly, the uncritical acceptance of a foreign culture at the expense of one's own also produces cultural paralysis since the ensuing suffocation of one's roots prevents a creative response to the traits taken over from another civilization. Finding a 'middle' position is the way out of the dilemma. To put it in terms of the deep hospitality theory sketched in the present inquiry, both the refusal and the embracing of other civilizations create severe difficulties for the position of the host. The parallels to the hosting or not hosting of words and strangers are striking. On the one hand, the complete and uncritical espousal of foreign ideas erases the host; the 'guested' culture takes over. On the other hand, radical rejection bans the guest and turns the host into the master of a home soon to crumble.

Zurayq is being rightly perceived as a Neo-Kantian (see Kassab, 1999). Nevertheless, his attempts to mediate between the opposing poles of the binaries he analyses also reveal a Hegelian streak. Ultimately, the extremes are not there to showcase the dilemmas he identified but to offer a spectrum on which civilizations may calibrate their exact position. It allows them to seek at different times the vicinity to one or the other pole to suit their needs without losing their unique 'character', what Zurayq called 'shakhsiyya'. When Zurayq wrote Fī Ma'rakat al-Ḥaḍāra (On the Fight for Civilization, 1964), his sight was on the Arab world. Nevertheless, what he says about the need to 'fight' applies to all civilizations, mainly since his understanding of fighting implies critical self-examination and examination of other civilizations. No civilization can survive as a stand-alone. It is precisely the encounter with other civilizations which secures one's future by responding freely and creatively to them. Self-preservation and the preservation of other civilizations are therefore inseparable in this world view. They are the soil upon which cultures thrive, and none is hostage to others or itself. They are in a continuous stream of exchanges and thus become civilizations on the move.

---

[27]   See Faris (1988, pp. 24–25), Ibrahim M. Abu-Rabi' (2004, pp. 296–318), and Kassab (2009, pp. 65–74).

From Hosting Words to Hosting Civilizations

To go back to sectarian tensions, the goal is to make the Shi'ite become the guardian of the Sunni Muslim and *vice versa*. This entails fighting in Zurayqian fashion for the other community's right to its narrative and thus preserving their own identity. As hostage civilizations they needed a negative foil to make sense of who and what they were. However, by becoming each other's host-guests they add a dimension to their self-understanding that says they could not be who and what they are without the existence of the other. After all, the other view could hold a *shakhsiyya* trait that has escaped them or can become an innovative further development, which might need reviewing, or was simply lost in their tradition. Similarly, at the level of civilizations with no common legacy, each holds both unique and shared features that may help other world civilizations sustain each other mutually or, better even, become each other's sustenance. Slavic culture and Slavic languages are hardly ever seen as repositories of human experience and wisdom in a Western context; this is another relationship in need of deep hospitality.[28] However, a look at, for instance, Bulgarian 'съхранител' (*sahranitel*, with the meanings of 'guardian', 'custodian', 'protector', and 'keeper' reveals the root 'храна' (*hrana*, meaning 'food'), derived from Proto-Slavic **xorna* and possibly related to Proto-Indo-European **ǵr̥h₂nóm* (grain).[29] The same root is also contained in Bulgarian охрана (*ohrana*, meaning 'protection', 'safeguard', 'safe conduct') and съхранение (*sahranenie*, 'safe-keeping'). The guardian is thus the one who keeps you safe by 'nourishing' you.

We are a long way from a world where civilizations are each other's cultural and spiritual 'food'. If they were, no one would lack physical food either. Nevertheless, one ought to hope and dream. Hope is not a sign of weakness but, as Kant put it, an ethical obligation. It prepares the ground for change. And dreams? They sustain hope.

---

[28] Benveniste includes some Slavic terms in his chapter on Hospitality: '*hostis* in Latin corresponds to *gasts* of Gothic and to *gostĭ* of Old Slavonic, which also presents *gos-podi* 'master', formed like *hospes*' (2016, p. 65). Derrida adds '*hospodar*', i.e., 'prince', 'lord' (2000b, pp. 13–14). '*Gospod*' ('Lord') is also the term used for God.

[29] See https://en.wiktionary.org/wiki/Reconstruction:Proto-Slavic/ xorna. All Slavic languages have terms with the root '*hrana*' connoting protection, guardianship, or preservation. Serbian thus uses the word '*сахрана*' (*sahrana*) for burial with the meaning of interring and thus safekeeping the deceased body.

Tamara Albertini

References

Ibrahim M. Abu-Rabi', *Contemporary Arab Thought. Studies in Post-1967 Arab Intellectual History* (London, Sterling, Virginia: Pluto Press, 2004).

Ellie Anderson, 'From Existential Alterity to Ethical Reciprocity: Beauvoir's Alternative to Levinas', *Continental Philosophy Review*, 52 (2019), 171–189.

Avempace [Ibn Bajja], 'The Governance of the Solitary', in Ralph Lerner and Muhsin Mahdi (eds.), *Medieval Political Philosophy* (Ithaca: Cornell University Press, 1963), 122–133.

Émile Benveniste, 'Hospitality', in Elizabeth Palmer (trans.), *Dictionary of Indo-European Concepts and Society* (Chicago: HAU Books, 2016), 61–73.

Lewis Edwin Hahn, Randall E. Auxier, and Lucian W. Stone, Jr. (eds.), *The Philosophy of Seyyed Hossein Nasr* (Chicago and La Salle, Illinois: Open Court, 2001).

Scott Davidson, 'The Ethics of Translation in Ricoeur and Levinas', *Analecta Hermeneutica*, 4 (2012), 1–14.

Jacques Derrida, *Adieu to Emmanuel Levinas*, Pascale-Anne Brault and Michael Naas (trans.), (Stanford: Stanford University Press, 1999).

Jacques Derrida, *Of Hospitality*, Rachel Bowlby (trans.), (Stanford: Stanford University Press, 2000a).

Jacques Derrida, 'Hostipitality', *Angelaki: Journal of the Theoretical Humanities*, 5 (2000b), 3–18.

Farah Diba-Pahlavi, *Erinnerungen*, Karla Bartosch, Frida Hagestolz, Tina Bunge, and Regina G. Sturm (trans.), (Bergisch Gladbach: Gustav Lübbe Verlag, 2004).

Hani A. Faris, 'Constantine K. Zurayk: Advocate of Rationalism in Modern Arab Thought', in George N. Atiyeh and Ibrahim M. Oweiss (eds.), *Arab Civilization. Challenges and Responses. Studies in Honor of Constantine K. Zurayk* (New York: State University of New York Press, 1988), 1–41.

S.A. Farmer, *Syncretism in the West: Pico's 900 Theses (1486). The Evolution of Traditional Religious and Philosophical Systems, Medieval and Renaissance Texts and Studies vol. 167*, (Tempe, Arizona: 1998).

James Hatley, 'Generations: Levinas in the Jewish Context', *Philosophy & Rhetoric*, 38 (2005), 173–189.

G.W.F. Hegel, *Philosophy of Right*, T. M. Knox (trans.), (London, Oxford: Oxford University Press, 1967).

G.W.F. Hegel, *Phenomenology of Spirit*, A.V. Miller (trans.), (Oxford: Oxford University Press, 1977).

B. Heller and N.A. Stillmann, 'Luḳmān', in P. Bearman, Th. Bianquis, C.E. Bosworth, E. van Donzel, W.P. Heinrichs (eds.), *Encyclopaedia of Islam*, second edition, accessed online on 7 October 2022 at https://referenceworks.brillonline.com/ entries/encyclopaedia-of-islam-2/lukman-COM_0586?s.num=0 &s.f.s2_parent=s.f.book.encyclopaedia-of-islam-2&s.q=lukman.

Martin Heidegger, *What is Called Thinking?*, Fred D. Wieck and J. Glenn Gray (trans.), (New York, Evanston, and London: Harper and Row, 1968).

Samuel P. Huntington, 'The Clash of Civilizations?', *Foreign Affairs*, 72 (1993), 22–49.

Samuel P. Huntington, *The Clash of Civilizations and the Remaking of World Order* (New York: Simon & Schuster, 1996).

Elizabeth Suzanne Kassab, *Contemporary Arab Thought. Cultural Critique in Comparative Perspective* (New York: Columbia University Press, 2009).

Elizabeth Suzanne Kassab, 'An Arab Neo-Kantian Philosophy of Culture: Constantine Zurayk on Culture, Reason, and Ethics', *Philosophy East and West*, 49 (1999), 494–512.

Claire Elise Katz, *Levinas, Judaism, and the Feminine: The Silent Footsteps of Rebecca* (Bloomington: Indiana University Press, 2003).

Claire Elise Katz, 'Levinas – Between Philosophy and Rhetoric: The "Teaching" of Levinas's Scriptural References', *Philosophy & Rhetoric*, 38 (2005), 59–172.

Peter Kingsley, *Ancient Philosophy, Mystery, and Magic. Empedocles and Pythagorean Tradition* (Oxford: Clarendon Press 1995).

Edward William Lane, *Arabic-English Lexicon* (London: Willams & Norgate, 1863). Also available online at http://www.tyndalearchive.com/TABS/Lane/.

Mohamad Zaidin Mohamad, Sofyuddin Yusof, Ahmad Zahid Salleh, and Abdillah Hisham, 'Dialogue among Civilizations: A Historical Perspective', *International Journal of Publication and Social Studies*, 2 (2017), 34–39.

Sheila Murnagham, *Disguise and Recognition in The Odyssey* (New Jersey: Princeton University Press, 1987).

Mauricio Pagano, 'Recognition and Hospitality', *RAPHISA. Review of Anthropology and Philosophy of the Sacrum*, 6 (2019), 85–93.

Asín Palacios, *The Mystical Philosophy of Ibn Masarra and His Followers*, Elmer H. Douglas and Howard W. Yoder (eds.), (Leiden: E.J. Brill, 1978).

Tamara Albertini

Julian Pitt-Rivers, 'The Law of Hospitality', in *The Fate of Shechem or The Politics of Sex: Essays in the Anthropology of the Mediterranean* (Cambridge: Cambridge University Press, 1977), 94–112.

Paul Ricoeur, *On Translation*, Eileen Brennan (trans.), (New York: Routledge, 2006).

Bertrand Russell, *A History of Western Philosophy* (New York: Simon and Schuster, 1967).

Edward W. Said, 'The Myth of the 'Clash of Civilizations'', lecture, University of Massachusetts (1996), available at https://www.youtube.com/watch?v=aPS-pONiEG8.

Sonya Lynn Scheel, 'French Language Purism: French Linguistic Development and Current National Attitudes', PhD dissertation, University of Oregon (1998), available at http://hdl.handle.net/1794/5916.

Dylan Shaul, 'Recognition and Hospitality: Hegel and Derrida', *Symposium*, 23 (2019), 159–182.

Mona Siddiqi, *Hospitality and Islam: Welcoming in God's Name* (New Haven and London: Yale University Press, 2015).

Andrew Shryock, 'Hospitality Lessons: Learning the Shared Language of Derrida and the Balga Bedouin', *Paragraph*, 32 (2009), 32–50.

Winkler, 'Dwelling and Hospitality: Heidegger and Hölderlin', *Research in Phenomenology*, 47 (2017), 366–387.

Christopher Wise, *Derrida, Africa, and the Middle East* (New York, NY: Palgrave Macmillan, 2009).

Qustantin Zurayq, *Fī Maʿrakat al-Ḥaḍāra: Dirāsa fī Māhiya al-Ḥaḍāra wa Aḥwāliha wa fī al-Wāqi* (On the Fight for Civilization: A Study in the Nature of Civilization, and in the Current Situation) (Beirut: Dār al-ʿIlm li al-Malāyin, 1964).

Index of Names